Interpersonal Psychoanalytic Perspectives on Relevance, Dismissal and Self-Definition

of related interest

The Therapist's Encounters with Revenge and Forgiveness
Mary Sherill Durham
ISBN 1 85302 815 0

Between Therapists
The Processing of Transference/Countertransference Material
Edited by Arthur Robbins
ISBN 1 85302 832 0

The Challenge of Psychoanalysis and Psychotherapy
Solutions for the Future
Edited by Stefan de Schill and Serge Lebouici
ISBN 1 85302 477 5

Attachment and Interaction
Mario Marrone
ISBN 1 85302 586 0 pb
ISBN 1 85302 587 9 hb
International Library of Group Analysis 3

Suicidal Behaviour
The Search for Psychic Economy
Jürgen Kind
ISBN 1 85302 788 X

Dialogue in the Analytic Setting
Selected Papers of Louis Zinkin on Jung and Group Analysis
Edited by Hindle Zinkin, Rosemary Gordon and Jane Haynes
ISBN 1 85302 610 7

Interpersonal Psychoanalytic Perspectives on Relevance, Dismissal and Self-Definition

Arthur H. Feiner

Foreword by Edgar A. Levenson

Jessica Kingsley Publishers
London and Philadelphia

The lyric from *She Touched Me*, written by I. Levin and M. Schafer, is quoted with the kind permission of M. Schafer.

The extract from *The Visit* by Friedrich Dürrenmatt, published by Jonathan Cape, is reproduced with the kind permission of Rachel Calder at the Tessa Soyle Agency.

The extract from the poem *A Dedication to My Wife* by T.S. Eliot is reproduced with the kind permission of Faber and Faber and Harcourt.

First published in the United Kingdom in 2000 by
Jessica Kingsley Publishers Ltd,
116 Pentonville Road, London
N1 9JB, England
and
325 Chestnut Street,
Philadelphia PA 19106, USA.

www.jkp.com

Library of Congress Cataloging in Publication Data

Feiner, Arthur H., 1922–

Interpersonal psychoanalytic perspectives on relevance, dismissal and self-definition / Arthur Feiner.

p. cm.

Includes bibliographical references and index.

ISBN 1-85302-864-9 (pbk. : alk paper)

1. Psychoanalysis. 2. Relevance. 3. Self-perception. I. Title.

RC506.F3186 2000

616.89'17--dc21 00-030148

British Library Cataloguing in Publication Data

A CIP catalogue record of this book is available from the British Library

ISBN 1 85302 864 9

Printed and Bound in Great Britain by
Athenaeum Press, Gateshead, Tyne and Wear

Contents

For Alice and Lisa, Lori and John

Acknowledgments

I must acknowledge my gratitude to the editors of *Contemporary Psychoanalysis* where I published, during the course of several years, the material from Chapter 1, 'Bewitched, Bothered, and Bewildered;' Chapter 2, 'Out of Our Minds;' Chapter 3, 'Laughter Among the Pear Trees;' Chapter 5, 'Touch and the Genesis of Hope;' Chapter 6, 'Countertransference and Misreading;' Chapter 7, 'The Thrill of Error;' and Chapter 8, 'Contradictions in the Supervisory Process.'

Chapter 4, 'Restlessness of the Spirit,' is an edited and rewritten version of an essay published in the *International Forum of Psychoanalysis* edited by Jan Stensson. To Dr. Stensson and his co-editor Mona Serenius at Scandinavian University Press, I am grateful for permission to use some of my original material. I also wish to thank the editors of Jessica Kingsley Publishers, especially Helen Parry, Christine Firth and Della Gray for their editorial guidance in the production of this book. And I must thank Carolyn Parqueth and Lisa Bazlen for putting the manuscript on floppy disks.

Finally, during the course of many years of analytic work, I have had the extremely good fortune to discuss many of the subtle, elusive problems of practice with a broad group of colleagues. I have learned from the comments of all them, especially when, as sometimes happened, there was little agreement. In joint efforts, personal discussions, and publications, no one has been more scientifically astute, consistently original, stimulating, challenging and insightful than Edgar Levenson. My debt to him is immeasurable, and I trust it shows. Also influential were Nathan Stockhamer, Lawrence Epstein, Earl Witenberg, Robert Langs, Robert Marshall, Nick Dellis, Murray Krim and Darlene Ehrenberg. I am no less grateful to the patients who trusted me with their feelings and their unique ways of expressing them, along with their rectifications, assuring me, despite my inadequacies, of the feeling of relevance that they strived for so painstakingly.

Foreword

Edgar A. Levenson

I am honored to be introducing this long-overdue collection of Arthur Feiner's writings. This format has permitted him to flesh out and elaborate the theoretical and clinical themes which have distinguished his individual papers; simultaneously, by some legerdemain, he has managed to maintain the combination of solid scholarship and antic humor which caused me, on another occasion (his retiring from the editorship of *Contemporary Psychoanalysis*), to call him a cross between Isaiah Berlin (one of his favorite philosophers) and Zorba the Greek!

I must first confess my own bias. Arthur and I have a long history of collaboration that goes back to the early 1950s College Drop-out Project at the William Alanson White Psychoanalytic Institute, and we have, over the years, shared many ideas and co-authored a few papers. Since a great many of my articles have been published in *Contemporary Psychoanalysis* under his editorial stewardship, and since Arthur personally, at considerable sacrifice of his time and effort, edited and published my last book, it is evident that I am hardly unbiased in both my gratitude to him and my admiration of his thinking (and good taste in authors!). All that notwithstanding, I am convinced that he is one of our most original and creative thinkers, highly appreciated by readers of *Contemporary Psychoanalysis*, but deserving of a much wider audience.

According to my reading of his book – which must inevitably be a 'misprision' as he uses the term; i.e., a creative and idiosyncratic misreading – its main thrust is clinical. I believe that his primary inquiry is into the nature of the dialogic encounter, what advances it and what, under the guise of understanding or interpretation, interferes with it. The assumption is that this 'I–Thou' process is the essence of the therapeutic. As do most interpersonalists, Feiner believes that therapeutic action is not qualitatively different from any other variety of authentic experience; that it does not depend on mutative interpretation, but on the consensual field of patient and therapist, and how it is conceptualized and used.

Running through almost all his writings, is a continuous thread of interest in the nature of the countertransference; or, in more precise interpersonal terms, the nature of the analyst's participation, deliberate and inadvertent, in the therapy process. He is, in this sense, entirely within the interpersonal tradition as it came to fruition at the William Alanson White Psychoanalytic Institute. H.S. Sullivan, Erich Fromm, Clara Thompson, followed closely by Edward Tauber, Janet Rioch, Rose Spiegel and Ralph Crowley constituted the first wave of interpersonal authors. In the early 1970s, a second group consisting of Feiner, Stockhamer, Levenson, Epstein, D. Ehrenberg and E. Singer continued the focus on the participant-observer analyst (Levenson 1972; Ehrenberg 1974; Epstein & Feiner 1979; Singer 1965; Schecter 1972; Wolstein 1964).

There have been several waves since – a tidal rush – of many original and provocative writings in the general realm of interpersonalism, and, more specifically, in the area of countertransference. The corpus of interpersonal writings on counter-transference range from meticulously 'neutral' inquiries into the particulars of analyst/patient interaction to more imaginative – and looser – usage of the analyst's experience as grist for the psychoanalytic mill.

Feiner, it seems to me, has been less interested in the specifics of interaction than in the analyst's tacit assumptions about what he/she was doing and why. Although he obviously respects the singularity of each analytic encounter, he also reflects a certain Frommian concern for the larger socio-cultural issues which, albeit delineating the interaction, are so pervasive and covert as to be hardly noticed. What is it to be a patient? What is it to be an analyst? What do we believe cure is? What is 'mental health'? What do we want from the patient? What is it to help?

While some of us elaborated the old paradigms, and some of us ventured into new models, Feiner's work has been distinguished and defined by a striking Appolonion-Dionysian split: the juxtaposition of literate, carefully thought out, sophisticated theoretical presentations, and the playful, punning, poetry-quoting, lyric-singing, jostling kind of praxis which Feiner demonstrates in almost every chapter. I believe that this reflects suspicion that language, in its formal presentation, often serves as an instrument of influence and control; that when we talk with each other, we attempt to mold the other person to our safe sense of the world, our security system. For language to be an instrument of change rather than persuasion or control, something different has to happen.

I believe he is on to something very interesting. We have all had the experience of a song lyric popping unbidden into mind and then opening up a train of emotion-laden associations and memories in much the same way a taste (Proust's madeleines) or scent will set off associations. This seems to be some kind of hippocampal release, not cortical, and the emotional impact is intense. I believe that his emphasis on misreadings, humor, play, puns, tunes, lyrics and touching is a way of bypassing the obsessional and controlling use of language. I do know, by the way, that he also wrote parodies of pop ballads for entertainment at the W.A. White Institute's graduation ceremonies and celebrations. That the words must match the music isn't a bad injunction for psychoanalysts to follow.

This impressionistic use of language clarified for me several clinical observations I had never been able to put in context. For example, I have observed that depressed, masochistic patients take very well to being 'kidded', teased; although one would ordinarily predict the most dire consequences of such genial sadism. Why? I also remember, working with my first supervisor at the White Institute, Meyer Maskin, who was a sardonic, Oscar Wilde-ish sort. I was seeing a very dependent adolescent boy with an extremely controlling, over-protective and infantilizing mother. I would point this out to him in appropriate psychoanalytic lingo with absolutely no discernible effect. Maskin, enveloped in a cloud of cigarette smoke, drawled, 'Say to him, "Gosh, your mother sounds like an awful bitch."' When I did, the patient almost fell out of the chair, and did begin to resist her incursions. It might not have been a nice thing to say or a nice way to say it, but it struck me then that form was, indeed, content; and that there were odd, off-beat ways of putting things which made a great difference; i.e., there is an emotional language which gets closer to the bone.

Feiner's work is most particularly distinguished and defined by his singular assertion that psychoanalysis is a form of poetry, and that poësis is a supernal playfulness. I believe in his youth, Arthur wrote poetry. He certainly read it, and his papers are generously sprinkled with quotations, from Dante to Yeats. His conjoining of poetry and psychoanalysis is no mere metaphor:

> I believe psychoanalytic issues parallel those of poetry... 'Poetic history', Harold Bloom writes, is 'indistinguishable from poetic influence, since strong poets make that history by misreading each other, so as to clear imaginative space for themselves.' (Feiner 1979, pp.125–126) (Bloom 1973, p.5)

or:

> If a patient's neurotic way of life and the communications he makes about it are seen as his 'creative' or even 'poetic' statements attempting to swerve himself from *his* precursors, then that swerving way, on the part of the therapist, that clearing of imaginative space, becomes a corrective gesture which makes change possible. (Feiner 1977, p.125)

Psychoanalysis has, since its inception, struggled with the dialectic between two aspects of the process, what I have called the axis of poësis and the axis of pragmatics; namely, what the patient, and the therapist, bring to the process out of their imagination, their flow of consciousness (Levenson, 1988a, p.214). Free-association, dreams, sudden memories fall into the first category. The behavior of the patient in his/her own world, i.e., the matrix of social existence, the way the patient negotiates the world out there, and the way this pragmatic is replayed in the therapy with the therapist is the essence of the second category. Freudians have leaned towards poësis, interpersonalists towards pragmatics. Each position is insufficient in itself, and successful therapy must be a tightrope walk. Most of us, in the interpersonal tradition, have – perhaps as a kind of antithesis to the Freudian's dream world – leaned in the direction of the 'interpersonal field' as the field of intersubjective behavior, with the transference/countertransference conceived of as an enactment or a reenactment (i.e., behavior, not fantasy). Each position, alas, begins as a therapeutic instrument and ends as a countertransference.

Feiner's passion for the poetic, the imaginary, the play of language is a welcome counterpoint to those primarily interested in the nuances of literal experience. He has left his mark on the psychoanalytic literature and I believe that this original and stimulating book will consolidate and advance his reputation. His own lines make a fitting conclusion:

> ...I think that if anything is taken in by the patient it is the therapist's willingness to hear non-dismissively, and to use his imagination in an uncompartmentalized way; to tolerate imperfection and the complications of ambivalence; to admit plausibility to the patient's view without necessarily agreeing with it, and in a judicious way, to look honestly, courageously at himself, at his fantasy, at his errors, at what is going on between him and the patient; and finally to expose his pleasure and playfulness in an exploratory process of a great deal of uncertainty – which I think engenders hope, a sense of vitality, possibility, and surely detoxifies the felt banality and the tedium 'of our life's way' (*di nostra vita*) making it interesting. (Feiner 1988, p.644)

How could it be said better? Can't one see Berlin and Zorba dancing off together?

References

Bloom, H. (1973) *The Anxiety of Influence.* New York: Oxford University Press.

Ehrenberg, D. (1974) "The intimate edge in therapeutic relatedness." *Contemporary Psychoanalysis 11,* 320–332.

Epstein, L. and Feiner, A. (1979) *Countertransference: The Therapist's Contribution to Treatment.* New York: Jason Aronson.

Feiner, A. (1978) "Countertransference and the anxiety of influence." In *Countertransference: The Therapist's Contribution to Treatment.* New York: Jason Aronson, pp.105–128.

Feiner, A. (1988) "Countertransference and misreading." *Contemporary Psychoanalysis 24,* 612–649.

Levenson, E. (1972) *The Fallacy of Understanding.* New York City: Basic Books.

Levenson, E. (1988a) "Real frogs in imaginary gardens: facts and fantasies in psychoanalysis." *Psychoanalytic Inquiry 8*, 4, 552–556.

Schecter, D. (1972) "Two of Sullivan's conceptions." *Contemporary Psychoanalysis 8*, 71–75.

Singer, E. (1965) *Key Concepts in Psychotherapy.* New York: Random House.

Wolstein, B. (1964) *Transference.* New York: Grune and Stratton.

Introduction

The themes of relevance and dismissal, their varied nuances, and (especially), how people define themselves, keep recurring throughout this book. For a long time they have been dominant in my analytic work and supervision. They are the how not the what of patient struggles. They are no strangers to psychoanalytic thinking and I make no claim for discovery. Surely, they are not all there is to psychoanalysis. It would be absurd to claim totality. But, they recur nevertheless.

In interpersonal psychoanalysis, for an intimately engaged, collaborative self – as Sullivan (1973) conceptualized it – there is the centrality of connectedness with all its myriad varieties. Relevance and dismissal fall under this umbrella, for without the conviction of relevance, without the feeling of mattering, no intimate way of relating is possible. With impactlessness comes a defensiveness against an assumed vulnerability. Even the likelihood of communal feeling tends to be banished from consciousness. Still, in my work, it may mean that patients give back what they come to believe is my preoccupation. All patients do that in their analyses, often reflecting their analysts' theories. And so, sometimes, it seems that the therapeutic data prove the theory.

The desire for relevance and mattering is the feeling expressed by patients who have been left with the idea that they have been diminished in their relationships with significant others. Their feelings, their desires, in essence, their rights to be who they are, have been made largely irrelevant. The inevitable behavior by others that accounted for this was a seemingly dismissiveness that ultimately was absorbed as part of the patients' definitions of themselves, which in turn affects how they function. In essence, like the protagonist in Ralph Ellison's (1947) famous novel, patients get to feel, to define themselves as invisible.

The experiences of anger and rage, anxiety and depression follow a belief that one is impactless, that one has been dismissed. In fact, respect, i.e., seeing a person as he or she really is, tenderness, care, and relevance are more than qualities of compassion. They are standards of relatedness that too often individuals and groups fail to observe. The threat to individuals who believe that their right to be who they are in a differentiated, autonomous way has been negated, is to their mortality. To experience being ignored is to feel being at the mercy of things, or of being made into a thing oneself. It happened with slavery, and with all official exclusionist and exterminationist policies throughout history. Whom we wish to destroy, or, less destructively, whom we would ignore or deny, we first make invisible. In interpersonal situations it may not be consciously deliberate.

Self-definition is another concept that begs explanation. I am not referring to an abstract idea although the words are abstractions from something that actually exists. Sullivan (1964, p.217) often referred to a man's 'conception of himself' in contrast to his conception of others. He wrote of the self 'having content,' which accounts for a person's functioning. I think self-definition can be inferred from behavior. It is known by other concepts such as ideology, belief system or structure, including even, that fancy German expression *Weltanschauung* (world-philosophy), and it is evident in how people behave. But behavior is not derivative of self-definition. They are identical, which explains in part why change is difficult. Although much of it is out of awareness, as are often the feelings that are coincident with it, self- definition is never too far, or remote from revelation. But that requires a sensitive, detailed, non-dismissive inquiry.

While people do appear differently with different others, careful scrutiny suggests a few basic organizing principles. These are what I am referring to and I try to make it clear in this book. Self-definition is like one of those garish, global, multifaceted, mirrored chandeliers that revolve endlessly in dance halls reflecting the colored spotlights focused on it. The globe has its own structure, and yet, like Sullivan's (1947, p.10) idea of 'reflected appraisals,' gives back appropriate color as it turns.

Here is an example: During an initial interview, a successful 45-year-old businessman tells me that he feels he must be a caretaker to members of his immediate family, his manic-depressive ex-wife and members of hers, his extended family – and anyone else who approaches him in need. All he wants in return is acknowledgment that he is a giving person, that what he has done for them has had value. It is a matter of simple gratitude. When this is not forthcoming he feels intense rage, so much so, and so often, that he does not want to go home. All of this is told in a plaintive tone, in sharp contrast to the affable way he introduces himself, communicates his success in business, and social matters. His expectation, he says softly, with supplication, as though he were in a confessional booth in St. Peter's, represents a dirtiness or evil inside him. He believes that it is an evil that he inherited from his alcoholic and abusive father, who had a string attached to all his apologetic generosities, and who chronically expressed his cynical disappointment with the world.

Early on, the patient says, almost in tears, he was the mainstay of his nuclear family. Apparently, his role has not changed. Since age 9 he has been solving others' problems. Like his father, he says, he gets furious, and then depressed when he is not thanked for his effort – by his self-preoccupied current wife, his seriously depressed ex-wife, his dysfunctional brother, either of his two young-adult children, his golfing companions, even his many employees. He says, now with bitterness and self-contempt, this desire for gratitude is like prostitution. What he wants most of all is some peace, some quiet, where he could do nothing, and answer to no one.

Analysts of all schools would encourage the patient to explore his thoughts on how it is that he is rarely thanked. They would nurture his curiosity about his feeling rage when he believes he has made little impact; that he really does not matter; that despite his ever-present helping hand, he is made to feel irrelevant; that his needs are of no importance. They would inquire about his attitude toward his father – whether he responded to his father's requests, and with what feeling. And they would be interested in his compulsion to volunteer caretaking when someone in need approaches. What makes it necessarily his responsibility? What is it like to be an iron man? Is it related to his experience with his parents? Was his father's alcoholism involved? In what way? How is this connected to his definition of himself as a man, a son, a husband, a parent? Is there something of interest in his father's relationship to his mother? Where was she during his childhood? Was she passively incompetent? If so, in what way? Was his first wife seen similarly? When did she develop her symptoms? And the feelings of evil, where do they come from? Was there contempt in his attitudes towards his alcoholic parent and his dysfunctional mother? What is there in his ungratified feelings that make him so self-denigrating? Does his rage further degrade him in that he believes he cannot contain the feeling so that returning home is additionally threatening? Is there no expectation of comfort and support at home? There are a lot more questions to be asked, all germane, not necessarily in the order presented.

Authenticity as a quality of enactment has been the interest of interpersonal psychoanalysis since its inception. In psychoanalysis, it means that the analyst's words and communications faithfully recapitulate and represent the quality of the relationship established with the patient. Non-dismissiveness comes across in attitude, choice of imagery, tone of voice, as much as it does in words and intent. Messages sent are not necessarily messages received.

It is not easy to describe, which may explain why so many descriptions of therapist–patient interaction fall flat. Authenticity is a lot easier to observe in some pop ballads. In these, form and content are more than parallel, lyrics and music do more than fit together, they recapitulate each other. The best works of songwriters are perfect marriages of words and melody, both accurately reflecting intent.

For a patient in analysis to experience actual relevance, the analyst must function as non-dismissively as his words imply. If a patient says she is angry because the analyst started the session late, and to her that means he does not take her seriously, a denial will repeat the conditions of her vulnerability and her assumed victimization. This, to her, justifies her anger. A slippery exchange as to the analyst's respect for the patient's point of view, with the concurrent appeal of an interpretation that anchors the patient's feelings in the past, seems equally duplicitous. To me, it looks like the analyst is playing the 'expert' who knows best, with the patient's feelings effectively dismissed. In contrast, an inquiry into the patient's feelings and her perception that gave birth to them, will not reiterate a denial of her right to have them. In fact, it will be an experience of having been treated seriously and relevantly. The patient may even discover the appropriate interpretation herself.

But this book is not intended as a guide on the technique of psychoanalytic therapy – interpersonal style. Nor is it an exegesis of the history and development of the interpersonal movement.

The chapters here are all revisits to essays that I wrote during the 1990s. I have expanded, revised, and tried to clarify some of the material, and cut a lot of other stuff that I thought superfluous, repetitious, or needed entirely new treatment. A decade is a long time in psychoanalysis, and ordinarily, we would expect that as times change, we would change with them. It is true that there are some ideas here I no longer claim, and several I might wish to express differently. But, by and large, the importance of relevance and self-definition as fundamental notions of a way of being in this world with others preoccupy me still, as they did in the past.

I would hope this book makes the reader more curious about the curious profession of psychoanalysis, especially about those interactions between analyst and patient that facilitate change. There is no question that every school of analytic thinking has its failures as well as its well-earned successes. And, so it seems to me, there must be something about the process of change that all analytic procedures share, regardless of the received theoretical constructs that attempt to explain them. I do not think we know what that is precisely. Unfortunately, full comprehension about the facilitation of therapeutic change eludes us still. If we were as scrupulous about that mystery, the 'how' of change, as we are with our varied metaphors about 'what it all means' we would be a lot more advanced and secure in our efforts.

Since there are two people in any analytic consulting room, I have addressed some of the chapters to one of the participants and some to the other. The book is broken down along these lines. But the chapters appear in no specially arranged order, either thematic or chronological. Chapters 1 and 2 express some of the basic or core ideas in interpersonal psychoanalysis that guide me, as differentiated from classical theory.

Chapter 3 is a discussion of vengefulness, vindictiveness, responses to dismissal, and the problems of vindication. Chapter 4 is an examination of the restlessness and tension that brings patients to therapy, the difficulty in their resolution, and the attention to and striving for salvation. Chapter 5 refers to the experience of hope and its relationship to touch, something analysts rarely pay attention to.

The second part of the book is focused on the experiences of the analyst. Chapter 6 addresses the analyst's deliberate attempt at 'misreading,' as distinct from interpretation, as an interpersonal way of intervention. Chapter 7 discusses the usefulness of the analyst's errors and their correction being at least as significant as their commission. Chapter 8 looks at some of the difficulties and contradictions in the supervisory experience of student-analysts that is to encourage their professional competence.

The predominant writers who have informed and guided my work, broadened my thinking, and the way I look at patients and the analytic process, have been Harry Stack Sullivan, Erich Fromm, Frieda Fromm-Reichmann, and Clara Thompson. While each wrote and practiced in his or her own unique way, all shared several attitudes. These included a rejection of the libido and drive theories of classical psychoanalysis, as well as the concept of the structures of the mind. Still, they retained and advanced many basic psychoanalytic ideas that had originated with Freud and Ferenczi. These were the notion of unconscious processes; the significance of the history and patterning of feelings and their expression; the importance of memories and reveries; the usefulness of dreams as communication; and, particularly, the scrutiny paid to the relationship the patient establishes with the therapist; and the patient's reluctances and resistances to therapeutic change. One thing is patently evident in all their thinking. While aware that any particular feeling, and the emotion it came from, depended on activity in several specific brain systems interacting with body organs, they did not negate the primacy of that feeling as an interpersonal and social phenomenon, real or illusory. In other words, to them, nothing is born in a vacuum so that there is no such thing as disembodied feelings. To comprehend them the analyst must scrutinize the interpersonal field in which they occur. And that requires a detailed inquiry. With full awareness of the analyst's participation there is also a focus on his or her impact.

Other analysts, like wise aunts and uncles who taught me how to hear and how to speak, and listen to myself, include Clara Rabinowitz, Rose Spiegel, Harry Bone, Alberta Szalita, Geneva Goodrich, Edwin Kasin and Joseph Steinert. Their influence and clinical acumen are evident on every page.

Finally, since the original pieces were written on different occasions, there may be some repetition. I apologize for that.

References

Ellison, R. (1947[1995]) *Invisible Man.* New York: Vintage Books.

Sullivan, H. (1947) *Basic Conceptions of Modern Psychiatry.* Washington D.C.: The William Alanson White Psychiatric Founation.

Sullivan, H. (1953) *The Interpersonal Theory of Psychiatry.* New York: W.W. Norton.

Sullivan, H. (1964) *The Fusion of Psychiatry and Social Science.* New York: W.W. Norton.

PART ONE

The Patient

Chapter 1

Bewitched, Bothered, and Bewildered[1]

Some Core Issues

Much of what I do as a psychoanalyst is marked by severe uncertainty and an embarrassing, slow recognition of my ignorance. It would be reassuring if I had a broad fixed set of guidelines to follow, but as an interpersonalist I do not. And I am sure many of my interpersonal colleagues share these sentiments.

Traditionally, psychoanalysts defined psychoanalysis by creating it, laying down rules and constraints, even rituals or ceremonies. With the flowering of interpersonalism in the mid-twentieth century, by contrast, a new psychoanalysis came about through efforts to define it. By so doing, as happened similarly in the concurrent move in art to abstract expressionism, interpersonal psychoanalytic efforts shifted from labeling and explaining to a description of experience. This was a conceptual change that advanced technique and practice as well. If libido theory was ignored, the assumed unicausality of neuroses abandoned, and the labels for the structure of the mind dropped from the vocabulary, what kind of confidence could a radical group of interpersonalists have in psychotherapy as a relief from barriers to expansive growth and change? Actually, what was objected to was not the idea of unconscious processes, but the correlatively held reifying notion that analysts could examine these processes as though they were studying three-dimensional objects in space. Sullivan (1964 [1950]) had commented wryly:

> the postulate of the unconscious has...nothing in the world the matter with it. As soon as you begin to arrange the furniture in something that cannot be directly experienced, you are engaged in a work that requires more than parlor magic...don't be tempted to tell the world all about the unconscious because someone is almost certain to ask you how you found out.' (Sullivan 1964, p.204)

The leaders of the movement – Sullivan, Fromm, Fromm-Reichmann, and Thompson – had begun their careers in an orthodox or classical way, but their growing interest in clinical authenticity – that is, what they said they did was no different from what they did – introduced a radical but uncertain perspective to their work. The focus turned from what it all meant to what was going on. The technique of inquiry, with the encouragement of curiosity, instead of free association, became the impelling force for self-scrutiny. Since technique and theory were seen as interdependent and interpenetrating, splitting or separating them, i.e., discussing them in isolation, would have given a false impression of the interpersonal position. They assumed that how analysts function, and how they speak about it, ought to be the same even though communicating what actually goes on in practice is extremely difficult.

Some of the basic canon never changed. What really did? Concepts like unconscious processing and the affecting power of resistance, transference, and countertransference (going on between analyst and patient, out of awareness and shaping the interaction between them), and the requisite need for their analyses, remained core, and are constant to this day. Their contents may be different (as they would be in different schools of thinking), but their forms are not. Most analysts tend to refer to these processes one way or other. As Freud suggested, they determine any analytic endeavor, regardless of metaphor. They remain organic aspects of all analytic procedure. So what was different? And does the difference characterize a new, viable position worthy of its own name? Or is it all nothing but old digested ideas?

With an emphasis on process, interpersonalists did offer their own stamp, shifting analytic investigation from the search for the what (the classification) to the study of the how (the experience). Therein lies interpersonalism's transformative contribution, and what is currently basic to it as a body of knowledge, a research tool, and a treatment technique. It is in its study of the how that interpersonalism is practiced – interpersonally. The analyst offers an ear that listens non-dismissively, and a self-reflective mind that contemplates and queries the patient's perceptions, and whatever is attendant on them – thoughts, feelings, attitudes, beliefs, without contradiction, correction, or, in the case of patient's hostile recriminations or attack, without retaliation, particularly so if they are about the therapist or the therapy.

Nothing characterizes the revisionist quality of interpersonalist thinking and feeling better and more succinctly than Isaiah Berlin's (1979) familiar hedgehog and fox metaphor, which he borrowed from the Greek poet Archilochus, one of whose lines reads: 'The fox knows many things, but the hedgehog knows but one big thing.' Berlin pointed out that there are those who relate everything to a central vision or system, more or less coherent and articulate, that is a single organizing principle, in terms of which, all they are and say has significance. In sharp contrast, there are those who pursue many ends, entertaining ideas which are centrifugal rather than centripetal, move on many levels, seizing the essence of a variety of experiences. It is the difference between the monist and pluralist attitudes (Berlin 1979, p.22). He warns that the dichotomy, like all oversimple classifications, becomes, if pressed, artificial and pushed to absurdity. It was the fixed centrality of the monist position of orthodox psychoanalysis, its emphasis on the Oedipus complex and drive theory, that the interpersonalists sought to revise.

Despite demurrers by the literary critic Frank Kermode, when presenting his Eighteenth Ernest Jones Lecture in 1984, that he, as an outsider to psychoanalysis, could comment only superficially on a few things of interest to an analytic audience, he presented, without awareness, some of the essentials of interpersonal theory. He did not know it, but he focused, in fact, on those ideas that specifically contribute to its inherent revisionary radicalism. If ever there was a misprision of a received body of thinking, interpersonalism is surely the apotheosis and, unknowingly, Kermode (1989) showed it eloquently.

With the shift from the what to the how interpersonalists had questioned whether reducing a patient's expression of feelings to a colorful metaphor really helped. In the development of classical theory, assumptions about history, its mechanistic, deterministic influence, had been carried over from the nineteenth century's natural sciences. Still, even during Freud's time, other assumptions about the perception of reality and causality had emerged. Early in the first half of the twentieth century there had arrived Einstein, Bohr, and Heisenberg. In the 1930s, in response to what he considered stagnation in analytic technique, Strachey (1934) had introduced the word 'mutative' when referring descriptively to interpretations. But it seems he believed that supposed, hypothetical mind structures – which, in fact, were little more than useful metaphors – could be changed by astute verbalisms.

If we presume that the past determines the present directly, we are prone to ask how things got to be the way they are, that is, what events contributed, and we assume that to be sufficiently explanatory. Yet if we split the way things are from the way they came to be, we subject ourselves possibly to discarding the Darwinian tradition itself, and that would mean a further remove from modern science. Interpersonalism follows a different track. It assumes an evolving interconnection between the growing person and the surround, that shows itself in his experience of feelings. With this in mind, there looms an enrichment that is possible only with a studied inquiry that expands the analytic interaction beyond listening to associations. Change is now facilitated by the inquiry itself, not by the naming or the interpretation. Therefore, interpersonalists pay attention to the immediate field or context of occurrence and all its complexity, especially the analyst's participation in it. This is a revisionary change from the diachronic point of view, a study of things in their coming to be as they are, to the synchronic point of view, the study of things as they are, in all their idiosyncrasy and mess (Kermode 1989).

Interpersonalists agree that understanding is subject to time and change, and that no past is fixed. In fact, the past can no longer be separated from the present. As interpersonalists, we view patients from within our own self-definitions, as they do their past and present, and these are subject to change. Therefore, the past becomes, in this view, inextricably woven with the present. Even past meaning changes, since the past is a creation of the present, and cannot be detached from it. In this way, the past is a product of the moment. And here is the interpersonal rub: If the past becomes a construction of the present, are least in part, we must take into account, in addition to the historical data, the self-definition and participation of the observer as well as the observed. Thus the interpersonalist's emphasis on the how is not to ignore the past, but to use it differently to gain some comprehension about an individual's present that is in flux – a better word might be 'anticipation' – but to avoid imposing anything in place of discovery and expansion (Kermode 1989, p.146). This is the search for feelings and how they have evolved, not events.

It was interpersonalism that rejected imposition. But so would have Freud, who asserted that observation is the only legitimacy of science. Kermode (1989) says that Freud would have eschewed the doctrine that the innocent eye sees nothing. How then, not to impose? Since the blank screen is impossible, and the anonymity of the analyst a myth, interpersonalists, admitting their presence and influence, seek to harness it all by monitoring it. In fact, they assume the efficaciousness of the therapy evolves out of the scrutinized relationship itself, its quality, its enactments, more so than the words exchanged and the so-called insights achieved.

Sullivan (1954) concluded that the data of psychiatry 'arise only in participant observation.' What he meant was that no one can stand off to one side and observe what someone else is doing without becoming personally implicated in the operation. The idea follows Heisenberg's principle of uncertainty (Pais 1991).

Here is the way participant-observation played out. Where previously the analyst studied an 'other,' now there are two people observed in mutual influence. The principal instrument of observation is the analyst's self – the analyst as person. The data are not solely from the subject, nor are they from the observer, but in the situation that is created by the two. Where formerly there had been the free associations of one, necessitating a receptive, passive analyst waiting for the pure 'metal' of the patient before making an interpretation, now there is inquiry, and importantly, a mutual monitoring of the thoughts, feelings, and narratives of the participants in response to each other. The analytic interviewer has one recurrent thought (among others): Do I understand what the patient means by what the patient is saying? Do the patient's remarks need spelling out? Clearly, there is no tacit agreement as to understanding.

Where there had been an attempt at encouraging the patient's remembering with an elegant reconstituting of events, i.e., the analyst listening to what the patient had experienced with feeling, we now focus on what the patient's feelings have experienced, along with their derivative imagery. Where there had been implicit supplications for ultimate adjustment, that is, a coming to terms following restitution or repair of the patient's damaged past, there now is a respect for differentiatedness, especially private experience, in the context of connectedness, along with a regard for the necessity of enduring (Feiner 1988; Levenson 1991a). Where there had been a scrutiny of internality, i.e., conflicts and the upheaval of drives, their fusion and defusion, and, later, anxiety, there now is a concentration on the adaptational aspects of self-definition with all its conscious and unconscious facets influencing the necessities of choice, especially with the analyst. All of this is to be analyzed and commented about (Levenson 1991a).

Essentially, where there had been a display of authoritative expertise, a putative knowledge of unconscious structures, and, one supposes, of being an arbiter of mental health, and, later, of having an alleged sophistication about problems in living, there is now our naked admission of not-knowing, and of our availability for search. And, while these revisions seem to represent the heart of interpersonal psychoanalysis, there may even be more to acknowledge.

Appropriately, the founder of psychoanalysis said that the analytic relationship was based on truth – an absence of sham or deceit (Freud 1937, p.248). In our modern, indeterminate age, the interpersonalist wonders 'what truth, and whose?' Furthermore, interpersonalists consider the possibility that the 'truth' of the interpretation of events may not even be what is relevant between analyst and patient. Feelings can be only expressed or not, they cannot be argued about. They are neither right nor wrong. Memory, or the analyst's study of a person's history, is the examination of history as it is felt.

Still, if there is no ultimate 'truth,' is there some kind of state, seemingly relevant, which, when encountered, engenders feelings of self-integration and of union, contact and connectedness, at the same time? At the least, is there something that precludes discontinuity, alienation, and deracination? Could this be something like the authenticity sought by analyst and patient in contrast to the patient's all too familiar consanguineous and social experience? Is this the relative still point (as T.S. Eliot called it),[2] recognizable more in the analyst's enactment of inclusion and attitude of non-dismissiveness, than in his words, and the attempt (not necessarily the success) at resolving distance, and discontinuity through mutual commentary (Feiner 1970)? Intimacy, as Levenson (1974) puts it, is a way of relating, evidently not a state of grace. Surely, it is this 'way' that engenders contact and connectedness, those antidotes to isolation and insularity. And is this coincident with the quality of exploration of self-definition in safety, which itself is behavior, i.e., dialogue instead of sequential utterances? I shall try to illustrate, but, first, a digression.

Sometimes, when I was 8 or 9, during the summertime, my parents would take me to the movies. It was during the Great Depression, and baby-sitters had not been invented for our proletarian class. The films my parents liked, which were probably a relief from their poor, drab lives, and which, I suppose, kept me quietly enthralled, were gangster-musicals, like the ones with Joan Blondell and Dick Powell. The stories were always the same. She played the part of an impoverished dancer, and he a struggling singer in a night-club owned by a powerful mobster called 'Ace.' You recognized Ace because he wore a diamond ring on his pinky, smoked fat cigars, and called people 'Sport.' Typically, after a late show at the club, Dick would walk Joan home, and she would say something allegedly romantic like, 'It's only you I like, you big lug.' It was the way Hollywood portrayed young, struggling people speaking tenderly to each other in those days. Then she would say, 'Would you like to come up for a nightcap?' Since it was summer I thought that sounded pretty dumb, because I thought she meant a hat. As I remember it, upstairs, in her (*sic*) opulent, forty-foot living room, with fire roaring in the fireplace, and bar decorously appurtenanced with Baccarat crystal, she would purr something like, 'Excuse me, while I get into something more comfortable.' Whereupon, Dick would start crooning something like, 'There Must Be Happiness Ahead.' And my all-knowing and all-seeing mother would lean across me and whisper to my father, 'Uh…oh!' As I recall, my father just grunted. 'Uh…oh!' must have meant something, but I did not have the vaguest idea what they were murmuring about. Nor did I ever catch on to the con that was occurring on the screen, offered as stimulating and gratifying entertainment to an economically depressed, but eagerly willing audience.

I assume today that my parents were exchanging nothing more cryptic than that they had evidently surmised what was being alluded to (but they, like everyone else, were conned by the screen's ambiance), and that a part of their exchange, sotto voce, was that I, the child, was not to be privy to it. Of course, I felt left out. But while there was this exclusion, there was no con. I still felt connected to them, enjoying the fascinating film and the experience (usually of youth and goodness triumphing over evil).

Furthermore, with them in general, as I remember it, there were never false titillations, or stimulation with an impending disaster, were I to seek gratification. There were no alternations between stimulation and frustration; no switching of emotional wave-lengths during conversation (e.g., from serious to humorous, or from triviality to seriousness). As I recall, there was no simultaneous insistence of unrelated topics (i.e., no tangentialism). And there was a minimum calling attention to something about me that I had revealed out-of-awareness, something that was at variance with what I knew about myself. Well, hardly ever. Maybe! – maybe they had little imagination; of course, they were not saints. But, by and large, there was no con (Laing 1961; Levenson 1972; Searles 1965).

I believe that to know the 'what' of my parents' thoughts is less important than to know and appreciate the 'how' of them – how they were with each other and with me, and especially how I experienced them, and felt about it. It is not that what they said or did not say did not matter (the 'uh-ohs' aroused my interest), but it was considerably less important than how authentic and reliable they were, as well as non-dismissive or diminishing of my reality.

How does this apply to interpersonal psychoanalysis?

Here is a patient's contrasting example:[3]

> I had a dream about being stuck by virtue of being in analysis. My analyst had aroused my desire to be saved, or rescued, but he couldn't or wouldn't fulfill it.
>
> Yet it was a hope. It was awakened and reawakened by him, or by the setting, so I was stuck, waiting for deliverance which I knew would never come.
>
> I told him, as a joke and fantasy, that I had witnessed many touching scenes in the waiting room of the suite of offices he shares with two colleagues. I said I had encountered the elderly parents of his colleagues' patients asking for their sons' and daughters' forgiveness, and that everyone, including the analysts, wept at these healing reunions-reconciliations which these analysts had engineered.
>
> It was merely coincidence that these scenes vanished into thin air whenever my analyst opened the door of his office to usher in the next patient – me.
>
> My analyst replied that perhaps I didn't really believe that he had no magic. Perhaps I believed he was "conning" me, simply withholding a solution to my perennial insularity, my isolation and rage, so as to keep his practice full.
>
> We had spoken, in a session several months prior to this, of my experience as a child of having been conned by my mother repeatedly. I now realized that I had, in fact, an ongoing fear of being conned, that I believed I was surrounded by potential con artists much of the time and that "analysis," whatever that term means, might itself be a hideous con.

It seems that for this patient the word 'con' refers to both conning and mystifying processes. As I have written (see note 1), I view conning as a conscious process. Mystification is the result of communication in the context of the anxiety of the mystifier (Ferenczi 1955; Laing 1965).

The patient continues:

On leaving his office I had the subsequent thought that though he was not a con artist, he too must have been conned by the Great-Analytic-Process-Bitch-Goddess. He was spending his declining years in slavery to some bullshit 'analytic process.'

I realized, after thoughts like this, that my mind was continually coming up with con scenarios of which my analyst and my analysis were very much a part.

For example, when he recently had to have surgery: In my fantasy I wondered if the surgery were a ruse. He would enter the lobby of the hospital but leave by a back door and fly off to the Caribbean for a week with his beautiful, blonde mistress – or in pursuit of one.

When I was vacationing in Canada recently, thinking often about my mother and my history with her, which has been a primary focus of my analysis for the past year, I realized how comforting it was to be in an environment – nature, that is – that I could trust.

The water of the pond would not only be there from one day to the next, but its temperature would be relatively constant. The grass in the meadow would be the grass in the meadow. The farmer down the road would be the farmer down the road.

None of these things would be other than what they appeared to be. The water of the pond wouldn't disappear or freeze in the middle of August. Or, suddenly boil. The farmer down the road was unlikely to be a former prime minister who had retired in disgrace and was staying up late at night planning his political rehabilitation, or dreaming of a sex change operation.

I think one of the problems of having been successfully conned as a child is that as an adult it is painful, and enraging to wake up fully to the fact that one had been taken for such a ride. One really doesn't want, in one's heart, to believe it.

Though one can, logically, take steps to protect oneself in the present, there is nothing one can do to reverse the past deception. How could I have been so blind? How could I have been such a stupid, gullible child? But, I loved and needed her. Surely other children would have been wiser, would have seen through her gross deceptions, would never have wanted to be taken in, or believe these lies? Or, would have had the support of another parent, which I did not.

One would prefer to believe that one had misunderstood her, or that there was some hidden aim in her lies, some guiding intelligence that would one day reveal a beneficial purpose to them. But, the beautiful safe deposit box is empty, and it is unlikely that it ever contained much that was of any value. This, and the awareness that she got away with it, is infuriating and painful. As a child I was bewildered.

> I don't want to suggest that her cons were isolated events. Everything my mother did, in retrospect, seemed a con, or a con within a con. It was as if she woke every morning thinking: 'How will I pull the wool over their eyes today? Will I be crazy, or only pretend to be crazy? What would be most efficient?'
>
> But, I will mention one obvious con or delusion that occurred when I was approximately 5 or 6 years old.
>
> During my early childhood, my mother would frequently wander through the downstairs of the house singing Broadway show tunes. Her voice was terrible, and as she sang she would pose very theatrically, looking up at the ceiling as if to the heavens, or to nameless faces in an imaginary balcony. She had a weird smile on her face, and an unnatural glint in her eyes, and as a small child I couldn't imagine what or whom she was looking at.
>
> One day, during this period, my mother took me aside and told me, as if in confidence, that had her mother not prevented her (since her mother did not think the Broadway stage was a suitable career for a 'good' girl), she, with her singing voice, and acting skills, would have been a great star on the Broadway musical stage, and most likely, would have gone to Hollywood.
>
> On hearing this, I assumed we might have been living in a splendid mansion in California with servants, or, on the contrary, that she might never have married my father (where had he been in all this?).
>
> She would later say that I had destroyed her voice, because I complained of her singing in the house, and, stopping at my request, her voice then 'went' completely. I gave her the benefit of the doubt.
>
> Perhaps in the past her voice had once been beautiful, I conjectured. My mother actually had been a fashion model. She had been a beautiful woman. Her physical beauty in and of itself had not been a delusion.

Children, who are realistically dependent, and whose worldly experiences are limited, are vulnerable to the inauthentic or the adulterated. In the beginning their response is usually confusion. They can be taken in endlessly, even growing up preferring the sham, since it is familiar, and becomes part of their self-definitions, and, consequently, part of their expectations of the world. In this way, later, they are attracted to the con, and in the process, con themselves, since expectations, however painful, are assumed to be reasonable because they fit their self-definitions. These include the suppression of their rage. The developing limited or warped organization is something they become intimately familiar with. It explains why those who grow up integrating this kind of self-definition have difficulty appreciating and extracting enjoyment from something honest and straightforward. The experience of that kind of relatedness is strange or foreign, even possibly humiliating. Sometimes they are simply blind to it, necessarily inattentive because it would be too disrupting. Sometimes they doubt it possible, or are suspicious of it. There is no 'there, there' for them. There is only their vulnerability, their anticipated victimization, their assumed, fantasized entitlement, even their self-aggrandizement.

Most people have limited knowledge about themselves, not because they are afraid to know, afraid to move, but primarily, because they are forbidden to know. This is the essence of the mystification experience. That is, not knowing is part of self-definition, and negating that would wreak havoc. It is a reminder of earlier denigration, and would provoke humiliation. Even learning can be processed and integrated this way. This is evident when black students doing excellent work are sometimes denigrated by peers with 'she's acting white.' More than hostility, it implies that doing excellent work, being rewarded in a white world, is not part of self-definition. And one dare not assume the futility of such pretension.

Some even need the other's confusion (anyone's) so as to maintain sanity (Laing 1967; Levenson 1972). Some analysts seem to continue to persuade their patients, via so-called interpretive gesture, that what the patients believe is not actual reality, not metaphoric for feelings that have been, or, most important, are being experienced, but is solely their own distortion. The issues of early central nervous system wiring, subsequent mapping, safety and survival, self-definition and organization may be largely ignored, with the therapist, as Levenson points out, blind (during the session) to the enactment of the content of the patient's report. This synecdoche, this attention to the part standing in for a whole (the way things are enacted reflecting homologously the anecdote), is a critical aspect of the interpersonal orientation.

In the patient's report presented here, one wonders about the conspicuous absence of the father in the commentary. The patient mentions it in passing, but the analyst must consider whether this implies a more seriously limiting psychic structure than is evident in the patient's self-referring complaints. One also questions whether the patient's assumption of the description of 'con' (as a conscious process) is a safe way for the patient to maintain some kind of relationship with his mother. Either he does that or, facing her massive self-deception or madness, he is entirely without connection, abysmally alone.

There is also my con of the patient, as well as the reader. Sure, the patient refers to me as egregiously virile, but as a con artist, nevertheless. The request for the summary, my telling him its purpose, i.e., for a paper, is, despite my honesty, a rupture of the analytic frame, and a blatant exploitation. Where did this dismissive impulse come from in me? To state simply and straightforwardly that I envy the patient's imagistic facility and expressiveness belabors the obvious. Was it my need to flesh out a paper? To please my colleagues? Was it my laziness, my reluctance to write in the first place, my doubts about my originality, or of having little to say? Finally, did my lack of confidence in my memory of the details of the sessions round out the enactment of the countertransference? None of these thoughts were in awareness when I made my request. Their contemplation and consideration by me and the patient makes the analysis manifest. It becomes the negation of the mystification and the con.

Therapists fall into patterns or roles related isomorphically to the patient's self-definition and current feelings necessary for the patient's homeostasis. Basic to interpersonal analysis is the discussion of these processes. These require therapists' active inquiry, but again, with their awareness of their assumptions. The point is, it is not their elimination that is important, it is their analyses in dialogue (not monologue in disguise). Furthermore, a comprehension of how the analysis (and the analyst) is being used, and a commentary about what is going on, takes precedence over content and its interpretation.

Sometimes, either naively (or perhaps grandiosely), in an explicit way, or, perhaps, benignly, implicitly, through acceptance and attention, therapists con the patient into believing that the past, somehow, someday, can be cured, glossed over by being remembered, now to be transcended by being ignored. The issues of the restoration of alleged past events, or repair of the damage resulting from early experience, that are, paradoxically, comparably parallel to persuasive editorializing or sermonizing, result in the same con. That is, 'Now, with this rational insight about yourself, this understanding of your past, and your conflicts, you can be "different."' This is as much a lie as telling someone they can change their eye-color. But the lie itself is not the only destructive element. With the patient's resulting confusion, his sense of betrayal, and the implicit request or expectation for disavowal of his appropriate, vengeful anger, his self-definition involving dreaded experiences of invasiveness (confirming his helplessness, hopelessness, or sense of inadequacy), is reaffirmed. The bothered victim, as in the Hart lyric, just feels bewitched and bewildered, even disconnected. It is a new con, confirming the old and one's readiness to being conned again.

The patient is then in that bind that prevents him fulfilling his own authentic autonomy and differentiatedness, on the one hand, and his desire to maintain a reciprocally altruistic connection on the other. Therein is conceived subversion of the desire to grow, to be oneself, with self-defeat devolving into the desire to maintain a comfortable, safe connection by virtue of staying where one is. The analyst hears pleas amounting to, 'If you are like me, you like me.' With the recognition of difference or asymmetry, the patient experiences threat and anxiety.

Laing (1961, p.135) refers to this as an untenable position. No matter how one feels or acts, no matter what meaning one attributes to a situation, one's feelings about oneself lack validity. In effect, any situation (e.g., the analytic one) becomes robbed of meaning, so that one is completely mystified, and alienated, with the essence of the felt experience being discontinuity and concurrent (but suppressed) rage. An anastomotic experience with others becomes impossible. Communal sensibility is destroyed.

Sometimes, referring to their efforts on stage, actors will say, 'It was beginning to "sing",' when they believe they were in touch with something in life. When it is over, it is a painful loss. In a similar way, for analysts, some sessions 'sing,' through mutual exchange, or articulation of immediate experience. When the session ends, there is a distressful sense of loss, because the 'singing' has put the analyst, like the actor, in touch with some part of the patient's life, via the inquiry, and the discussion about it – the enactment. It is the opposite of the inauthentic and the discontinuous – it is the still point. Our collective desire for this feeling explains, somewhat, why so many of us do things like climb rocks and mountains of ice, sail alone around the world in a rowboat, or wait at four in the morning, up to our waist in some godforsaken swamp, for the return nesting of a rare bird. As my patient wisely observed, there is no con in nature.

So where are we? Could not all the things I see as vital core for an interpersonal psychoanalysis be jettisoned, just like what I consider the obsolete ballast of the past? Could we not substitute other issues, seemingly just as relevant – those, perhaps, that will emerge with our thinking and what is current in science over time, particularly our understanding of neural science – how the brain functions and how consciousness evolves?

Does not my rhetoric reveal my prejudices – about sensual contact, authenticity, communal consciousness, selfhood – and the nature of my peculiar experiences, my self-definition? Perhaps I con myself, even though I believe my interests are worldly, broadening membership in a community, in contrast to what I view as the solipsisms and platitudes of others, especially their infatuation with their own thinking, their own metaphors, all of which encourage solitary, insular existence. My understanding of my countertransference enactment indicates a conning of the patient described here, that he picked up perceptively and incorporated in his typescript, almost as if he had had a dream about me.

I see my interests rooted in neural biology – Darwinian, selectionist (attentive and inattentive), interactional – and fundamental to the evolution of consciousness, part of nature in mind. Freud seems to have said the same thing, and may have said it more elegantly than all the interpersonal literature, with greater eloquence and flourish, and, more completely. True, Freud's rhetoric was marvellous, but, it seemed to me, always left us with stereotypes, those 'usual suspects' to be rounded up at case conferences and conventions. It seemed to me his was a rhetoric about universals. Even so, perhaps my rhetoric is just shallow and about the trivial, reflecting metaphorically what is my fantasy.

Of course, the scrutiny of the past as explanation of the present may be an allusion to the present, whether the participants know it or not. That would be so if memory of the past is a function of the present. Analysts of all stripes sense that in the mundane commentary, fantasy, dream report, or otherwise – the police officer, the firefighter, the teacher, the hairdresser, the architect, and the surgeon (or any figure) may stand for the analyst, and the patient's expectation of the analytic function identified with the work of the figure. And (we hope), all analysts tend to see all commentary as derivative of the adaptive task of being in the analytic relationship, in a particular time and setting, as well as how these are managed (Langs 1995).

One area that is rarely discussed by psychoanalysts, however, is their playfulness or playful activities with patients, even though jokes and humor are no strangers to psychoanalysis or psychodiagnosis (Freud 1905; Richman 1996). It is important from the point of view of coparticipation since play and playfulness are in the context of reciprocal influence (Ehrenberg 1990). They can be viewed under the rubric of humor or comedy.

Like tragedy, comedy and humor are releasing and transforming. They have a leavening effect in human affairs (Schimel 1975). From license comes renewed confidence in ourselves, especially in our integration. It ushers in candor, that is, a realistic appraisal of our vulnerability. It includes jokes, puns, one-liners, self-criticism and self-scrutiny, parody, satire, irony, all in a hopeful, perhaps even affectionate context. The man who fearfully warns comrades in battle to be careful, is not the same as the man who looks out of his foxhole under mortar fire and says: 'Holy shit, we can get killed here!' Nor is the son who answers a screaming father, with 'Yes dad,' the same as mine who, when I yelled about something, walked up to me slowly and said, in whatever Oxonian splendor he could muster, 'You rang, sir?' Many years ago, I remember being told as a student that Nicholas Murray Butler, then chancellor of a famous university, raged at, and actually struck with his umbrella, some students who were picketing on campus in protest to a visiting diplomat from fascist Italy. When he dropped the umbrella, one of the battered students picked it up, and, handing it to the chancellor, said politely, 'Your sword, sir.'

Freud once told his patient, the imagist poet HD, after she had expressed some fancy metaphor in French, that he would appreciate it if she spoke in English or German, since the prosthesis he wore in his mouth was terribly inefficient in Romance languages.

Playfulness is more ongoing, I think, than one-liners or puns. Certainly there is more emphasis in it on continuity and unfolding. It stimulates reflection and dialogue between therapist and patient. Elaborating a fantasy encourages openness, but one-liners do remind people that they are human, and that openness is possible for them. The comedic also encourages us to look at our ways of living exactly as they are, not mechanized, or guarded against with our private, tyrannical shoulds, oughts and musts. The comedic idea also transcends tedium and monotonousness. With comedy we sometimes can respond to a repetitive complaint that no amount of insightful wisdom could interrupt (Schimel 1975). If we do get off the bus long enough to look at ourselves, we are helped to correct our pretentiousness.

If the world is seen as insensitive, inhuman, and alienated, then the comic spirit is what Wylie Sypher (1956) has called the 'ultimate civilizer.' Comedy is also charitable in its stripping us of our affectations, checking our sentimentalism, watching over our vanity, pompousness, smugness, hubris, and officiousness. And it is charitable in that disdain can be issued in a single stroke of laughter.

And what is it that we laugh at? Surely, it is not the person. Surely, it is not meant to wound, except those ready-made gestures and values that keep people off or closeted. If a human lives by formula, a formula necessary for survival to be sure, one that was forged in the process of growing and learning, then that person does not live life with animation, but lives a series of banal repetitions. And the goal of psychoanalysis is the antithesis of repetition. We have learned, of course, just calling it that does not negate it.

The comedic moment can occur whenever it is evident that individuals seem to exist as though they could not function as a human being. Where intelligence, creative spirit, or one's sense of one's evident potential is wanting, it is useful if laughter makes its entry. The opposite – in the complaining, the self-pity, the fault however trifling, the fear, the rage – is also true. For therein no laughter has dominion. The point of all this is that the comedic requires us to look at ourselves and each other skeptically. And I believe that is a healthy thing. In our upbringing we had to become what we became. That removes us from one aspect of responsibility. In the present, with a skeptic's eye cast on our lot, we can expand our thinking about our ways of living. But we must assume the responsibility for it, and the risk in doing it.

Playfulness, if authentic, is inherently spontaneous. For the analyst, it clearly is not impulsive. Impulsivity refers to a discharge of an inner force without regard for consequences or social context. Impulsivity is diagnosable when one is swayed immediately by feeling or sudden impulse. Spontaneity, in contrast, refers to a voluntary, unconstrained action without premeditation, but which is wholly in keeping with one's social awareness and relatedness. With impulsivity the focus is on the discharge. With spontaneity the focus is on the lack of planning of action, the freedom to imagine, or to feel, but with an eye on social connection. Playfulness, like any creative gesture, derives from our deepest resources – our vitality, our vivaciousness, our capacity to see different levels of reality at the same time, different meanings and nuances, different feelings in relation to another person, event, or idea. First we risk entertaining the ideas, then we juggle them, and then we order them and integrate them in our minds. The act of playing therefore, helps us integrate ourselves by containing all these things, by combining and communicating them in new ways.

In playfulness we suspend disbelief. We mean what we say, and we do not mean it at all. It is like the writer's playing with words. I mean Shakespeare's punning, the poet's use of alliterations, tropes, metaphors and such, all that word craft that interrupts our complacency and heightens our awareness. Figurative language disregards the literal meaning of words in order to show or imply a relationship between diverse things. It is the same with sound, but we are not so attentive, or even conscious, of the lyricist's playful simplicity (our ears cannot have it otherwise – it must be simple). Here is an example suggesting the poignancy of lonesomeness. One Rodgers and Hart ballad goes like this: 'Spring is here, etc., etc.; Why doesn't the breeze delight me, etc., etc.; Maybe it's because nobody loves me, etc., etc.;' and ends with: 'Spring is here, I hear.' When I was a small child my grandmother would put her two hands on my face, and with her face close to mine, would say, 'Your mother and father are a pair, but you're a peach.' The point of all this is that the playful engagement of the patient points her in an expansive direction.

Here is an example:

A female patient (an expert in the field of pop music) who has been unremittingly depressed and furious for three years, comes in and says angrily, tearfully:

> I need a romance. (*tears, sobs*) I am in so much pain. I'm hopeless. It's all hopeless. I'm dreadful.

The fact is our relationship has not been a 'romance.' In fact, she has been continuously vituperative toward me and denigrating of the analysis. I say something like: 'What do you think your romance needs?'

Still in tears, she says:

'Well, my romance sure doesn't need a castle rising in Spain.' (It is a quote from a 1935 Rodgers and Hart song.) Seriously, I say something like: 'I think it doesn't need a patient writhing in pain either.'

She breaks out laughing and says:

> Gee it's good to come here. I remember for so long I hated your fucking guts. After every session I would think of cutting my wrists, or jumping from a bridge. I just hated life.

Is this playfulness? Did I chance on an intimate language that transcended her interminable self-loathing, so that we shared for one shining moment, something different? That is, did something new, something expansive, facilitate the next issue, which she goes on to describe as, 'What makes anyone attractive to someone else? What can I do about it? And what inhibits me from doing something about it?' And all this is in the context of some attractive fellow choosing her friend instead of her at a party. Did the transference shift to something more safe since I spoke her 'language'?

Maybe!

Perhaps it was just punning on my part, a clever witticism, perhaps a countertransference discharge to relieve my boredom, or a defense against her interminable attacks. Or it actually was some fortunate, adventitious bridge to contact, one which she and I had refused to cross for so long. I would like to think it was the latter. That is, I had listened to her version of her abusive, lonesome, depressed history all these years, and, having digested her dark, ugly biography, was I now saying in effect, 'Enough already, time to let go, time to change, let's get romantic'? And, did I do it in such a way that I encouraged her? Or, did I behave sadistically so that a masochistic self-definition was gratified?

In playfulness we look for and expect fun, we expect to achieve pleasure. It comes out of the clinical effort that went before (Ehrenberg 1990). In the action there is a mutuality in the experience of what is going on, affectively and cognitively. When analysts play analytically they must participate, with the responsibility to monitor themselves, as well as their patients, and what is transpiring between them.

But for this an analyst needs a solid personality structure of his or her own, so that the flood of experiences or fantasies with which he is confronted, do not undermine it (Szalita 1955). It is like a comedian actor, seemingly lost in a double or triple take, but knowing precisely where he is on stage, in his lines, and what cue is imminent. It requires considerable tolerance for the irrational, the unknown, the ambiguous, and the unpredictable in the patient, and similarly the nonrational in the analyst.

Here is another example:

A 57-year-old woman, who has had many years of stormy therapy characterized by near psychotic depressions, eating binges, phobic responses, promiscuity, and inappropriate material indulgence (she does not wear the ten or more fur coats she owns, because, as she says, she does not enjoy wearing them) complains about her explosive, unpredictable husband. He is about twelve years her senior. The incident is typical.

At the start of the session (in a fury) she says:

> That R. is crazy. He's irrational. He's nuts. I sent him to the store for soup greens. And when he comes back there is no dill. So I say there's no dill. I ask him, 'Did you ask for it?' And that crazy man says he's going back and punch the grocer. 'I'll kill that bastard,' he says. I tell him 'You crazy fool, did you ask for dill?' He says no and go drop dead, hit your head against the wall, you know, his usual stuff. I said, 'Do you think the grocer can read minds?' And he stormed out cursing me.

Now I had heard similar episodes like this before. I had nothing to say although I believed something needed to be said.

So I said something like: 'Listen, for my own edification what's soup greens?'

She says (gently, but not patronizingly):

> Well, there's carrots, two, an onion and leeks. We don't eat leeks because they're too dirty, too hard to clean... If you like I'll bring you the leeks in a bag, next time I get soup greens.

At this point I started to think like I used to many years ago:

> Oh boy, now we're getting into analysis. Leeks! What symbolism! And in a bag. Wow! I wondered, was she offering, perhaps insisting on analytic potency? Ah! the leeks are magical nurturance.

Then she said: 'And there's parsley.'

I said: 'What?' (I was probably lost in my enthusiasm for my fantasy of the cliché analyticese.)

She said (singing): 'Parsley, sage, rosemary, and thyme.' She then laughs.

And I said: 'Now that's what Simon says.'

She laughs again (she is no longer in a fury) and we begin to discuss how she believes she often behaves like a fool, or feels like one, or is arrogant, and is never prepared for R.'s rages. She says she never was prepared for the world by her parents while growing up. During early adolescence, for example, she remembers being left in situations by her mother which were literally dangerous, or at best inappropriate. But always she felt too stupid to protest. She says she just froze in fear, and assumed she was inadequate.

Was she 'mothering' me? Was she 'preparing' me the way my mother had not – homologously – the way hers did not? Did my pun, using the composer's name as a double entendre (referring to the children's game), set up the possibility of her associational trend (i.e., the subtext goes: we're all the children of our parents and repetitively imitative of the ways of living we had to learn in growing up)?

I know these two examples end up in balladry, and I suppose my patients tune into my unconscious, as well, if not better, than I do theirs. One of my teachers taught that the patient's unconscious becomes the receptacle of the analyst's theory. He said that Freudian patients have Oedipal dreams and Sullivanian patients have dreams about their self-systems. Mine have dreams of differentiatedness, relevance and self-definition.

Here is another example. It is another attempt at playfulness by me and a patient:

A woman in her early fifties is asked by her son to pick up his mother-in-law on her way home after her session with me. The mother-in-law lives in the Bronx. The session seems to be a desultory, rambling one, with my feeling pretty much out of it, getting a little sleepy and bored. It is only 2:00 p.m. and I had plenty of sleep the night before. So I say something like: 'Are you distressed or tense about something?' (Some analysts automatically assume that the analyst's sleepiness in similar situations is a defensive response to a patient's unexpressed murderous rage directed toward them. I know my own characteristic response under those conditions is some variation of tension. It is not boredom and/or sleepiness. I know I sometimes get drowsy when there is an experience on my part of distance, or no contact, that is, when there is a felt absence. Of course, one might say that in that context the analyst has been killed off or abandoned. But that is metaphoric. Unless an inquiry establishes the reason in the patient for the analyst's defensive somnolent detachment, a lot of guessing can be imputed to a person who hasn't the foggiest notion about his or her own unconscious state. Therefore I opt for the word 'distress,' assuming that an intense, out-of-awareness, untoward feeling – probably extreme anxiety – is preventing contact. I do know it is the absent contact, for whatever reason, to which I am responding.)

She replies: 'As a matter of fact I am.'

And she proceeds to tell me of her son's request.

(I am no longer sleepy.) I say: 'Well, what do you think is frightening about it?'

She says: 'Well, it's the Bronx. God, you know, The Bronx! Some
place way up there off Gunhill Road. 238th Street.'

I believe I made some kind of helpless shrugging gesture, communicating I think, well, you just have to grin and bear it; or, don't do it.

She says reassuringly: 'Well, it is a Jewish neighborhood.'

I say: 'Oh, a Jewish neighborhood? Listen whoever went into a Jewish neighborhood and said, "Watch out there goes an accountant!?"'

She laughs and says: 'Yeah, watch out there goes a medical student.'

Now my one-liner was a quote from the comedian Jackie Mason. I queried her about the reference to the medical student. She insisted it was from Mason's show and began discussing her relationship with her brother, a lawyer; her son, a lawyer; her husband, a shop-keeper, and her feelings about status, her own, especially in comparison to her son's mother-in-law. I thought the medical student reference was an exercise in can-you-top-this! But I was not sure. Mason could have changed the line to get a better laugh.

In another session I used the words 'receptacle' and 'vessel' to describe the way she denied her own ideas, relying as she did on others' opinions. She responded back with: 'Oh yeah, the vessel with the pestle has the pill with the poison.'

And then we chanted in unison: 'And the flagon with the dragon has the brew that is true.'

After the laughter, we discussed her confusion about assertion and aggression. If one experiences oneself as a vessel, information advanced by others, uncritically accepted advice as to feelings, perceptions, and behavior – like the pill in the verse line – may or not be useful. Their poisonous potential lies not in their chemical composition but in the repeated acts of undiscriminating acceptance. Each time a 'pill' is dropped in this way, its presence guarantees an absence of one's own creative activity. Consequently no pattern of learning is established. There is no experience of history save a lot of accumulated events, with the recurrent feeling of being ill prepared, of being empty, and of memorial fluidity. It is this that is the poison.

In the same way a dragon on the surface of a flagon is only an image in ceramic. Its fiery ferociousness is imagistic and illusory since it rests harmlessly in clay. Therefore, the brew that this flagon contains is true. The light verse is a diagnosis of the patient's state, and indicates her way to change (Richman 1996).

We might have achieved this without the playfulness and the two catchy lines. I have no reason to believe otherwise. As it happened, there must have been subtle language interactions in the past that presaged this ostensible intimate way of relating. The shared experiences had evoked feelings that were now so familiar to both of us that only a hint of a cue was enough to set off a meaningful exchange. The abbreviation in the communicative context induces predictability, which can be a test of a shared cultural background, as happens with colloquialisms and humor, and as an indication of mutual openness in therapy as well. It occurs, I believe, when the serious and the playful tenderly touch hands.

To be useful, playful interactions should occur spontaneously. When expressed by the analyst do these gestures imply sensitivity to issues extant in the patient? If so, playfulness and its relaxed, sparkling repartee are respectful of the analytic process. Stylistically there must be good fit; that is there needs to be authenticity for patient, analyst and the technique that serves them.

But there can be miscommunication and, obviously, the move to engage the patient this way may be derivative of countertransferential feeling. It is true that many countertransference reactions are likely to occur during fallow periods, sometimes called resistive. Yet they can function at such times to make contact, and to break into the resistance by surprise (Tauber 1954). What is this surprise about? Surprise, life is not necessarily toxic! Surprise, one can loosen up! Surprise, one can be expansive! Surprise, it is not fatal to feel, think, contemplate, explore, experiment with fantasy, be curious! Surprise, it is not disastrous to be visionary. In fact that reflects the best of humankind. And for the analyst, the surprise, the use of countertransference data, restores hopefulness, an antidote to cynicism. This, I believe, comes about in the free play with, or, in the presence of another who does not intrude. For then the duality of symbol and real can be sustained, their difference suspended. What happens, I think, is that the fear of being known, of being found, of losing one's boundaries through engulfment, and losing one's sanity, is dissipated. I think this is the essential power of playfulness.

The monitoring and processing starts with an analysis of the timing. When and how did it begin? Why especially at this moment? Why not yesterday, or tomorrow? What is experienced by the patient, and analyst, and what is learned? Finally, where does playfulness take us? Where does it lead? Does it open new areas of interest? Is it indulgent, for either analyst or patient, simply a discharge? Or is there a shift in content or style? And is this a genuine useful activity? It is one thing to feel good, another to make feeling good functionally useful. It is all in the inquiry and the self-scrutiny, i.e., all in an interpersonal effort, a radical way of exploring the patient's reality, that is real (Levenson 1989). These are the preeminent issues for us with regard to playfulness. But, of course, it is that way with all analytic data.

Interpersonal psychoanalysis addresses the individual's purposes of the present, the adaptive intentions of the patient and the way his or her expressions affect the analyst, and how these are representative of self-definition. The interpersonalist knows that any one communicative gesture may represent a whole, being a strand in the patterned fabric of communication of self.

In a safe setting, when the analyst sticks to inquiry, showing a 'deliberate' failure to fulfill the patient's wish for clarity, for naming or classifying, swerving when necessary from the patient's intended aim or meaning, the patient is pushed 'to fall back on his or her own resources and begins to arrive at his or her own construction of the world' (Levenson 1994, p.704).

With this idea, Levenson echoed percipiently the doctor in Shakespeare's *Macbeth*, responding to Macbeth's query about his wife, who suffers 'a mind diseased from memory in sorrow.' Macbeth wanted the doctor to 'raze out troubles for the brain… [and] cleanse the bosom.' The doctor replied, presaging today's psychoanalytic wisdom, 'Therein the patient must minister to herself' (Act V, Scene 3, 48). Self-ministering with courage and hope moves the patient, and all evolves to that instant (there is really no precise moment, especially, of recognition) of a qualitative leap, a transformation of a structure into something entirely new. The leap is a leap of faith into a new way of living, a new way of defining oneself, that was previously unknown, and oddly, may still be without the rudder of awareness. But it did not exist before. The experience is somewhat like clinging to the side of a cliff, and, to one's own surprise, screwing up one's courage to let go and fly. Changes in perception lead to changes in conception, and, subsequently, to changes in self-definition.

Like the juxtaposed notes or colors in impressionist music or painting, the pattern of interaction that reaches the ear and eye of experience is created by the proximity, by the influence of the interweaving of the contributions of patient and analyst. In the case example early in this chapter, the con theme threads its way from patient's report of his mother, to analyst, to reader. It becomes interpersonally psychoanalytic when the whole tangled skein of thoughts and feelings is brought into awareness in the session (Levenson 1996). But, the interpersonal psychoanalytic process, with its monitoring of the feelings of the patient and analyst, its special attention to transference and countertransference data, is not simply an accumulation of material in awareness, like an in-gathering or an additive process. Mutual involvement in a collaborative effort, the opening of oneself to another, produces mutual impact.

Expanding on an early contribution about mutual analysis by Ferenczi (1985), i.e., by patient and analyst simultaneously, Franklin (1994) cogently points out that serious impediments to the therapeutic process often stem from therapists' difficulty in recognizing entrenched problems in their own personality. They arise during the therapeutic interaction. These are not the common garden variety of assumed countertransference responses that intrude regularly in the engagement, that are usually eliminated with awareness, but more fundamental difficulties that require change or, at minimum, some sensitivity as to their limiting influence. It is what Freud (1910) meant by the comment that the analyst goes 'no further than his own complexes and resistances permit...that he shall begin his practice with a self-analysis and continually carry it deeper while he is making his own observations on his patient' (p.145). Franklin's (1994) point is that during any psychoanalysis the analyst can develop a 'companion self' that can be depended on as a loyal, understanding, compassionate friend, regardless of what emerges from within. In fact, sometimes, during interpersonal therapy, the patient turns out to be the most useful agent for the analyst's self-understanding (Ferenczi 1985; Franklin 1994; Searles 1975; Singer 1971).

With the interpersonalist's willingness to inquire, the moment anything occurs, that is, to comment, and call attention to the process itself, with an emphasis on the analyst's intervention and how it is received, so that the analyst and patient can examine their connectedness in all its facets. They then take their rightful places among the 'crooked timber of humanity.' This phrase is the title of a collection of essays by Isaiah Berlin. Berlin took it from his preferred rendering of a favorite quotation from Kant: 'Out of the crooked timber of humanity no straight thing was ever made' (Berlin 1992, p.vii). I note it here to emphasize the interpersonal psychoanalytic focus on the patient's and analyst's particularity.

The interpersonal psychoanalytic proceeding is an authentic enactment, in contrast to the patient's lifelong experience with tangentialisms and to feeling dismissed and irrelevant, upon which his characteristic self-definition is erected. It is the mutuality in interpersonal psychoanalysis that makes a new structure possible.

References

Berlin, I. (1979) "The hedgehog and the fox." In *Russian Thinkers.* New York: Pelican. First published as "Lev Tolstoy's skepticism." In *Oxford Slavonic Papers* 2 (1951). Reprinted under its present title, New York: Simon and Schuster (1953).

Berlin, I. (1992) *The Crooked Timber of Humanity.* New York: Vintage.

Ehrenberg, D. (1990) "Playfulness in the psychoanalytic relationship." *Contemporary Psychoanalysis 26,* 74–95.

Feiner, A. (1970) "Toward an understanding of the experience of inauthenticity." *Contemporary Psychoanalysis 7,* 64–83.

Feiner, A. (1988) "Countertransference and misreading." *Contemporary Psychoanalysis 24,* 612–649.

Ferenczi, S. (1955) "Confusion of tongues between adults and the child." In *The Problems and Methods of Psychoanalysis,* vol. 3. New York: Basic Books.

Ferenczi, S. (1985) *The Clinical Diary of Sandor Ferenczi,* ed. J. Dupont. Cambridge, MA: Harvard University Press.

Franklin, G. (1994) "Dual therapy: personality change in the therapist while working with patients." *Israel Journal of Psychiatry 31,* 86–93.

Freud, S. (1905) "Jokes and their relationship to the unconscious." *Standard Edition 8,* 9–236. London: Hogarth Press.

Freud, S. (1910) "The future prospects of psycho-analytic therapy." *Standard Edition 11,* 139–151. London: Hogarth Press.

Freud, S. (1937) "Analysis terminable and interminable." *Standard Edition 23,* 216–253. London: Hogarth Press.

Hart, L. (1986 [1941]) "Bewitched, bothered and bewildered." In *The Complete Lyrics of Lorenz Hart.* New York: Alfred A. Knopf.

Kermode, F. (1989) "Freud and interpretation." In *An Appetite for Poetry.* Cambridge, MA: Harvard University Press. Also in *International Review of Psycho-Analysis 12,* 3–12 (1985).

Laing, R. (1961) *The Self and Others.* London: Tavistock.

Laing, R. (1965) "Mystification, confusion, and conflict." In I. Boszormeny-Nagy and J.L. Framo (eds) *Intensive Family Therapy.* New York: Harper & Row.

Laing, R. (1967) *The Politics of Experience.* New York: Pantheon.

Langs, R. (1995) *Clinical Practice and the Architecture of the Mind.* London: Karnac.

Levenson, E. (1972) *The Fallacy of Understanding.* New York: Basic Books.

Levenson, E. (1974) "Changing concepts of intimacy in psychoanalytic practice." *Contemporary Psychoanalysis 10,* 359–369.

Levenson, E. (1989) "Whatever happened to the cat?" *Contemporary Psychoanalysis 25,* 537–553.

Levenson, E. (1991a) "Back to the future." *Contemporary Psychoanalytic Review 6,* 27–43.

Levenson, E. (1994) "Beyond countertransference." *Contemporary Psychoanalysis 30,* 691–707.

Levenson, E. (1996) "Aspects of self-revelation and self-disclosure." *Contemporary Psychoanalysis 32*, 237–248.

Richman, J. (1996) "Jokes as a projective technique." *American Journal of Psychotherapy 50*, 336–346.

Schimel, J. (1975) "The function of wit and humor in psychoanalysis." *Journal of the American Academy of Psychoanalysis 6*, 369–379.

Searles, H. (1965) "The effort to drive the other person crazy." In *Collected Papers on Schizophrenia Related Subjects.* New York: International Universities Press.

Searles, H. (1975) "The patient as therapist to his analyst." In P. Giovacchini (ed) *Tactics and Techniques in Psychoanalytic Therapy* Vol. 2. New York: Jason Aronson.

Singer, E. (1971) "The patient aids the analyst." In B. Landis and E. Tauber (eds) *In the Name of Life: Essays in Honor of Erich Fromm.* New York: Holt, Rinehart and Winston.

Strachey, J. (1934) "The nature of the therapeutic action of psychoanalysis." *International Journal of Psycho-Analysis 15*, 117–126.

Sullivan, H. (1964 [1950]) "The illusion of personal individuality." *Psychiatry 13*, 317–332 (1950). Also in *The Fusion of Psychiatry and Social Sciences.* New York: W.W. Norton (1964).

Sullivan, H. (1954) *The Psychiatric Interview.* New York: W.W. Norton.

Sypher, W. (1956) "Introduction to comedy." In *An Essay on Comedy by George Meredith, and Laughter by Henri Bergson.* New York: Doubleday.

Szalita, A.B. (1955) "The 'intuitive process' and its relation to work with schizophrenics." *Journal of the American Psychoanalytic Association 111*, 7–18.

Tauber, E. (1954) "Exploring the use of countertransference data." *Psychiatry 17*, 331–336.

Notes

1 This is the title of a song by R. Rodgers and L. Hart, from their production *Pal Joey* (1941). It is sung by the female lead expressing, in most of the lyric, hopeless, helpless love for a con artist. Similarly, it is the feeling a child has for a conning or mystifying parent, the victim experiencing a double-binding humiliation, loving the parent, which permits the interaction, and continuing the love in bewilderment and anger. Conning is a deliberate bamboozling. One is fooled, bewitched. Befuddling and bewilderment occur as the result of a behavioral gesture that carries with it the anxiety of the mystifier. The felt experience of mystification is almost a by-product of the other's self-deception. It is conditioned by the context of dismissiveness and irrelevance.

2 T.S. Eliot's 'still point' in *Four Quartets* (in which the spiritual struggle of the poem echoes the poet's spiritual struggle in his life) is an absolute epiphany, a reverberation of an incarnation to which everything returns – the Crucifixion. I have borrowed the sense of the 'pure' or 'nakedness' about it, which is the antithesis of mystification. That is, the expression of the right words in a relationship is the same as the pursuit of the actual feelings. Things are what they are, and what they appear to be without anxiety.

3 These extensive quotes are a reconstructed narrative of the contents of many sessions. They are printed with permission, after revisions of the patient's typescript (requested by the analyst) to assure privacy and continuity.

Chapter 2

Out of Our Minds

In a seminar, a long time ago, a student, echoing Freud's remark about the 'impossible profession,' said that we were out of our minds practicing it. I thought it was an apt double entendre capturing our praxis and our feeling.

There is a delightful, charming anecdote in the physics Nobel prize-winner Richard Feynman's (1988) collection of reminiscences that instructs us how science functions, in part. It is about Feynman's father who pointed out that calling a bird a Spencer's warbler in English, a *chutto lapittida* in Italian, a *chung-long-tah* in Chinese, or a *katano takedo* in Japanese, adds nothing to our scientific knowledge about the bird. All we learn is what humans in different places call it. If we want to know something about the Spencer's warbler we have to scrutinize it and observe what it is doing (Feynman 1988, pp.13–14).

Naming or labeling should rightfully establish a relationship between us and that which is named. If it does not it cannot lead to knowledge. At the heart of interpersonal psychoanalysis lies its observing function, exercised in the metaphor of the observed. This is neither reductionistic to, nor substitutive with, the metaphors of a metapsychology external to the observed phenomena. In fact, simply naming may lead to misunderstanding. For example, an attribution based on the self-indulgent conceit that we know what the other feels can result in miscategorizing and distancing. Assuming we know what anyone feels can be an egregious kind of inauthentic communication (Feiner 1970). This would be antithetical to the aim of psychoanalytic interaction. Of course, there are certain moments or settings, such as in the operating room, or sailing, when proper naming is vital about communication so as to facilitate movement or prevent disaster, but it does not add to knowledge.

Sullivan put it properly when he wrote that the individual is the 'entity we infer so as to explain interpersonal events and relations' (Sullivan 1964, p.33). Interpersonal refers to participation, not sequential utterances and gestures. A good, perhaps precious, description might be the choreography of the dyad.

The bifurcation of psychoanalytic knowledge into clinical praxis and a theory of man, or a metapsychology, derives from an all-too convenient illusion that theory represents congruence with knowledge. We often talk among ourselves as if theory were knowledge itself. It is not, regardless of the way it is organized or the school of thinking that it represents. It is metaphor or, more often, myth. This is not to say that theory or metaphor are not useful in helping us organize our thinking, our relatedness to patients, but too often we assume it represents ultimate truth, and as a consequence, the patient gets lost.

The word theory comes from the Greek *theoria* which means 'viewing.' If theory is little more than metaphoric thought, that is, a way of looking at observable data, it cannot be knowledge of how the world actually is, how people function with each other. It is steps removed. We are appropriately humbled by the fact that just like our patients we tend to assume that the contents of our thinking is an accurate, realistic, fundamental description of the world as it is. Despite that incautious assumption, the actual lawfulness of the world tends to inhibit us from learning about it and how it operates with ever increasing, ultimate accuracy. No matter how perfectly tuned our instruments of observation become, there seems to be an irreducible uncertainty in our simultaneous measurement of properties. Our active observation produces an inevitable and indeterminable change in structure and relationships (Heisenberg 1927, Letter to Pauli quoted by Pais 1991). This notion is directly applicable to an appreciation of the interpersonal position since it implies that the act of measuring or describing the data changes the data in some way, so that the presence of the observer has some impact that must be accounted for.

This idea of indeterminacy seems to negate our inherited, nineteenth-century, Cartesian image of what we do: an objective observer separated and quite distinct from an observed object, with the observer-analyst knowing the truth about the observed-patient. One theory of patients' experience may be more appealingly comprehensive than another, but that does not mean it is more fundamental. This would explain why there is value in having different formulations of the same human phenomenon, because different versions bring to mind different mental pictures, and thus help us make discoveries. As Nils Bohr put it, in quantum theory, particle and wave behavior are mutually exclusive, yet both are necessary for a complete description of all phenomena (quoted in Pais 1991, p.23).

I do not mean this as sophomoric jousting. I do mean that patient and colleague amendments and suggestions can have something to do with the enhancement and expansion of the process, if we are not threatened and our minds are not clouded by feelings of unsafety. It could be that this is one reason why everybody in all psychoanalytic schools of thinking has success, and all have failures. I believe our failures should be studied by more than one pair of eyes or ears.

A lot of writing in our profession is sort of like, 'Here's how I do it.' It is not designed to let you in. There are many reasons for this, positive and negative. Positively, there is our desire to teach and pass on the keys to the inherent difficulties, and ubiquitous limitations in analytic work. There is also the legitimately earned felt experience of euphoria over effecting change. It is a good feeling to work past a barrier. But a lot of 'Here's how I do it' papers seem only to beg praise, rarely conveying discovery. I respect the difficulties and the achievements, but I think a lot of the writing is self-serving at best, or self-aggrandizing at worst. Some of it naively refers to the ground of therapy not its figure, the kind of stuff that lets it happen: warmth, acceptance, establishing safety, curiosity, associating, remembering. Or it tells of seemingly one-session cures. The analyst reports that he told the patient he does not like to be shouted at, whereupon the patient tearfully has what is called 'many painful associations or memories.' That 'painfulness' has now been injected into the analytic exchange somehow is ignored. Sometimes some of it is shamelessly like the rediscovery of the wheel. A new label is assigned and it is assumed the verbal newness is a discovery. Or, some of it is about the patient's alleged insides, with the analyst's presence or influence nowhere in sight, certainly not acknowledged.

My problem with this is that I just do not learn from someone else's success, except in some general way. Success surely shows how clever one is for having worked something out. I believe we should also notice how clever or creative patients are in their search for safety, and their claims for relevance, or notice the simplicity of it all, and therefore, the great beauty of the lawfulness of integration, or defensiveness. Perhaps wonder is a more appropriate word since some defensiveness is revolting. The variety, application, and compass, as well as the internal coherence of people's defensiveness, represents an amazing energetic display.

Maybe I am just stubborn and dense. Reminding each other of our success supports our hope, and suppresses our cynicism, which is fine, but I do not think it is enough. Ultimately, learning must be internalized, not imitative. Imitation is actually the beginning of learning. We should build on that until we integrate it so it is part of ourselves. That is why I think analysts can learn mostly from their errors, especially about themselves and their technique, as artists do (Feiner 1991a; Levenson 1992).

One of the more useful interactions of interpersonal analysis is patient rectification (Langs 1981). The patient's sensitivity to our errors can be used to supervise ourselves by our recognizing to what our patients are actually responding. It is also an opportunity for the therapist to function non-dismissively.

There is a value in learning what stopped the flow of the process so we can get it moving again.

That is why I think that if we reverse the conventional wisdom about theory before practice we shall be in a more secure position to understand better what people do around us. From practice, with all its imperfections, we might be able to derive that kind of theory which would open us to a greater comprehension of human behavior. It could be that Freud (1910) and the rest of us have been asking the wrong question. Better stated, we have been asking the right question, but we have been thinking of it backwards (Witenberg 1993). We might try thinking of technique, not as a logical extension of theory, but rather the other way around. In this way, we could address the commonalties of therapeutic interaction, from an interpersonal point of view, since 'interpersonal' is the single shared defining characteristic of all psychoanalytic therapy, regardless of school, assumptions, or loyalties. In the consulting room, all analysts, whether they describe it this way or not, function in an 'interpersonal' way. It is in their interpersonal engagement that human beings show themselves with such remarkable consistency and tenacity. The data of that interpersonal field, in which personality is made manifest, and which is made up of two or more people, 'all but one of whom may be more or less completely illusory' (Sullivan 1964, p.33), are from what we might derive more viable analytic theory (especially of therapeutic change) and finally bring it into conformity with modern science in general, and neural science in particular.

We could even speculate that theories of technique of psychoanalytic practice may be no different than metapsycholological theories, but at least they have a firmer grounding in observable operations between human beings (Klein 1976), rather than metaphoric fantasy.

With this in mind it is possible to keep our focus on the interpersonal field, namely the interpenetrating of forces that engage in the contact-presence of the analyst together with the individual-in-treatment. In fact, I believe it is necessary to do this, as it is useful to be alert to one's own assumptions, and spell out one's own experience. Since interaction does effect changes in feeling, and, ultimately, behavior, knowing our assumptions, even if articulated naively but honestly and clearly to ourselves, must influence the shape of our inquiry. Obviously ideology never vacates inquiry. And inquiry is not about the what but about the how, the description of events, not their meaning. Furthermore, it is the inquiring itself that is a force for change, not necessarily its rhetoric, since inquiry is selective and interpretive in its own way, avoiding what the father of Professor Feynman warned against, and it is a collaborative process.

Now this interactive idea raises what looks like a curious, unresolvable contradiction. Does not the suggestion that the analyst go where the patient is and keep looking (Havens 1974) imply two separate, ontologically distinct, heterogeneous individuals? And does not my variation of the interpersonal position insist on holistic interpenetrating, each party affecting the other? If the interaction is seen as a class of events of which the patient is only an example (Levenson 1982), it does not fix into oneness the identities of the two parts, analyst and patient. The 'whole,' the 'oneness' is the focus of processes – temporarily. To go where the patient is, is to choose to go, and in the process of reaching the patient, both analyst and patient are influenced and changed. One could claim that even the assertion of the analyst's choosing has been influenced by the other. From the point of view of the systemic process that is true. From the point of view of stage, however, someone initiating an inquiry is another matter. It is a contradiction that has no resolution. Following Bohr's concept of complimentarity, a full description of the phenomena necessitates both perspectives.

At the heart of all things in human living, all our felt reality, there are inescapable opposites or contradictions. I had a supervisor once who told me that despite whatever we observe on the surface there is underneath the exact opposite. It was sort of like scratch a saint and you will find a devil. I believed my revered teacher was right, but the notion troubled me until I added the notions of anxiety, safety and context. It seemed to me that the prescription was too mechanistic for me to do anything with it, that is, for me to respond to the patient in some viable, constructive way. Once I introduced the idea of anxiety, or better, the search for safety, in keeping with self-definition, I could ask myself a different question. This is: What would the patient be doing were he or she not anxious or phobic, or he or she not in a search of safety in the particular way I was observing as part of our relationship? What was the necessity for what was observed on the surface? How did that come about, and under what conditions could it be abated?

Engels (1954) played with this ancient idea about contradiction (it derives from Heraclitus) in the middle of the nineteenth century. He called it the 'unity of opposites.' The process of change, Engels insisted, can be described as the 'negation of the negation.' To effect change in human behavior, for example, the negation of closeness, i.e., distance, is to seek paradox. How can 'distancing' negate 'distance' so as to achieve the closeness desired by two people, that has been negated by 'distancing?' It is a most tricky tango. Niels Bohr called it 'complimentarity' in the 1920s, and demonstrated its validity in quantum theory. Bohr came to the conclusion that there is no ultimate truth. Since we cannot know the meaning of an essence, to describe experience, he called for clarity of expression, and the need for the unambiguous use of words. His was a search for what is going on (Pais 1991, pp.445–446).

What are the data of psychoanalysis, and how does the interpersonalist see them? How does data come about? Is the reportage of events (e.g., 'I made love with Hepzibah' or, 'So I asked my husband what exactly did you say to your son?', the equivalent of analytic data, or does something have to be done with it to make it data? To reportage, the analyst can only listen. It is what the patient wants to talk about. Analytic data come about via the inquiry and are a vector function of the interaction of the reportage and the inquiring of the analyst (Levenson 1981).

In an inquiry there can be no tacit agreement as to understanding. When a patient says, 'I became involved with Frank, but did not like him that much,' I want to know what the words mean, and in what way. And, what does 'but' signify in that sentence? In other words, I want to know what I am supposed to hear. The point is that analysts should know why they are in the room. I wonder why I am being told this anecdote or that complaint, on this particular day (why not last week?). Do I understand what is being said, and to what purpose? This idea has as many variations as there are disciplines. The principle in psychoanalysis is 'function before content'; in architecture it is 'form follows function'; in philosophy it is 'existence before essence.' The conscious or unconscious assumption on the part of analysts that they know what the patient experiences better than the patient, seems to me to be a repetition of the original dismissal in the patient's history.

It is not always immediately clear what motivates behavior. Someone could receive the Medal of Honor because they are suicidal; or stupid; or grandiose; or lucky; or opportunistic in that they were in the wrong place at the right time; or because they were courageous. Often we really do not know why they, or, more likely, their widow or widower was awarded the medal. Obviously, context determines meaning.

Analytic work may be seen as problem solving, although I like to think it is useful to see the patient's difficulties as puzzling instead of problematic. I prefer that analytic work be transformational in the sense that it is hoped some move is made from a change in perception to a change in conception and, subsequently, to self-definition. These probably go on at the same time, and the differences are barely perceptible.

There is nothing new about the idea of transformation versus reformation. Reform goes by other names such as adaptation, adjustment, negotiation and the like. In a negative sense, it is agreeing with analysts' prejudices because of their persuasiveness.

The influence on my own training by Erich Fromm was that analysis was indeed radical, perhaps even revolutionary. To call itself analysis, the work should be more than the analysis of resistance and transference. Those were givens following Freud's definition. I learned that it should also aim toward some transformational aspect of a person's view of himself and the world around. It means a transformation in self-definition.

Sullivan, working with extremely disturbed people, sometimes used the phrase 'going concern' to describe a hoped-for goal. His rhetoric reflected Depression era socio-economics. Fromm's emphasis was different. He did not eschew functioning, but he did search for transformation – and authenticity. This comes about, not by the exchange of correct metaphors, persuasion, or education, but via an ultimate interchange, rendering analyst and patient accessible in union (Feiner 1991b). I have suggested (along with others) that it happens with an analysis of the verbal exchange itself (Feiner 1970; Laing, Phillipson and Lee 1966; Levenson 1972). The setting is contact, the implicit goal is union (Dr. Fromm's word), with analysis being the continuous analysis of the analysis. Union or intimacy is not a state of grace, just a way of relating (Levenson 1974). It is like stepping with the patient into a reverse, ever-expanding and widening funnel during the inquiring, and wondering about fantasy and feelings. And then, inquiring about the feeling about inquiring about the feeling. (What is it like talking about how you felt about this with me?)

I assume that were we to view ourselves through a so-called interpersonal lens we would see each other struggling with the following issues.

I think there is a biological, evolutionary basis for interactive, interpersonal existence: from an exchange of protein between protozoa; then up the phylogenetic scale to an exchange of tissue; to primate back-scratching; and ultimately to the exchange of experience and communication of feelings between humans. In essence, always interactive or interpersonal, this contact is coincident with organizing and maintaining communal life. In the analytic setting we observe the pressure to make contact as a desire for union. Union is seen as an overarching principle of existence that includes an awareness of separateness or differentiatedness without isolation or insularity and connectedness without intrusion, fusion, or engulfment. A union requires reliable, optimal boundaries, with mutual agreement that in the context of union there will be no ostracizing, no exile, no abandonment; no intrusion or invasion. There is agreement to disagree. But most important, even in momentary disagreement, there will be relevance and non-dismissiveness (Feiner 1991a). Without the framework of union and relevance there can be no intimate way of relating. Studies of monkeys and couples seem to indicate that without contact, without affiliation, immune systems are weakened. The quality of the contact is of significance, not only in terms of the experience of the lowering of stress, or an increase in tension or anxiety, but also that the contact meets the specific needs of each party.

For psychoanalysis, I believe the exaggerated, mechanistic emphasis on the unique, independent self has been misplaced. I do not mean to lessen the value of selfhood, but it seems to me that the image of selfhood without contact, without union, reflects an empty, reified, isolated, and consequently meaningless, dislocated experience. Another way of saying it is that the particularity of individuals can only be discovered, and expanded within the located framework of a relationship. An intimate way of relating is precisely the instrument to accomplish this. And the rooting of a person in a relationship surely prevents the disabling terror of dislocation, of not belonging, of even evaporating.

I had a patient once who complained that I was afraid of her dependence on me. My response was to analyze the dependency. I had thought that my having the lap of a good daddy in place of the original bad one she had described angrily, was what I believed her words indicated she wanted. I did not think it was necessarily in the best interest of her 'analysis.' I think now that she was right, but for the wrong reason, and her rightness should not have been dismissed by me. Her need to belong was being frustrated, not because of my fear, but because of my ignorance. I could not get to that failing in myself, and all its implications, because I had failed to comprehend her implicit fear of being without rootedness, location or place (the Greeks called it *nostos*) – that she felt she was always in danger of dissipating like fog, was veritably impactless, and was always faced with the threat of loneliness. She needed the grounding, the cohesiveness, the belonging to place. What she had taken as my fear was really my obtuseness, that I and she may have been afraid to face. Had that been discussed openly, the rest could be analyzed. Had I asked simply and with clarity what I had said or done in session that evoked the bad feelings in her, I might not have failed her.

Sullivan's (1953) 'good-me,' 'bad-me,' 'not-me,' his tripartite conception of the personifications of the self and its integration in a system that provides satisfaction and security, is good as far as it goes in self-definition. The 'good-me' refers to the personification, or the organization of the self, that learns to organize interactions so that satisfactions are enhanced by the felt experience of tenderness. It is like those that come to the infant because the mothering one is pleased and expresses, therefore, her pleasure with the infant. It leaves one with the feeling of having been approved and of being of some worth.

The 'bad-me' personification is based historically on an induction of an increasing gradient of anxiety, the result of disapproval (perhaps misinterpreted) of the infant's behavior.

The 'not-me' personification comes about gradually as the result of persistent, severe experiences with anxiety. It is made up of poorly grasped aspects of living, usually regarded as dreadful, and later in life is connected to feelings of awe, horror, loathing, and dread. It is experienced in nightmares, and states of severe disturbance.

Some time before this book was contemplated I began thinking about an anti-self personification (Feiner 1991a). I think there is a marked difference between the idea that one is bad because one has transgressed, and the idea that one is worthless or not relevant, and without impact. I believe this anti-self notion could be added to the interpersonal system, with all its nuances. I see the anti-self as a fundamental, personal conviction that some humans develop, following extreme, extended experiences of being made to feel non-relevant and having one's desires or thoughts dismissed. That includes one's inherent needs, one's feelings, one's values, and one's ideas. One is treated as though one does not have a right to any of these. One takes on a self-definition of irrelevance, of not mattering. The commanding force of the self-definition is similar to that of being right-handed or blue-eyed. Interpersonal relationships as a consequence, become burdened with, and characterized by it. Since a structural self-definition is laid down early in life, no matter how many times there may be encouragement and/or success in the present, it is doubtful whether one can change this basic conviction about one's self without a lot of analytic work.

I do not think people change any internal organization by virtue of reassuring reminders of day-to-day successes or an exchange of words about role models. Reminding a young boy with a graffiti spray can that he too can be like Denzel Washington, Michael Jordan, or Frederick C. Douglass matters little. Recall how it felt like being compared to one's parent's favorite nephew. The presentation of role models is actually a reminder of failure. That one could be like Booker T. Washington is probably a lie. The encouragement does not address one's feeling and self-definition. It is more likely heard as deceitful criticism. It is like persuasive lectures. They tickle but do not transform. In fact, in the anti-self schema all learning becomes a stimulus for a reminder of accountability and responsibility, and therefore new opportunities for the emergence of an anti-self feeling.

Accolades are rarely treated realistically. They are seen grandiosely or it is believed others do not mean it. It is all sham one way or the other – e.g., about compliments, a patient replies to the analyst, 'They are all dopes.' One is left with the unsteady, stressful question about what one could possibly do for an encore since one got away with it this time. A cumulative, successful self cannot be effective in changing self-definition, since the anti-self self-definition negates patterning and the integration of experience. All experience therefore, remains discrete, and compartmentalized. The good feeling of success is only in the moment. New learning, the analytic process itself, carries a burden of proof, since patients are always confronted with their dismissible self since that is who they are (I emphasize it is not just what they feel like). Patients are these worthless creatures, the idea of which they see as part of them, like anatomy, and they are totally convinced that they must demonstrate otherwise, but cannot. To learn anything in an anti-self system cannot be an achievement, only a humiliating reminder that one did not know it beforehand. The anti-self definition gets in the way of any celebration of learning or discovery, the celebration of intimate contact with either materials or people, or even one's self.

Analysts also show this in their all too often collapse before the rectification or rageful critiques of certain patients. I do not mean this in an absolute sense, but some analysts struggle with a touch of the hidden anti-self when the patient expresses criticism, dissatisfaction, or especially hatred and suspiciousness, e.g., that the analyst is interested only in the possibly exploitative nature of the relationship: the fee, the time, or the analyst's self-serving status. To the patient, one is not being taken seriously, or, better put, one's seriousness has been dismissed. In all of us there have been moments when we were brushed with the hurt of non-relevance. So the analyst is faced with the probable, horrifying truth in his own mind that he may be a bad analyst, or, indeed, a faker (Epstein 1982). But the patient is offering mutual diagnoses and, oddly, mutual therapy. Notice me, treat me relevantly and we shall both be better for it. It sounds sweet and simple. When 'Notice me!' is communicated in an actively angry, destructive mode, it is extremely difficult to respond constructively, and analysts' denials as to their imperfections further exacerbate the patients' not trusting their own perceptions.

A person saddled with this kind of self-conviction because of personal history is endlessly in doubt, and tediously available to humiliation and shame, as well as feeling suspicious. Thus, in some way, people also feel that they deserve what they get. With some people their own dismissive attitudes and behavior are precisely expressed to evoke this feeling in others. But counter-hate, counter-assertion – by themselves – miss the point. They are really counter-dismissal. What is required is the converse – negation of non-relevance and dismissiveness, not 'You're doing this to me,' or even sophisticated interpretations that cut into the patients and direct them away from what they consider the validity of their feeling, only to experience a current dismissal.

This is not simply a self-centered, self-approving, self-feeding operation, neither for analyst nor patient. To effect change in an anti-self system requires the dignity of broader contact, that includes safety and the freedom to express all feelings and the right to be noticed, to be taken seriously. And this need to be noticed is one way of experiencing and expressing non-dismissiveness. In fact, it is dismissal's opposite. I think the sense of dismissal accounts for so much angry aggression in some patients. I believe that the anger that is expressed not only serves the purpose of guarding against some feeling of dislocation or not belonging, or even disorganization, but also is a kind of pseudo-self-therapy, the message of which is, 'I will not be dismissed, I will be noticed! I will have impact, even if I have to exploit your system, or punch you in the nose, or urinate or scribble graffiti all over your walls.'

Anger itself can be toxic, and in some quantities leads to one's being overwhelmed and isolated by the feelings themselves. But the expression of anger has this self-therapeutic value. Therefore, I think, an analyst might use the idea of the expression of anger judiciously. Patients, for example, may be signaling their desire for some sort of authentic affective response from the analyst. I think a lot of patients' critiques and corrections and suggestions have to do with an attempt at making the analyst and the analysis relevant. Patients also may be trying to find out, albeit in primitive ways, whether one is a self, in a relationship.

In contrast, we are all familiar with the feeling we have when the student or the patient (especially the student) comments that we have been helpful. That feeling is a good one. I do not think it has to do with the specifics of help, since sometimes we have not the vaguest notion how we have been that way. Nor does it have to do with our need for applause. But we do get a glow, an internal one that indicates that we have been told that we have been relevant.

Many of our convictions are expressed in words rather than in authentic enactment. We say things to patients, but alas, they are only words. Even though they are correct they lack authenticity. When I was an intern at a veterans' hospital many, many years ago, I once tried to convince a paranoid fellow that the antennae of the doctors' cars, which he saw arriving in the mornings, were not tuned to his thoughts, as he had insisted, because the doctors had other interests, other lives. I was hot for the self and differentiatedness in those days. In some insensitive, pseudo-sophisticated way I added that I did not think he was that important to them anyway. This was true – an idea I had borrowed from John Rosen, someone with whom I had brief contact at that time. I think now that while correct it was invalid and terribly hurtful in its pointlessness. It is true he was not that important to them, but it is also true that his delusion expressed his ambivalent desire that he be noticed by them, or anyone – I suppose me – something of which I was unaware or afraid. My ignorance was fueled by the self-evident fact that I was 'seeing' him every day for 'psychotherapy.' Since I knew so little, I reasoned, how could he believe I was actually tuned in on him the way he insisted? But my patient's metaphoric expression of his feeling would be in keeping with his desire to be and feel relevant. And so my violent patient Anthony, who may have had to be afraid of what he wanted so desperately, simply said, out of his own internal wisdom, and sensitive awareness of my fears and naive limitations – he said it, as I recall, with a Robert De Niro grin in an affectionate, tender way – 'You say that doc; you say that.' (I now think he was saying, also, 'You say that, but I know you really are interested in me.') One can see how authorities sometimes cavalierly throw the difficult and innocent ones to the lowliest and ignorant ones. I doubt my assignment was inspirational. More likely it was attempt to get rid of two annoyances, the patient and me.

My next point is that I think the interpersonal situation is essentially dialogic and dialectical. By this I mean that an interpersonal analytic situation, to be genuinely interpersonal, is not an additive process in which one says something to another and the other says something in response. If that were the case, patients would do much better were they to read the good books, or go to appropriate lectures, or hire smart tutors. The nature of the relationship is the therapeutic experience, and it is a four-part exchange. It is what happened with my patient Anthony. The patient presents a positive yes, and a negative yes; and a positive no, and a negative no, with regard to his or her desire, intention, or experience. It is not simply that positive and/or negative elements ought to be scrutinized, it is that positive elements of contact, as well as negative, and positive elements of distancing, as well as negative, should be as well. To my mind it is the thrust of the therapy to facilitate moving the exchange to a different, higher level of organization.

The crucial issues of union and the quality of contact within union serve as an umbrella for everything else. But this does not mean that the analyst thinks of that only and/or always. In fact, it is too abstract. It does mean that his or her dialectical inquiry should be in keeping with a genuine dialogic attitude. Ultimately, this has to do also with the interpenetrating of the two – the patient and the analyst, an interpenetrating that accounts for the influence of the analyst on the patient's response and, of course, vice versa (Feiner 1991a).

There seems to be some mythology around the idea that if analysts maintain silence and anonymity, and are receptive, they will get pure ore from the patient. But there is silence itself; the analysts' implicit attitude in greeting, for example: their expression; their furniture; the color of their clothing; the look in their eyes; the tone of their voice; all of which must have some communicative, influencing effect on the patient's response. A dialogue is not simply sequential utterances: A. says something, B. says something. A dialogue is an attending to the relevance, if not the position, the history, the subculture, the reality of the other and the way the analyst is being used. It is not that patronizing, perspective business, that quickly dispenses with the patient's point of view, with, 'Oh yes, I can see how you might think I did not care, but really I do care'; and explicitly goes on to an interpretation of the patient's fantasy: 'You must be repeating something here.' I would probably say something like, 'You're right I forgot, and in that I dismissed you, and I'm sorry. I shouldn't. What did you feel…? What did you think…? What's it like to have an analyst who…?' A way of relating in the family setting of realistic dependency initiated the difficulties a patient endures in the first place. An intimate way of relating that would be safe and gratifying, the setting that he or she ambivalently strives for, is needed to facilitate the change that is necessary.

If one's difficulties were engendered by dismissal, an experience of non-dismissal may relieve them – not words about it.

I believe people struggle with contradictions, as I have observed them in therapy, and they struggle with them for one purpose only, and that is the purpose of survival in some learned, organized way. One could easily replace the nouns that I use to label what I perceive as struggles so as to organize. Others would do just as well. Contradictions are distinct from contraries. Contradictions make for tensions, but both elements are tenable in their unity. They are neither compromised nor balanced. Contraries are antagonistic, and are designed to eliminate each other.

One of these fundamental contradictions is about compassion and standards. This is really an arbitrary label. I could just as easily have used thought and feeling, separation and connection. The Greeks and Shakespeare and Herman Melville and Freud, and many others, wrote about it. Our compassion routinely comes into conflict with the rules and standards by which we live. The reason why I think it fundamental is that the resolution, transient and otherwise, of this contradiction goes into the formation of the self-definition that the patient brings to psychoanalysis.

It is true that we live with our best foot forward, especially in the transferential aspects of psychoanalytic therapy. By this I mean we do as we must in terms of our self-definition, so as to make any relationship work, so as to survive (Feiner 1983). One thing I have had a lot of difficulty with is the idea that some patients try to destroy the therapy. This conclusion on the part of therapists is based on their correct awareness that patients fear change, and recreate the past in the present. The leap from these valid observations to a conclusion about motivated, deliberate destructiveness results in adversarialness. It ignores the patient's need to re-do the past (in fact, what else can the patient do?) for the purpose of mastery (or curing it), and to lower the tension level around a threat to the survival of a self-definition that has worked in some way thus far. If we look at what is going on from the point of view of stage, there is a truth in the conclusion. But from the point of view of the growth process, the patient is struggling to change and maintain safety, at the same time. The same obtains for the analyst. Do we not want to maintain our own safety? And does that not inhibit us from looking, sharing, experiencing, exploring?

Living with our best foot forward also means that historically we continuously make choices for which we are accountable. We are made by, and make, the influences around us. We are influenced, and selectively engage the influence. We are actors in our own evolution. These choices can be explained in terms of the past (sometimes we do this to bypass accountability), as well as in terms of the present. The analyst can try to 'understand,' but ultimately the patient is responsible and accountable despite any compassionate framework of understanding.

It is not easy to convey this to someone. Inevitably, in a dependent mode particularly, any suggestion of accountability is received as criticism or attack. (A simple greeting can have the same effect – rather like a burn victim's response to the initial touch of the doctor.) To some, responsibility means blame.

Here is an example: A patient of mine, a British psychiatrist, has what he considers to be an original idea and he wants to write about it. The idea is credible, and furthermore, emanates quite appropriately from the data of his engagement with a patient. He says he is so afraid of being banal that he cannot write the paper. He talks to me about his idea, which I find interesting and something worth writing about. It is what I think of as 'from the bottom up,' from the patient's data, in contrast to 'from the top down.' But alas, he cannot produce a manuscript. After a period of time, he changes the topic to something about his dissatisfaction with his wife; his hungry interest in other, exciting women. (I wonder am I losing my excitement for him?)

This is a man who has great difficulty accepting responsibility and accountability for any of his feelings and their contradictory aspects. We spent a month – I think wastefully – discussing the number I needed to assign him as a diagnostic coding for his insurance company. It turned out that there was no number with which he would have been satisfied. I told him to pick any number he wanted and I would discuss it. In effect, he wanted the insurance compensation, to which he was entitled, of course, but he also wanted me and the insurance company to think of him without a code number. His concern was not his humanity (that is, not being objectified as a number) or his privacy or confidentiality. His concern was what I thought about him, and his not being exposed (to himself) or spotted. When I heard the remarks about his proposed paper – and I must say I was genuinely enthusiastic since I did think the patient had given him a highly individual and informative way of expressing a problem that the patient shared with many others – I was aware that he was talking to me as his analyst, and as a prospective editor, at the same time. Both were real. As an editor, I know that the remark that one is afraid of not being original, or any other way this is expressed, is a sure sign of a beginner. But it is really no shame to avoid being straightforward in print because that is dangerous. It is revealing, and one's fear usually is expressed as a fear of being obvious. Strong feelings beget strong defenses. I know this and it evokes my sympathies, having been here. It takes some experience with the pain and resentment of rejection before one risks the vulnerability of putting down one's thoughts on paper candidly in any form, and then working very hard to forge them into an acceptable piece of work. That is craft. It is difficult time-consuming effort.

But he was talking to me as his analyst so that I was faced with the issue of working through his refusal to accept responsibility and be accountable for his desire and his behavior. Of course, he felt intimidated, his problem being rooted in the past with authority figures, he being a lousy student before university, a fair one during, and later in medical school, despite evident abilities, and fearful now, as always, of being laughed at and humiliated – in essence, not being taken seriously. His desire to be original and creative, without risking the work to do so, is glossed over in part by what is called, in literary circles, the pathetic fallacy. (The patient does not want to be trite or self-evident. Who can object?) This struggle may be based on ignorance, but it is an ignorance that is the result of the persistent, patent refusal of responsibility, and the difficulty in risking exposure.

And so, with my patient I had a double problem of trying in some way to get to the accountability issue without dissuading him from the idea that I appreciated his risk. He had the legitimate desire to be relevant, and have some point, wanting to be seen by colleagues as though he were doing something meaningful.

I am afraid I failed despite my being aware of all this. Maybe I just did not convey enough compassion for what seems to have been a syndrome belonging to his early adolescent era. Perhaps I was not sensitive enough to the nature of class or authority relations in his country of origin, and how they affected his family dynamics in terms of his creative attempts and impotence. I saw the technical issue as similar to tossing a pebble into an otherwise quiescent pool. I assumed that I could work from the outer ripple in to the center, the outer being the issue of writing, next the burden of accountability and risk of exposure, and at the center the issue of relevance or need. First, I told him that all writers have at one time or another, asked the same question of themselves. (There is the danger of relativism in this communication in that it tends to get away from his experience.) Second, writers know that essays do not come full blown, like Athena out of Zeus's head. Most go through three or five or more versions, with the bulk of the effort and the shaping in the editing and the revising. Third, if his discussion is authentic and accurate, in terms of what his patient has stated about himself, it would be impossible for it to be trivial. Alas, possibly, because of my masked contempt, and impatience, I was playing educator or social worker. It was not my job to educate. Would that not have humiliated him? I think it did.

That was not the point, he said. He was only afraid that he really had nothing more than transparent rhetoric with which to tell his trashable story and I was not getting it. I reiterated my awareness of his tension and appropriate concern; that maybe he wanted to be sure he was relevant. To no avail. He insisted on pointing out his fear of banality – that is all there was to it. 'You see doctor,' he said, with the polite urbanity of a Security Council member, 'I don't do it.' (Foolishly, I did not stay with the simplest issue: his fear.) As I recall, my recognition and admission of those faults in me that irritated him came much too late. After all, how could he take himself seriously if I did not take myself too? How could he trust his thoughts and perceptions if he picked up my contempt, only to have me deny it?

I must say by this time I was thinking that indeed he was banal, and I said that I thought this was his convenient way of reassigning the responsibility for his effort. In a funny way, he just was not doing his homework, a phrase he had heard from me many times before, and which he echoed. Therefore, since he could not produce anything, he would not be exposed. I think this latter gem was a little harsh – true, but off the mark. My impatience with this kind of defense was getting in the way. I was doing what his family did, particularly his rich, powerful, professionally well-known father, and his two verbally gifted and successful elder brothers, one a writer, the other an academic. He countered with: 'I don't understand your language, I never heard of such an expression as "reassigning responsibility," no one talks like you.' This was no compliment. I had just missed the boat. 'No one talks like you' meant, I suppose, 'If I had a sensitive analyst he'd address something else, like my feeling and its history, especially about you.' It could have meant also, that I was reassigning responsibility to him.

At this point I was thoroughly and deservedly defeated, and deferred to his expression of more feeling. Unfortunately, I did not ask, 'What's it feel like to have an analyst who talks the way I do?' In so doing I would have opened up a whole new discussion of his feelings about being in therapy. He changed the subject to a problem he recognized he had in terms of his voracious desires for the variety of women he had met in the past, and his wish that he remain married tenderly, and not hurt his wife. In essence, my failure had been dismissed but I was now being given another chance with new content. It was not simply a shift in potency. The contradictions were evident. Freedom without constraint? Commitment without fidelity? Pulitzer prizes without manuscripts? There was no 'I am a man who...' Only, 'Tell me who I am. Tell me what's right so I can get away with it, or not do it at all. Tell me how to be straightforward.' Implicitly, 'Show me that it is possible by being that way.'

He wanted to please me. His dilemma was that if he pleased me he believed he would lose his identity, that minimum of bootleg independence that he thought he had achieved. After all, he was on his own in the New World. Would I not be pleased if he wrote an original paper? Even a paper that would not radically transform our field? Who has ever written a paper like that? Would I not be pleased if he wrote a credible paper? As an editor? As an analyst? What was so terrible about that? But it would not change his self-definition.

It is only his internal struggle that is of any consequence and which he has yet to resolve. He must risk pleasing me, risk not pleasing me, risk not pleasing himself, and risk exposure if he is to change, if he is to be himself. Ultimately, even pleasing me may be humiliating since I would have the pleasure, and he would continue on now as the scion, the 'son' of a good paternal figure.

In verbal exchange I have never been able to go beyond this with this man. I have found that after I get my ideas expressed, by my backing off, they seem in some magical way to take root. In three or four weeks, even months, the sense of what I have said comes back to me in his words. It is as though a lot of struggle goes on internally, out of awareness, which is in keeping with his desire not to be dismissed and humiliated – engulfed or overwhelmed by the hysterical mother and the dominating, former Commando officer, now prominent father of yesteryear, by whom he always felt dismissed, and of whom he was always fearful. This could be simply because the man is not without talent, or gifts, and is, in the long run, a rather honest chap. In fact, throughout his hospital circles he is known as articulate, dedicated, serious, and perceptive.

In the past, he has dealt with issues of differentiatedness and sameness in similar fashion. He would engage me for months on end disputing what I had to suggest. I never make ex-cathedra interpretations. In fact, most of my so-called interpretations or comments are phrased in the form of tentative questions, such as: 'Do you think it might have something to do with...?' or, 'Do you think it would be useful if you looked at...?' I usually sound pretty simple and puzzled. What I usually have to suggest, according to him, has nothing to do with him, or never quite captures his feelings.

Six months later, down the pike, it turned out that what I had to say was indeed useful and what I had suggested was of significance after all, perhaps to be amended or reemphasized in a different way, his way, but meaningful nevertheless. The point is that all of this talk with me is an enactment of the very things that are being discussed by him. That is, the content of the session is a recapitulation of the relationship and vice versa (Levenson 1972). We are talking about self-definition, differentiatedness, and/or a fear of exposure, or fusion *vis-à-vis* his family, his teachers, his past lovers, his wife, his hospital colleagues, his analyst. The nature of our talking about it presents him with the very problem about which he is talking. Therefore, my acknowledgment of what he was critical about in me (e.g., my impatience, my contempt) was key to his learning how to trust his perceptions and his judgment, and become able to transcend his fears. Thus, his analysis is an enactment of the content he brings to it. And the analysis, ultimately, is about the analysis.

I think a lot of this becomes self-evident if we keep in mind that the belief system, or any set of convictions, most of which are out of awareness, has survival value. A patient once said to me about his neurotic behavior with others, 'It was like carrying suitcases filled with rocks. I've put them down and now I don't know what to do my hands.' Analysts write that patients 'take on' aspects of their parents (e.g., victims of abuse). They mean, to me, that patients assume self-definitions in the process of growth, and those with whom they are in intimate contact contribute to them. Self-definition has the quality of a religious belief that is not shaken easily. Change is similar to giving up a religion. It may even be experienced as an amputation. Self-definition simply is not dispossessed easily by any kind of intervention in the present. That is so because the belief system, which is part of self-definition, is laid down so early with such force, and such power, that it sometimes strikes me as grandiose, or at best illusory, that one would think that a bunch of words from one person would make another person change. When I say laid down, I mean neurally. And it comes about over time in embryological and early familial climates of contact – of which words or events are only a part. It is not what we have experienced with feeling that is important to register with our analysts, but what our feelings have experienced.

How could an analyst's words get through to these neural tracks? But they do, as part of an ongoing relationship. A patient of mine says that every time her husband leaves New York and flies to London, which he does routinely on business, she feels adrift, cast away. Yet she knows that if he stopped going she would find something else to trigger the feeling. She must find the mechanism in her, she says, so leave-taking does not have this dreaded gravitational pull. We have yet to examine the feeling experience of her mother's many admissions to a mental hospital, and its relation to her weekend separation from me. Does her husband miss her in London? Did her mother? Would her mother survive? Will I on the weekend?

I have gone through training, and particularly so in late years, asking myself why on earth should anyone change? For what reason? It is not that current life is not without frustration, not without pain, or tension, not without difficulties. Life is just not all ice-cream. It is not that one may want to improve or change. It is change life for what? And in what way? There's the rub. If, for example, one's self-definition disallows one to make errors, whether to fix approval, or to stave off internal or external disaster, how can we expect anyone with that kind of conviction to loosen up, without his first assuming the right and responsibility to make a correction. But it must take place in a setting where this is questioned, encouraged and expected; not only by one talking to the other, but as part of the setting, the entire context that includes the analyst's participation (Levenson 1993).

How can we expect radical change? It does happen – to our credit. Consciousness must represent self-definition. The implications of modern research in neuroscience indicate that even the self is physically comprehensible. We should study the effect of analytic interaction on neural circuits and their mappings. Do old firings die down (but are never eliminated) when new ones start? And where does all that take place? Externally they are initiated in the same interpersonal space where they originated back in childhood. That is, the space between oneself and others. Internally there is registry in neural circuitry. It is evidently the result of new, efficacious interaction that makes recategorization possible. I think it is about time to include comprehensive courses in neural science in the analytic training curriculum. This kind of study may lead us to a better understanding of the biological bases for temperament and interpersonal anxiety, and of concepts like character and personality as Levenson has discussed most eloquently (Levenson 1991).

Some time ago a sensitive, South American psychiatrist, the husband of a patient of mine, told her that he believed psychoanalysis was a dying profession. He (and she, later) may have been speaking transferentially, in that he thought I was dead to her and consequently she to him. And why the hell did I not liven her up? I suppose he meant in bed. As I recall, it was the reverse. In contrast, I believe interpersonal psychoanalysis with its emphasis on availability and accessibility, its intimate way in the thrust for union is coming into congruent alignment with modern science. It has never been more vivacious, not as a radical rattling of an older establishment, but as an eminently useful way of thinking and working. Part of a grand continuity, it is, after all, only four or five handshakes from the original source.

References

Engels, F. (1954) *Anti-Dühring.* Moscow: Foreign Languages Publishing House.

Epstein, L. (1982) "Adapting to the patient's therapeutic need in the psychoanalytic situation." *Contemporary Psychoanalysis 18,* 190–217.

Feiner, A. (1970) "Toward an understanding of the experience of inauthenticity." *Contemporary Psychoanalysis 7,* 64–83.

Feiner, A. (1983) "On the facilitation of the therapeutic symbiosis." *Contemporary Psychoanalysis 19,* 673–689.

Feiner, A. (1991a) "The analyst's participation in the patient's transference." *Contemporary Psychoanalysis 27,* 208–241.

Feiner, A. (1991b) "The thrill of error." *Contemporary Psychoanalysis 27,* 624–653.

Feynman, R.P. (1988) *What Do You Care, What Other People Think?* New York: W.W. Norton.

Freud, S. (1910) "The future prospects of psychoanalytic therapy." *Standard Edition* 11, 139–151. London: Hogarth Press.

Havens, L. (1974) "The existential use of the self." *American Journal of Psychiatry 131,* 1–10.

Heisenberg, W. (1927) Letter to W. Pauli. 23 February.

Klein, G. (1976) *Psychoanalytic Theory.* New York: International Universities Press.

Laing, R.D., Phillipson, H., and Lee, H.R. (1966) *Interpersonal Perception.* London: Tavistock.

Langs, R. (1981) *Resistances and Interventions.* New York: Jason Aronson.

Levenson, E. (1972) *The Fallacy of Understanding.* New York: Basic Books.

Levenson, E. (1974) "Changing concepts of intimacy in psychoanalytic practice." *Contemporary Psychoanalysis 10,* 359–369. Also in *The Purloined Self.* New York: Contemporary Psychoanalysis Books (1991).

Levenson, E. (1981) "Facts and fantasies: the nature of psychoanalytic data." *Contemporary Psychoanalysis 18,* 1–15. Also in *The Purloined Self.* New York: Contemporary Psychoanalysis Books (1991).

Levenson, E. (1982) 'Follow the Fox.' *Contemporary Psychoanalysis 18,* 1–15. Also in *The Purloined Self.* New York: Comtemporary Psychoanalysis Books.

Levenson, E. (1991b) *The Purloined Self.* New York: Contemporary Psychoanalysis Books.

Levenson, E. (1992) "Mistakes, errors and oversights." *Contemporary Psychoanalysis 28,* 555–571.

Levenson, E. (1993) "Shoot the messenger: Interpersonal aspects of the analyst's interpretations." *Contemporary Psychoanalysis 29,* 383–396.

Pais, A. (1991) *Niels Bohr's Times.* New York: Oxford.

Sullivan, H. (1953) *The Interpersonal Theory of Psychiatry.* New York: W.W. Norton.

Sullivan, H. (1964) *The Fusion of Psychiatry and Social Science.* New York: W.W. Norton.

Witenberg, E.A. (1993) "To the Editor." *Contemporary Psychoanalysis 29,* 371–372.

Chapter 3

Laughter Among the Pear Trees

Vengeance, Vindictiveness, and Vindication

Those of us who have been hurt by others know all about vengeful feelings. They are common enough. Dramatists and novelists have scrutinized them incisively. There are more than fifty expressions of vengeance in about twenty of Shakespeare's plays. In analytic literature they are usually characterized as a less than admirable form of retaliatory hostility, and as part of rage. We tend to attribute them to our more satanic, or sinful and evil natures. In our modern age of enlightenment, with our popular expectation of loving connectedness, we seem to be embarrassed by the rise of the feeling to consciousness. Perhaps it is the primitivity of the feeling that accounts for its being so down-played pejoratively. Only the Lord can state easily, 'Vengeance is mine.' To some, that kind of justice is too long term for satisfaction. To others, for the short term there is supposed to be a system for justice, which includes the police and the courts. But too often the judicial system is found wanting. As admonition, the quote from St. Paul suggests how uncomfortable we are with it. It is clearly a private justice, as Joyce Carol Oates (1999) emphasizes, committed when public justice is unavailable or untrustworthy.

Fromm (1964) comments that while rage results from wounded narcissism (p.75), vengefulness is in inverse proportion to productiveness, and that the very process of being productive makes us relegate injuries of the past to the dustbin (p.27). Accordingly, as we mature we are supposed to get over it. We seem to feel more content when we assume its appearance is attributed to the more disturbed. Nevertheless, our vengefulness, like our shadow, is there, as any violation against children (ours or others') abruptly reminds us, and, in fact, we know it colors all our discussions of capital punishment.

Among the several references in Freud's writing, one mentions vengefulness as having remained unconscious in certain women:

> who still cling to their first husbands in a state of bondage, but no longer through affection. They cannot get away from them, because they have not completed their revenge upon them, and in pronounced cases they have not even brought the impulses for vengeance to consciousness. (Freud 1918, p.208)

It is one thing to note there are those who base most of their existence on wishes for revenge, so that it becomes a focal expression of their self-definition. It is another to recognize vengefulness as part of human potential and a common aspect of interpersonal connectedness.

Of course, like any feeling, vengefulness or vindictiveness can serve a defensive function. Horney (1948) remarks that vindictiveness can provide a form of self-protection against hostility from others, as well as a kind of reactive wrath. It also can restore injured pride, and, in so doing, provide hope for someone's ultimate, vindictive triumph. Echoing Freud, Searles (1965) stresses its usefulness in guarding against the awareness of feelings of grief, and the pain of separation. He gives examples of patients whose vengeful feelings covered their grief after having been ostracized; or having suffered early loss of a maternal figure; or whose vengefulness helped suppress feelings of anxiety in anticipation of separation; or of having been deprived; or having been faced with dupliciti-ousness. These patients felt they were never appreciated, or were constantly misjudged, i.e., they were made to feel irrelevant, or dismissed. Their vengefulness helped them hold on to a connection, perhaps a needed relationship.

When a patient feels that the therapist is insufficiently available, arbitrary, or impotent in gratifying demands, even less accessible than is hoped for, all feelings about past transgressions return to consciousness, that is, especially those feelings about being disavowed, or having one's needs dismissed, and being made to feel irrelevant. The usual reaction is rage. Adler (1985) points to one patient's interpretation of someone's failing to gratify as abandonment, even as a threat to the patient's 'entitlement to survive.' The evoked rage has three sources for the borderline, Adler reports: (1) the therapist's 'holding' is never enough; (2) the patient expresses what he or she experiences by means of projection; (3) the therapist's capacities to be available are envied, and, as a consequence, hateful, destructive impulses surface (Adler 1985, pp.50–51).

Boris (1990) agrees with the insight of Freud's, that vengeance is related to dependent but harried, possessive connections. In his exegesis on envy and its pathological role in identification with vengeance, or, better, a lust for it, he attributes it as reactive to protracted torment, following infant failure to identify out of possessiveness. Boris gives envy a greedy, brooding, hateful face. He writes percipiently: 'When what the Other has, good or bad, can only inspire envy, the Other must either be kept from offering it, or punished for being able to offer it'

(Boris 1990, p.130). In essence, Boris says, this kind of vengeance is quid pro quo, and he uses the horror of Poe's 'The cask of amontillado' (Poe 1927) as illustrative of his meaning of the term.

> The thousand injuries of Fortunato I had borne as best I could; but when he ventured upon insult I vowed revenge. You, who know so well the nature of my soul, would not suppose, however, that I gave utterance to a threat. At length I would be avenged; this was a point definitively settled – but the very definitiveness with which it was resolved precluded the idea of risk. I must not only punish, but punish with impunity. A wrong is unredressed when retribution overtakes its redresser. It is equally unredressed when the avenger fails to make himself felt as such to him who has done the wrong. (Poe 1927, p.205)

Wounding as a primer for vengefulness has been trenchantly captured by many writers since Greek drama. Medea is prototypic. H. von Kleist's *Michael Kohlhaas* and F. Dürrenmatt's *The Visit* are classic examples.

Here is some dialogue from Dürrenmatt's tragi-comedy *The Visit* (1962, Act III, pp.66–67):

> *Claire Zachanassian:* It was winter, long ago, when I left this little town in a schoolgirl sailor suit and long red plaits, pregnant with only a short while to go, and the townsfolk sniggering at me. I sat in the Hamburg Express and shivered; but as I watched the silhouette of Petersens' Barn sinking away on the other side of the frost-flowers, I swore a vow to myself, I would come back again, one day. I've come back now. Now it is me imposing the conditions. Me driving the bargain...
>
> *Schoolmaster:* Madam Zachanassian! You're a woman whose love has been wounded. You make me think of a heroine from antiquity: of Medea. We feel for you, deeply; we understand; but because we do, we are inspired to prove you further: cast away those evil thoughts of revenge, don't try us till we break. Help these poor, weak yet worthy people lead a slightly more dignified life. Let your feelings for humanity prevail!
>
> *Claire Zachanassian:* Feeling for humanity, gentlemen, is cut for the purse of an ordinary millionaire; with financial resources like mine you can afford a new world order. The world turned me into a whore. I shall turn the world into a brothel. If you can't fork out when you want to dance, you have to put off dancing. You want to dance. They alone are eligible who pay. And I'm paying. Guellen for a murder, a boom for a body...

These classics, obviously, are about adult vengeance for protracted hurt. It is in this direction that I shall explore this issue, particularly with regard to analytic patients. All of this has been by way of an introduction to the following story:

The Parable of the Doctor

The Man lived with his Wife and two children in a verdant valley next to a range of snow-covered, impassable mountains. They had a large ranch that included acres of vineyards and orchards, a comfortable home, and led a comfortable life. But The Wife was never happy.

Each day she complained of her bruised heart, her anger, and her melancholy. She told The Man it had nothing to do with him, their children, their surroundings, or their way of living. She knew it had to do with The Doctor.

Many years before, in a distant country, The Doctor had been in charge of a death camp, and was responsible for the destruction of The Wife's family who had been his prisoners. He had done this, he had said later, because he was told to by the authorities. The Wife was haunted by the fact that The Doctor had escaped justice. It was this that prevented her from enjoying the good life around her.

The wind-sounds reverberating among the pear trees were like eerie, sibilant whispers about the lost laughter and freedom in her childhood. In fact, this discrepancy between her present life and the past of her childhood was a constant reminder of her earlier vulnerability and victimization. She even wondered whether she was still vulnerable, despite her new family attachments and their good life. Perhaps, with a change in the central government, she – all of them – could be victimized once again. Thus, she felt that her ability to enjoy life wholeheartedly in the present was one more thing The Doctor had stolen from her.

One day, her torment was dramatically increased when she learned that in a neighboring valley, separated by the mountains from the one in which she and her family had their home, The Doctor was now living. He too had pear trees; he too enjoyed the warm sunlight at noon, the local wines with his meals. It enraged her. Furthermore, The Doctor was now recognized as a venerated, senior citizen and local sage. He supported the choral societies, the churches, the synagogues. He bestowed generous gifts on all who came in need, young students, poets, musicians, artists. His reputation was heralded throughout the province so that he was known popularly as 'The Good Doctor.'

The Wife realized, in horror and shock, that he had gotten away with all his crimes. He was, she thought with utter dismay and bitterness, living with impunity.

From that day, when she strolled with her husband in the early evening through the orchard above their home, she heard not only the wind among the pear trees, but also The Doctor's laughter mixed with it. It echoed through the hills, as if it were able to travel over or through the mountain range. It could do this in some mysterious way that her almost consuming rage could not. And this rage only appeared in her dreams— never at her children, at her husband, or the men and women who worked on the ranch.

> The Man, whose background in no way resembled his wife's, could not hear The Doctor's laughter. He was always puzzled as to what he should do to help her. His tender support, and their material abundance and comfort, did little to assuage the pain of her past insult, or her daily unfulfilled desire for revenge.
>
> The Man thought of trying to find a passage over the mountains, or around them, so he could kill The Doctor. But, he knew, somehow, that while this deliberate act would have given him and his wife transient pleasure, it would simply turn The Doctor into a ghost that forever would have haunted his wife's dreams. The dead relatives could not be brought back to life, nor would the injured have become uninjured, nor the terrified have become less terrified.
>
> The Man was left with the nagging question, 'What is to be done?'

The elements in the parable are clear. There is the loving family and their viable, productive, good life in the present. All this is marred by the memory of the previous disavowal and dismissal of the family's humanity, resulting in their grotesque debasement and destruction. This had been due to the arbitrary, inhumane, destructiveness of the authorities. There is also present in the story the figure most responsible for that offensive devastation – The Doctor. As in Freud's (1918) terse remarks, there is The Wife's unrelenting, hateful bondage. It invades The Wife's dreams and affects her waking life with the painfully repeated cry for retributive justice.

Being hurt, violated, insulted, or injured, seems to be common enough. For those who have been made to feel diminished or irrelevant by parental, or communal, or organizational dismissiveness, it is easy to remember. The evil that men do is rarely forgotten, if at all. The analyst asks: How are the issues of reactive rage and differentiatedness to be faced and integrated in therapy? How do we respond to patients' wishes for vengeance and justice? How can we clear the air, and facilitate their coming to some safe place, so that something refreshingly new and integrative can begin? What is to be done with our own feelings, to which we are not immune, when they are stirred by the patient?

If the analyst suggests the need to 'understand' past disasters, hurts, invasions, violations, and abusiveness as derivative and functions of diseased and frightened minds, minds participating perhaps in the social evil, the analyst maintains the familial or communal collusion. It makes little difference if the analyst's posture is a function of ideology or defensiveness. While analysis of the countertransference will make the analyst's response less automatic, the effect will be the same. The persuasive display of a plea for compassion for the past, whatever the analyst's motivation, confronts the victim with an additional, burdensome inauthenticity. His hurt becomes, thereby, something in his stars, attributable to his luck, even his DNA. It now has been transformed into some collective, relativistic experience.

And, even if true, it seals over the reactive feelings. In so doing, the patient's viability as a related person, his presence, is denied again.

Our common experience is that back at the time when we were abusively derided and dismissed, we were made aware that the children of Armenia (today it is Rwanda or Kosovo), or even the family down the street, fared worse. When this happens in therapy, it is here we go again. We learn to thank the Lord for little blessings, compensate for our impediments, recognize that our rage is about a past hurt, learn to 'accept' ourselves and our fate, and try to forget, or let go of our uninfluenceable past, as friends and relatives recommend. The analyst does not realize we have already tried to do that with our symptomology, much of which has come about this way, and is substitutive.

If standards are trashed, we no longer dare to dream aloud, but keep our desires to ourselves. Ultimately, there is a reshattering of faith, as there had been when we were children. This followed then, the sense of the irrelevance of our needs and feelings. If there had been physical abuse or molestation, there is now little possibility of trusting life. In fact, we wind up hating it (Fromm 1964, p.30). And our minds are occupied with something we may call 'blackness,' which our analysts fail to understand.

As patients have said to me, it is a blackness of bad, destructive 'things,' horrible events, and wretched feelings, like hurt and vengeance. But, no words ever describe it adequately. It is not the blackness of emptiness, of the absence of light, a light that the optimistic analyst mistakenly may urge us to restore. This blackness is that of the physicists – super-denseness – like collapsed matter that needs a kind of revelation or release, or transformation. And that, requires time.

Here are Primo Levi's searing words of retribution:

> If I were a judge, even though repressing what hatred I might feel, I would not hesitate to inflict severe punishment or even death on the many culprits who still today live undisturbed on German soil or in other countries of suspect hospitality. (Levi 1988 pp.184–185)

And what did Levi place as epigraph for his last book? These lines:

> Since then, at an uncertain hour
> that agony returns,
> And till my ghastly tale is told
> This heart within me burns.
>
> (Samuel Taylor Coleridge)

Perhaps this hints at the release needed to come about. The finishing. The ghastly tale must be told. One cannot ignore, or bury the past, and leave all behind in forgiveness. Were one to do that, one would run the risk of betraying the sense of abuse inside oneself. Abused persons, who see themselves as a holdover from childhood, self-defined and personified that way, have an urgent desire for justice that has never been met, and that surely can never be met, simply by the act of differentiating or separating. There is no end to the torment in that, and there has to be an ending.

Analysts who facilitate differentiatedness, self-hood, or leave-taking with rhetorical persuasiveness, betray their patients by turning them into some abstract 'victim' out of the past. The abuse becomes a horrific shade, appearing and reappearing in dreams, day-fantasies, and reveries, as parts of horror stories. By abandoning one's inner sense of denigration in such a way, by being urged to move on, patients feel that they are surrendering to, and reaccepting the original insult that has never been properly exposed and authenticated, and worst of all, that they are letting the abuser get away with it.

Even with the fantasy that one could walk out into the sunlit streets, there is the coincident thought that, as one turns one's back, the abusive ones are about to blow one's brains out. As one patient pointed out, thinking about his parents:

> Even if I were to leave, as I'm leaving, they're probably getting drunk, having a fight, or thinking about whether to call their lawyer and have me removed from their wills! They may, in fact, be so preoccupied with themselves as to not even notice my leave-taking.

Since one was disavowed to begin with, one feels as irrelevant today as in the past. After all, one served as a faceless audience in the past, and now one remains that way with an analyst who does not seem to dispel the abstraction.

Nor is the attempt at sifting through the inner blackness relieving, no matter how assiduously it is done. (One patient reported that when she was 5 or 6 she was pushed from a moving car by her angry mother; another's father chronically criticized him bitterly for no apparent reason, in contrast to his arbitrarily approving of the patient's older brother.) The past cannot be excised.

The analyst's attempt at attributing memories of events to the fantasy, for example, of having 'swallowed cancer balls' or a patient's avoiding responses to news of natural disasters, or discussions of the Holocaust, only pads the inner experience with more camouflage, reifying it, perhaps with some exotic label, or even a dreadful memory of an alleged event.

Even the analyst's compassionate attempt to substitute concretely, in the present, what was supposedly missing in the past, evokes suspicion, and the anticipation of a new disillusionment. The analyst who, faced with the retributive feelings of the patient, tries to find some good amidst the evil, something reclaimable in the stagnancy of despair, by struggling with the alleged meaning of memory, too frequently loses sight of how it all felt, how life was actually lived, and carried out. There is nothing referent or metaphoric about dehumanizing non-relevance. Only the non-reductive expression of vengeful feelings without retaliation, along with the mournful state that follows, mournful over what was absent, can effect a release. If the patient has an opportunity to discuss feelings, particularly those directed toward the therapist – any feelings – in a carefully managed frame setting, there will be a multitude of recollections with reflection, so that their patterning can be established, and reintegrated in the safety of the therapeutic experience.

What is in the 'blackness,' or the 'cancer ball,' or the 'unnamable,' or the 'burning agony,' or the 'deadness,' or the 'emptiness', is most likely the vindictive rage, that needs no stranger's labels, clichés, interpretations, or constructions.

There is only one way to try to understand another person. It is to move into the recesses and nuances of their feelings about their life, so as to see the world through their eye-balls, and attempt to feel how it is to live it. Slowly some glim of understanding comes, but surprisingly, it is wordless. A strange thing happens then to some of us. We lose the urge to explain it because to explain it is to obfuscate it by creating distance between the experience and ourselves. The words do that. In fact, we tend to be suspicious of disquisitions made by some about others, and assume quite naturally, that they usually reveal more about the teller than they do about the subject. We see this in the attempted pseudoanalyses of presenters of cases before professional groups.

The patient does need the stranger's ear and authentic response. This is the analyst's regard for the nature of the patient's emotional responsiveness without the condescension of stereotyping. What is also necessary for the patient is the encouragement to talk about it in safety.

But, all this sets up a contradiction in patients' expectations. The emergent rage must be expressed, and although patients realize they now can tell their ghastly tale, they begin to understand, suddenly, that justice will not, cannot be done here. Since the therapeutic context is not the court-of-law the patient expected, there is the growing recognition that bearing witness in therapy is not enough. Furthermore, acknowledgment by the abusers ('Yes, I did this to you'), which is needed, obviously cannot be forthcoming while on the couch. It belongs in court, or better, in the public square.

The analyst inadvertently offers false relief, only to disappoint. The relief appropriate to therapy is not exactly what the patient had in mind. The inherent contradiction leads the patient to more disillusionment, and transient feelings of betrayal. Thus analysts soon become the immediate target, not because of their limited 'holding,' but because they fail to fulfill patients' retributive claims. All the analyst's trivial, natural imperfections make this convenient. And the analyst must hear it all out this way (Spotnitz 1976). This can happen only if the analyst is available to be the target, without retaliating, either grossly or subtly. Gross retaliatory gestures would be counter-aggressive attacks. Subtle forms reveal themselves in frame deviations, or abstract, intellectualized interpretations, or even affectlessness, or inauthentic unflappability. But, it is the analyst's ordinary failings that are most important. The analyst's queries are about whatever is said.

One patient, who was so generally rageful that he deliberately tried to function innocuously, almost invisibly, throughout his social contacts, during most sessions lay on the couch stiffly, with tightly clasped hands. Following one session, during which I told him I was confused by what he was talking about, he returned, saying he felt better and more relaxed since I was as confused as he, but that he still was angry because I was. If I were imperfect, he could be. He could even show a little anger. He could be angry about my imperfection. But that frightened him. If I were imperfect how could he get better.

A patient's aggression is not simply a reliving of an old hurt, as it has been called, a 'new edition,' but an aspect of a current, legitimate complaint, a current disillusionment, a current disappointment. What is necessary then, is the rare opportunity to express the hurt, the vengeful rage – with no vindication – with the in-built guarantee of no analytic counterattack. True, there must be agreement as to the hurt, but more important, there has to be the impunity. Then, inner self-abuse may cease, and the patient may be released from the blackness – whatever that may mean – with the mournful awareness that scars will remain. The violation has been done. It cannot be ignored, nor transcended. There will be no cosmetic surgery here. Scars will always be there, but they will not have the grip they once had.

One woman poignantly said to me, 'I have my work [obstetrics], and I have my art [watercolors and printmaking]. But there's still my blackness. Where's the rest of me? Isn't it in the blackness?'

One patient told me that her friends wondered why she should return from Florida (where she had a winter home), when, as she stated, she never talked with her hated husband who always remained behind. All the couple did was argue bitterly with each other, if they did speak. Then she said:

> I don't dare be mad at you either. It is poison. It will hurt. You haven't helped. I'm still married to that man. I detest him. Yet how can I leave that crazy old man? He is frail, and I'm not equipped to do so. And you?

(I thought if she expresses anger at me, which would help, she'll be 'marrying' me.) I said something like, 'Why do you think you can't be furious, and still be with your husband and me?' (I was thinking that protectively, for both of us, she's afraid to show me – another old man – her poison. Maybe she thought she couldn't trust me to take it, without retaliating.) She then said:

> You don't walk out on me the way my mother did. I would get bewildered when she did. She was irresponsible. The three of us [two siblings] were

> frightened, and I was crazy angry. I still am [patient is 62]. I don't do that – walk out.

(I thought, she doesn't stay either, she doesn't connect openly, though she tries. But she is probably afraid I will walk out if she expresses the rage.) I said something like: 'What makes you think you still have to hide the hatred?' She said: 'Would you walk out, would you? I'm not sure. Can I trust you?'

Another patient arrived in a sullen state and told the following anecdote. She had driven from the suburbs to the city to pick up her sister, who had had a colonoscopy. The traffic had been extremely heavy, and she had arrived at the doctor's office thirty minutes late, feeling irritated about the traffic, and worried about her sister, and the results of the examination. The sister expressed her annoyance at my patient's lateness, sarcastically saying something like: 'I've just had a colonoscopy and you're irritated about a little traffic!' Then the sister directed my patient to pay the $1,200 fee. When my patient hesitated, the sister said, 'Put it on your credit card; I'll pay you back when I get the insurance check. Besides, you'll get free air-mileage out of it.' The patient told me that she felt uneasy while taking her sister to her apartment. She thought there was something wrong with herself, something missing in her mind, not being smart or generous enough to volunteer the use of her credit card. Later, on the way back to the suburbs, she was disturbed by her preoccupation with fantasies of starving children. I suggested that she might be angry at her sister's apparent ungratefulness, and cavalier exploitation about the bill. (In addition, her sister had two affluent sons she could have called on for the ride, since they worked in the city.) I took my patient's fantasy as a metaphor for herself – starved for affection, appreciation, and relevance.

> If she had just said, 'I really appreciate your picking me up,' it would have been all right. She's exploitative. I was furious with her. But I don't dare be. After all, she's had two cancers. How could I complain? I thought there's something wrong with me. I still do. You haven't convinced me otherwise. Where was all the therapy? A lot of talk. I really feel that, but I know there's been change, by leaps and bounds. How could I get angry with her. She needs me. You haven't gotten me to be straight. I can't be myself. It is why I'm duplicitous with friends of mine, making believe I'm listening to their stupid stories. You haven't helped. I still can't be honest.

The patient went on like this for the entire session, warming up, I believe, to the idea of expressing the feeling against me, which she eventually did.

This kind of feeling toward the analyst surfaces, paradoxically, because of the implicit valuing in therapy. It is an experience in relevance and consciousness of self. The patient is compelled to remember that she is also a person, intently regarded, and listened to. This new experience paves the way for the awareness of feelings of unworthiness and anxiety mingling with the delight. The patient is fearful of being found ugly, embarrassed at being found lovely, and after all, reluctant to be found at all.

In Robert Shaw's (1968) *The Man in the Glass Booth*, an extremely affluent real-estate operator, a survivor of the Holocaust, plots to have himself kidnapped by Israeli agents and put on trial in Israel as a former Nazi murderer. After his shocking, public advocacy of Nazi ideology and behavior, without a shred of remorse, he is revealed as the person he really is. The judge asks for the point of it all and says he understands the man's concern for justice and law.

One patient fantasized that after his mother's death, no longer fearful, he might wander about enjoyably in his old home, for six months, examining all the objects there (none of which he could ever claim as his own), throwing some out, giving some to charity, retaining some others. Then, he thought, whatever creative gestures he could make could finally challenge his current self-definition.

In contrast, Tolstoy has Anna Karenina, in her final guilt and disintegration, say, as she thinks of her lover, 'I shall punish him and escape from them all and from myself.' Then she throws herself in front of a moving train.

What was about to destroy one's thinking processes before therapy was not the betrayal by parents, or by neighbors of the past, or the horrendous events that justified one's self-definition, but one's own retaliatory, rageful feelings that are inflamed. These are not at the thought of going on without vengefulness, but at the idea of letting them 'get away with it.'

One can begin to set aside the feelings as they rise to consciousness, only if they have been articulated securely. So it is not totally true that to understand is to transcend. Only with the other's acknowledgment can that begin to take place.

But suppose the analyst makes a plea for compassion, for understanding. The abuser, for example, one's father (the mother is recognized as collaborator), now may be ill; his respiration has deteriorated; he is fragile; wobbly on his feet; perhaps even a little demented. He sits in his chair in front of the TV mumbling about a family picnic. To simply maintain the natural compassion one has for a decrepit, tattered old man, tied to his cane like a dog to a leash, leaves the mocking laughter of the past echoing through the surrounding hills. Even with that recognition, one's inner blackness cannot go away, but lies there in unknown, threatening tumescence.

Fortunately, among us there are those who guard against the subverting power of the repetition of collective silence. They fight so that not a smidgen of hurtful abuse is ignored. To them, silence is symbolic of the current presence of the torturous past (Timmerman 1981, p.141). These people do not want to forget, nor forgive (p.136).

At the ceremonies for the fiftieth anniversary of the liberation of the Auschwitz-Birkenau complex, the largest of the Nazi death camps, Elie Wiesel, writer and Nobel Laureate, himself a survivor inmate, said, 'although we know that God is merciful, please God, do not have mercy for those people who created this place' (*New York Times*, January 27 1995).

With this in mind, we can appreciate why differentiatedness is so resisted, why letting go is so difficult, why patients are so obdurate in their clinging to inefficient, self-abusive ways. The act of separation from the past, even if genuine, really makes the past injustice, and the loss of whatever was good in the past, untransformable, irreversible, and irrevocable. It is similar to an amputation and the often resulting, hallucinated phantom limb, or the sudden death of a loved one.

If one simply accepts hurt it becomes fixed, the past becomes past, and in no way can one influence it any longer. Any fantasies of reparative justice must be buried with it. One patient told me he regretted the death – at 94 – of his hated father. For him the father's dying was premature. The patient no longer had a chance to achieve justice. The father had lived on another continent and there had not been adequate opportunity for confrontation during the analysis. My patient had not been ready. Before he was, the father had died.

One more point. For a patient to confront one parent is also problematic. Since the other was a collaborator, attacking one implies losing the other, that is, losing whatever the collaborator had to give.

Finally, for the analyst to assume that the rage over being treated irrelevantly might somehow be used 'creatively' in some automatic way is to misunderstand its origins, and, as a matter of fact, the nature of the creative act itself. The creative act is one of release. One cannot simply transfer energy from one set of fantasies that are destructive, and/or retributive, to another set of fantasies that are potentially creative. Waking, or in dreams, wholesome metaphors or symbols are not substituted for unwholesome processes or feelings, unless they are contaminated, or perverted by the context, or used for an ironic purpose. Then the meaning resides in the function, the how it is being used, not the property, not the what. Creative acts are themselves separations, leave-takings, departures, and syntheses. They require mastery over materials, availability, spontaneity, and concentration on what is considered a problem or puzzle, resulting in something new. It is true that the person will be present, somehow, in all his or her creative efforts, but not in any mechanistic way. For example, there is dreaminess, like sleep-walking, desire, and release in Schubert's piano sonatas; and the gazes of subjects do not meet in Degas's painting; T.S. Eliot made masterful poetry out of anti-Semitism. But whatever these observations tell us about the artists' personalities, the forms they used were for broad, complex, authoritative expressions. The simplistic biographical approach to 'seeing and hearing,' the focus on content, severely limits our appreciation of the process.

What then helps patients turn their backs on the disavowal and the treatment of non-relevance of the past? What facilitates change in self-definition? The productive life cannot be all there is to it, since it too can be reactively vengeful, and never autonomous of its vindictive origins. If we reemphasize that this is what is to be vindicated – the dehumanization that one experiences – we are reminded it is the conviction of an anti-self self-definition that keeps the flame for vindication burning. What others have done in hurt and denigration has been to reinforce this dreaded notion of not mattering in oneself, and it is the process of the analytic connection that can become an enactment of transforming this to its opposite. With all that, it does not remove others from the responsibility for their antihuman crimes. Radical change in the patient is one thing, the abusers' accountability is another.

Why is the analytic so important? Why, in an authentic analytic relationship, can the anti-self self-definition be discarded? It is true. In therapy, for the analysts to hear the patients and, ultimately, in the engagement, for the analysts to be the target of their feelings, the patients are helped to free themselves from the grip, and ossification of the anti-self self-definition. It is the analyst's 'hearing' and the quality of their response that encourages the patient's own adaptational alternatives. Why should this be so?

For one thing, the patient's feelings, disturbing to both participants, are occurring within the secure frame of an ongoing connection. To express feelings toward another, e.g., the anger of a patient toward the therapist, has certain advantages. First, the viable nature of the connection is affirmed, since there is no retaliation and the therapist is not destroyed, nor does he threaten abandonment. In this way, the expression is detoxifying. Second, the very enactment is a demonstration in relevance, in contrast to verbalisms that can be highly suspect. Third, with the rude awakening that justice can never be met in the therapy, and that there is an inherent contradiction in what analysis offers, the patient and therapist share what Niels Bohr (Pais 1991) has called a 'complementarity.' This is the most accurate model of the living process itself. It is the notion that what we know, always partial and incomplete, is comprised of multiple and mutually limiting points of view – at the same time. Only by building a composite picture, do we approach any clarity of the real world and its richness. Finally, this, I believe, is what Dr. Fromm intended, with his suggestion that productive work helps lay vengeful feelings to rest.

Thus, the patient is never consigned to an immutable category. In this way, the analysis and the expression of feelings itself becomes metaphor for the patient's actual nondismissiveness and relevance. And that relevancy, that is something new, is the fulfillment of the analyst's own self-definition.

References

Adler, G. (1985) *Borderline Psychopathology and its Treatment.* New York: Jason Aronson.

Boris, H. (1990) "Identification with a vengeance." *International Journal of Psycho-Analysis 71*, 127–140.

Dürrenmatt, F. (1990) *The Visit.* Tr. from the German: *Der Besuch der alten Dame.* London: Jonathan Cape.

Freud, S. (1918) "The taboo of virginity." *Standard Edition 11*, 193–208. London: Hogarth Press.

Fromm, E (1964) *The Heart of Man.* New York: Harper and Row.

Horney, K. (1948) "The value of vindictiveness." *American Journal of Psychoanalysis 8*, 3–12.

Levi, P. (1988) *The Drowned and the Saved.* New York: Summit.

Oates, J.C. (1999) *The New York Review of Books*, June 24.

Pais, A. (1991) *Niels Bohr's Times.* New York: Oxford University Press.

Poe, E.A. (1927) "The cask of amontillado." In *The Works of Edgar Allan Poe.* New York: Walter J. Black.

Searles, H. (1965) *Collected Papers on Schizophrenia and Related Subjects.* New York: International Universities Press.

Shaw, R. (1968) *The Man in the Glass Booth.* New York: Grove Press.

Spotnitz, H. (1976) *Psychotherapy of Preoedipal Conditions.* New York: Jason Aronson.

Timmerman, J. (1981) *Prisoner without a Name, Cell without a Number.* New York: Alfred A. Knopf.

Chapter 4

Restlessness of the Spirit

Exposure, Loss, Rage, and Salvation

In Chapter 3 I pointed out how the patient comes to realize that justice is not served on the couch. Not only is life often unfair, but also abusers too often get away with their crimes. The sad recognition is that the past leaves non-eradicable scars. No amount of analytic understanding removes anyone from the task of enduring. And that requires exposure, and change of self-definition.

One lasting psychoanalytic convention has been its adherence to determinism. Like the walls of austere Gothic buildings of worship, the doctrine has been buttressed by an abiding assumption with which it has been coexistent since its earliest beginnings: 'Where it was, there I (or you) shall be.' The tenet's persistence and tenacity color our analytic attitudes and our technique – directing our inquiry and influencing our understanding. It has been supported by 100 years of more or less respectable and energetic practice, which have given it its cachet. It represents a diachronic search for historical referents, or causes, the what of one's developing and current consciousness, not necessarily the how.

More than 160 years ago, Goethe wrote in his famous poem *Damon*, 'So musst du sein, dir kannst du nicht entfliehen' (So you must be – you cannot run away from yourself). It would seem that Goethe could not have conceived of change in self-definition. Still, Goethe had his restless protagonist, the opportunistic, deal-making Faust, finally (in Part II of the drama) renounce magic, confront nature in the present, identify with labor, and reject transcendence. In so doing, Goethe reversed the old apothegm to something radically new: 'Where I am, there it shall be' (Bloom 1991).

Similarly, in their jubilant parting with some of the received, traditional wisdom, and the presumed certainty of classical psychoanalysis during the early 1940s, the founders of interpersonalism, Sullivan, Thompson, Fromm, and Fromm-Reichmann, initiated a new tradition in analytic thinking and practice with their psychoanalytic variation of Goethe's aphorism.

Patients' memory of their history – a categorizing that was immensely valuable, and not to be ignored – came to be seen, in part, as a function of their current experience; which, in turn, was used by them to explain it. In addition, interpersonalists put themselves squarely in the patient's present, so that the field of interaction became the most important object of analytic scrutiny. Along with this was their abiding belief that values, learned in the course of one's interactions with others from the time of birth, were experienced internally as feelings. These feelings, as well as needs, influenced – and in turn, were influenced by – perceptions.

Let me reiterate what I have written earlier. In the classical tradition, we presume that the past determines the present directly, and we are prone to ask how things got to be the way they seem to be. We want to know what events contributed, and believe our inquiry will lead to a necessary and sufficient explanation. But, denying the past seemed like denying the unconscious itself, and left interpersonalism open to the criticism of superficiality. It is true that if we mechanistically split off the way things are from the way they came to be, we subject ourselves possibly to discarding the Darwinian tradition itself. Interpersonalists reasoned that if they began to assume an evolving interconnection, there loomed an enrichment of psychoanalysis that was possible with a kind of inquiry, the prime focus of which encourages curiosity. The emphasis was on what feelings have been experienced, in the present, as well as in the past, rather than what one had experienced with feeling. In this way, the past was not ignored. It was claimed, but in a new way. Change, they believed, was thereby facilitated by the inquiry itself, not by the naming.

Interpersonalists pay attention to the immediate field of occurrence with all its complexity, especially their participation in it. For technique, this is a revisionary change from the diachronic point of view, a study of things in their coming to be as they are, to the synchronic point of view, the study of things as they are, in all their idiosyncrasy and mess. It represents a radical shift in analytic investigation from the search for the what (the label or classification) to the study of the how (the experience). It is this that was interpersonalism's transformative contribution, and what is currently basic to it as a body of knowledge, a research tool, and a treatment technique. This way of thinking reflected interpersonalists' differentiation of reasons from causes, since meaning was understood by them as a product of the creation of a subject. Needs influenced perception, and perception affected behavior. Their radicalism – a derivation from Ferenczi – advanced a new way of exploring self-definition, and also asserted that somewhere, beyond the curtain of patients' translation of their memory and their interpretations of their current way of life, there lived a lonesome being yearning for connectedness. Interpersonalists assumed that the purpose of psychoanalysis was to help the patient find it.

Subsequent generations of interpersonalists have continued in this direction, expanding the canon, but not changing it.

Therapy has always required a setting, or context, in which the relevance of individuals' feelings and their restlessness, their feelings about themselves, their past and their future, are viewed as important and non-dismissible; their examination and expression are to be shared with another (the analyst), in an ambience of safety. This is often a welcome surprise for the patient, since these necessities do not seem to be too common in our world of trouble and ambiguity. Immediate survival, self-centeredness, ruthlessness, and opportunism, along with personal aggrandizement and ambition leading to celebrity, have tended to obscure, if not replace, communal spirit. What had been, in former times, a commonly shared anticipation of sensual contact, reliable tenderness and care, seems to be all too rare in our era. For example, we are as astonished that an entire French village would assiduously foil their Nazi occupiers so as to save the lives of many Jews, as are the villagers surprised when we call them heroes. For them it was just a matter of self-definition (Hallie 1994). Regardless of the functions of a relationship, that give it its contents, it is the relevance and/or non-dismissibility of the feelings of the person that are considered most significant in preventing disconnectedness. Furthermore, connectedness includes care and authenticity. Look at the two following examples from pop cinema.

The line everyone remembers from the movie *On the Waterfront* is, 'I could have been a contender.' It touches our frustrated, perhaps betrayed, sense of fulfilment, and our competitive desires for status and fame. But, we forget that a moment earlier, in the same scene, Marlon Brando plaintively tells Rod Steiger that as his brother he should have looked out for him. In this appeal for fraternal community and tender connection there is the antidote to dislocation. To be a 'contender' requires interpersonal relevance and care.

Entertaining and humorous is the scene in the film *Casablanca*, during which Major Strasser, the Nazi Waffen-SS officer, orders the local Vichy police chief, Captain Louis (Claude Raines), to close the hero Rick Blaine's (Humphrey Bogart) nightclub because it has been 'disorderly' (the patrons had been singing the *Marseillaise*). Louis says he has no reason. Strasser tells him to find one. When Captain Louis orders the nightclub closed, Rick approaches him at the bar and says he is shocked to find that gambling is going on. At this point one of Rick's croupiers approaches Captain Louis and gives him his winnings.

This scene was timely for us in 1942. We were at war with fascism – we were the good guys, but not doing as well as we could – and the film shored up our morale. We knew, especially, that Captain Louis really, really did not mean it. Captain Louis's swagger, his wry smile, the tilt of his captain's hat, and the twinkle in his eyes, presaged a benign outcome for our side. But, that was just a movie.

When a structurally equivalent, but inauthentic scenario takes place in family life there is no similar frame of reference. There are no good guys or bad guys – there are only children and parents. Nor is there any twinkle in anyone's eyes. Absent is the rootedness of a reliable connection to parental figures; missing are the outward signs, and the evolving inner capacity, both needed to predict favorable development. Wanting is a sense of relevance and safety, and trust in the ongoing nature of life. There remain only confusion, cynicism, discontinuity and dislocation. Add abuse of any kind to this melange, and we learn about the chronic felt experience psychoanalysts hear from so many patients about their internal 'blackness,' 'deadness,' 'emptiness,' 'cancer balls,' 'black holes,' 'rottenness,' 'sourness,' 'darkness,' and their feeling of despair.

Some case material will illustrate these issues.

A Clinical Vignette

All through childhood and early adolescence, one patient (41 years old, a classical scholar, an essayist, the editor of a literary quarterly, and the husband of a novelist. The couple has one child.), fantasized being adopted by a family who lived nearby, and with whose son he was friendly in school. He would wait until five o'clock each day and bike to his friend's house. Each night he would be asked to remain for dinner. Sadly, he says, he never would be invited to stay the night. He remembers, at eight o'clock he would mount his bike and 'go back to my depressed father and drunken, probably psychotic mother.'

In the middle of his analysis he had the following series of dreams:[1]

1. I am biking somewhere, someplace unknown, with another person who is also biking. It is dark, I don't know where we're going. The other man is homeless.
2. I'm with my son's friend, a 12-year-old, shy, young boy. He is thin and seems like a waif, all alone. I ask him where are his parents, thinking here's an abandoned kid. I wonder if I might take care of him.
3. I'm in a bicycle race going across the George Washington Bridge or perhaps the Tappan Zee Bridge from the Manhattan or Tarrytown side to Jersey or Rockland County. I'm doing very well. I'm in the top ten and it does not occur to me that it's necessary that I win. I do know and feel that whatever happens I will have done well and acquitted myself respectably. Suddenly the figure of the comedian actor Bill Murray appears. He happens to be an actor that I detest. This figure wreaks havoc in the race by making the bridge shake. The bridge shakes so much due to his perverse magic that we fall down. Even cars pull off the bridge. He is transformed so that his face becomes increasingly and ominously ape-like. The race is over because of his nihilistic, destructive action.

The patient says that the first dream is a reenactment of his past, a past from which he has not yet been saved.

The analyst wonders whether the analysis (biking somewhere unknown) is in the dark. And is the analyst ambiguous or unclear (homeless) about 'adopting' him? In some way has the analyst held out that promise?

The patient remarks that the second is a dream about feelings of abandonment. He wonders, in the dream, whether he can take care of an abandoned child (his feelings about himself), that is, can he make use of the analysis, and grow in a new way. But, while the child in the dream seems to be rootless, it is possible that he is not. Therefore, there is some indication of hopefulness about his resources; he might evolve and become less isolated and depressed.

The patient's comments about the third dream were as follows:

Here's the history I'm infused with. At some point in my childhood I was probably doing all right, and then my mother became crazy. Her demands and tangentialisms, that sometimes reached hysterical proportions, were a way of getting attention without any accountability for herself. This is typical of dysfunctional people who harbor rage against the functional ones. I see it every day at work, with publishers, in libraries, at music stores where I shop, walking in the park, everywhere.

When I was a kid we had a neighbor, a structural engineer who taught at one of the well-known schools of architecture. He traveled all over the world as consultant to various governments on projects like the construction of bridges or dams. My mother would disparage him endlessly pointing out that his job was of no significance; or, that the governments that hired him were corrupt; or, the places he traveled to were of no consequence.

Her attacks, as is typical of the hateful, raging dysfunctional, were against the enterprise of functionality, or the location where the enterprise takes place. They were not and could not be directly against the functional person. This would mean too much exposure for her. Her denigrations were always against an abstraction.

In the dream the 'Bill Murray' character destroys the race. He has no vision, no structure, no purpose. He is the disaster. He embodies it. He creates the disaster and he is the disaster. I think I picked him as standing for goofiness, ineptness and infantility which are qualities that I see as saying, 'Well, that's who I am.' But, I have been denying the emotional pain that goes with that. This is because of the frightening coldness, and the nihilistic rage I must face, as evidenced in the 'Bill Murray' character destroying the bridge. It's in me. My ineptness. My rage, my murderous malice. In my actual life, like the 'Bill Murray' character, my mother was a bomb. 'Biking' is living, thinking, being, in analysis or out. The bridge, which is really a metaphor for connectedness to family, places, creativity, or others, including the analyst, is destroyed in the dream, as my mother usually did in real life. My rage will hurt you and disconnect me from you.

> The enemy is dysfunctionality and how it is experienced by an isolated child with no support from a depressed father who is devoted to protecting his insane wife. It is even worshipped. In some way it is assumed better or safer to be disconnected than connected. Dysfunctionality can't be criticized. In fact, since it is worshipped, it is experienced as being on some 'higher' level. It is supreme because functionality is derogated. All resources of the family are sacrificed to dysfunctionality so that it becomes a faith, a mystery. One doesn't ask my father why did you marry (or stay with) this crazy woman? It evokes rage (How dare you?). I suspect it had something to do with his own sexual insecurity. Yet, if the question is not asked one feels inferior and one's own functionality is considered disloyal.
>
> My father was a wonderful tennis player. He had played in college and could have been a pro. My mother could hardly hold the racquet properly. Yet my father persistently and patiently had her take lessons from a friend, a famous pro whom he knew, so as to cover her awkwardness and her fears, which she never got over. She never improved. If she had tried to play the violin (which he did play well at one time) he would have bought her a Strad, or the equivalent.
>
> Ordinary people fear failure or disapproval. But that rests on their assumption of functionality. My mother wasn't able to try to participate. There was always something wrong. Something always made her upset. With that background how do I try to establish myself in the ordinary functional world? It is not the vagaries of existence that undermine one, it is the dysfunctional rage that determines the undermining. That's what I expect from others, and that's what I get.

Demonizing others is one common way of defining difference. Generally, demonization of others makes it easy to exclude them. We then tolerate our hostility and hatefulness that we assume is licensed, even commanded by divine authority (Pagels 1995). If we do find evil in ourselves we feel exposed. Then we are moved to deny or change it. What is ultimately banal about evil is its attack on the abstract, as the patient points out. It attacks the enterprise of others in collective or arbitrary ways. It attacks the location of their functionality, their communal relationships, their ethnicity and heritage, their religion, their racial backgrounds. These are abstract generalizations. Of course, groups are made up of individuals, but the individual, personal hurt is ignored. The impersonal callousness of this kind of evil is a function of its abstract, anti-human nature, which accounts for our shudder, and our astonishment.

From the time we are defined by others by being made to feel irrelevant, our organic, holistic, integrative tendencies facilitate our organizing a self-definition. Or, sometimes, unfortunately, an anti-self self-definition. This is, for the most part, out-of-awareness, with an inevitable residual sense of vacancy, self-denigration, and vulnerability.

Sometimes self-definition is revealed rigidly as, 'I know what I like and I know what I want.' The person probably is saying that they know what makes them feel good and safe. Knowing what makes one feel good is eminently appropriate (although it may be a defense of one's ignorance, and indicate one's quest for certainty), since it is part of self-definition that what one 'knows' makes for stability. This in turn makes one feel safe. Therefore, if being abused, feeling confusion, anticipating humiliation or alienation, is threatening, one's characteristic response to ambiguity, or the new, the radical, the shocking, and the disruptive, is invariably in favor of the familiar. The balanced, the organized, even the literal, or the concrete seals over the sense of vacancy. In marital therapy, for example, it is not uncommon for one spouse, speaking derisively and/or defensively, to state, 'I know what I heard!', with little thought as to possibilities of interpretation. That one has an interpretive lens before one's eyes (and filter anterior to one's ears) is not considered.

This part of self-definition is ultimately challenged by the experience of the inquiry in therapy through the self-awareness brought about by the engendering of curiosity, and self-scrutiny in the safe exchange. With the absence of historical reenactment in the connectedness of analysis, or, even when it fortuitously occurs, errors are rectified and apologized for by the analyst (especially for frame deviance), the possibility of hope is renewed. It is a hopefulness for possibility and the future (Kanwal 1995). If not, if there is a loss of hope again, or of faith, which is a new environmental failure, there is an investment in the status quo. And this unfortunate occurrence is supported by literalness or concreteness, the patient's refusal to conjecture or refusal to play (Kanwal 1995). Sometimes the patient relies on arbitrariness, or even a mystical conception of causality, and, ultimately, transcendence. In this way the patient's search for external reform takes precedence – a reform that serves his tranquillity, and fulfills the longing for whatever has been missed.

In a therapy that is transformative, patients recognize, as in the dreams presented above, that they have lived with a self-definition of being entitled to little but dysfunctionality in others or themselves. Patients see the need for a radical way of defining themselves. This is the beginning of the establishment of a new, autonomous 'I': i.e., I am, I see, I hear, I feel, I think, I learn, I desire, I give, I do, I receive. Indeed, this new 'I' can bring the patient into connection with others, if she wishes, so that further continuous evolving of the 'I' takes place. It is a reversal of Descartes's Cogito expressed as 'I am, therefore I think.' This 'I' is a moment by moment reconstruction on the basis of body image, history (old interpretations and new), current interactive feeling experiences with others, and one's intended future (Damasio 1994).

At this point one's hand now is on the knob of a door leading into an unknown space. But this is an unknown fraught with dangers, dangers of annihilation. Two feelings now occur, those of loss and rage. One is being urged to give up old, accepted inclinations, strengths and expectations, which, however limiting, have stood one in good stead for so many years, but have colored all perceptions. After all, the self that was constructed during the troubling years has had immense survival value. True, it may be inefficient, crippled, warped or deformed. But why give it up? It is the best, the only self one has. What is to replace it? The underlying restlessness becomes apparent.

Yes, it is a loss, the analyst admits, but time can be a refreshing river. The patient is the parents' son or daughter, but no longer their boy or girl. The point is that there is a stable continuity, and a generative discontinuity going on at the same time. And in that communication there is the implicit message that the analyst sees the patient differently; there is evident the patient's potential that evokes in the analyst an implicit demand, and encouragement, that the patient grow.

If there is agreement, based on all the trust, the impassioned, energetic exchanges, and the judicious encouragement from the analyst, as well as the presentation of the possibility of alternatives (not the alternatives themselves), then, along with anticipated loss, there emerges a panicky fear. One is expected to step into an unknown. It is similar to the felt, catastrophic reaction that some of us experience when looking down from an immense height into empty space. It is as if one were clinging to the side of a cliff and were being urged by a stranger to let go.

The rage is different. It comes into awareness as interior monologue whose expression is useful:

> If I am so worthwhile – and by words and actions, you (the analyst) reiterate I am – where were you, where was the world, when I was three or four or five or six? Where were you all when this started? I rage, rage against the injustice, the bad deal, the lousy hand. Fate didn't step up and slap or kick me. It stomped me all over. Why, you bastards? Now you're asking that I forget – now that I know (shall I say remember?). Now that I recognize my feelings in the patterning in the formative process you want me to forgive. I am supposed to give up what I worked so hard for. Where is avenging? Where is justice? Obviously, not here. So, fuck you! (Feiner 1995, p.161)

Yet, there must be the leap, the risk in faith, fostered and supported by the therapeutic connection, with a new-found ability to suffer the loss. There must be a move to a proper burial of past anti-selves, and an awakening of the mourning for what might have been. This is not the mourning of the loss of a past presence, e.g., the loss of a parent, a loved one, a pet, or the loss of a habitat, a place or event, or even an ideal – all of which one might wish to restore, repair, or return to. This mourning begins with the recognition of an absence – what was not there. It is most tenuous, painful, and difficult because it is of something vague, and not known, and, because it is mixed with murderous revenge. We mourn what was never there, what might have been. We mourn an unfulfilled wish with a strong, vengeful, almost all consuming desire for a justice that never comes (Feiner 1995). The patient described above hears the words of the analyst like some sirenic melody – a haunting incantation – going towards some other place, perhaps pointing to a 'higher' level of being; or, perhaps, like a reminder of the private, sensuous pleasure in being and being noticed. The patient is supposed to integrate the analyst's implicit urgings in the analytic atmosphere of relevance and safety. All anti-self feelings are to be dispensed with, the analytic echoing urges. But are they?

If the analyst tediously persists in going somewhere else, patients soon find that they cannot keep up, or believe that the place the analyst wants to go is actually forbidden to them. Either that, or they have no way, in their system, of understanding what the analyst is talking about. So they pull the analyst back to where they are. For example, depressed people hear things depressively, dependent people hear them dependently. It is as though they have no other way of being. Thus the analytic relationship recapitulates the patient's content (Levenson 1996).

If the analyst only communicates the value of the being of the patient, something that is necessary for the analysis to work, without somehow introducing the alternative that the patient could be otherwise, the patient will stay where he or she is – and then begin to resemble a cult member.

When analysts reveal clearly that they actually are analysts – not coaches, not advisors, not tutors – that they too are uncertain, and fallible, their otherness will be 'demonized.' Analysts will be attacked for analyzing, since their differentiatedness, their implicit demand that patients must rely on their own resources, becomes unbearable. In imitation, or idealization, or sameness, there is safety.

The admixture of the postures brings the patient to the moment of the leap. It is a leap from literalness, abandoning adjustment, or the necessity for reform (for oneself or for others), to accepting the need for, and the possibility of radicalization, of a change in self-definition, along with a reliance on one's own judgment. I think this is what Fromm meant when he lectured about analytic transformation in contrast to reformation (circa 1954). Analytic change is a change in structure, in self-system, which, when occurring, as Fromm advised, makes the psychoanalytic experience revolutionary. If the hope which had been abandoned and cast down is restored, reform is just not good enough (Kanwal 1995).

Along with vengeful feelings there is the insistent desire for justice, and then the disillusionment and unrelenting, profound, painful disappointment. Consequently, the rage turns toward the analyst who previously had been idealized (Feiner 1995). Sometimes, this is masked as an expression of fear, a fear of the analyst or some part of the analyst. Usually, the fear is of the analyst's expertise or lack of it. That is, the analyst's functionality, but especially his or her limitations. Or, it is a fear of losing the analyst.

The experience of – and associations to – the dreams (occurring in the course of one year) that follow are illustrative of my patient's struggle with these issues. The titles are his:

> *The Burial*
>
> In the dream I am presented with the task of giving aunt B.'s ashes a proper burial. An energetic, middle-aged, cheerful, stout woman with blond hair, who is somehow associated with the church and the cemetery, suggests matter-of-factly, that we simply bury them in the family plot. It's a very practical matter, easy to achieve. I reply that we must consult and possibly include my cousin A., aunt B.'s only child, and that we must get an Episcopal priest to officiate at the burial service.

The patient said that he thought the dream had to do with achieving closure, that is, putting the brutal past 'to rest'. Though a certain practical attitude and energy is needed, that is not sufficient. The feelings of the victims or victim (i.e., cousin A.) must be included, and the spirit of the deceased (in this case the patient calls her malevolent) must be sent on its way, or put to rest by someone who has the authority to send it on its way (i.e., a priest – that is, a belief system). The analyst (or best friend, close relative, or local civil court judge) does not have that authority. Therefore, the patient concludes, the analysis has limits. It cannot lay the past to rest. It cannot obliterate it. Nor can it cure it. The power for change must be felt internally.

> *The Big Bird-Contraption*
>
> I'm on an island beach looking out over a large body of water. High above the beach, just making its way out over the water, is an enormous flying contraption whose wings appear to be made of silk that is beige or golden in color. Roosting on the wings are exotic birds whose plumage is also this color. It's moving slowly out over the water. It's a remarkable sight.
>
> Yet it appears to be a ruse or a con. The contraption is being flown by a smuggler of exotic animals. The birds, who don't know any better, are being lured from their native habitat by this 'giant bird' which is heading north. There the real birds will be illegally sold into captivity.

> Before the contraption has gotten very far from land, it is shot down, perhaps by me or a young woman in uniform who is an island ranger. As the contraption falls toward the shallow water, the birds fly off unharmed, returning to the wild. Then out of the wreckage, unharmed, steps the pilot of the contraption. She is a short, middle-aged, plump Caribbean woman who is heavily made-up. She smiles, somewhat inanely, as if her smile might somehow conceal her guilt.
>
> The young woman ranger steps into the water, handcuffs the Caribbean woman, and leads her off, presumably, to jail. I call out angrily. 'You deserve to have your liver eaten out daily by one of the birds you tried to capture.'

The patient commented that he thought the meaning of the dream was clear. The giant, flying bird-contraption may be beautiful, but it is a con, and as a con it can be easily deflated (brought down to earth) by exposing the ruse that lies behind it. Fortunately, there is a viable representative of secular authority (the analyst) who can arrest the con-artist (self-deception or mother?) and take her to jail.

He states:

> The birds who are saved from exploitation, imprisonment and possible death, return to a place where they are safe, or at least safer. They might represent creative insights, ideas, or energies seduced by a mercenary spirit posing as something that appears at first to be creative, beautiful, even miraculous (e.g., my first book). Perhaps, it is the publishing business, or even marriage, or living in New York. The giant flying bird, though piloted by a Caribbean woman who could only be thought of as banal and transparent, is, after all, attractive enough to seduce and fool the birds (the phony mothering I received).
>
> Though it is clear at the end of the dream that the secular authorities (the analyst?) are well able to handle the creator of the con, the con or illusion, in and of itself, is not evil. Rather, it is the purpose to which it's being put. My calling out, 'You deserve to have your liver eaten out', is a sign of the degree to which I've suffered, of my murderous feelings, of my desire to see this woman suffer as I've suffered – even if, as I suspect, she does not know who Prometheus was.

> *The Carnival, or, The Happy Place*
>
> I see a carnival, merry-go-round, ferris wheel, people, families having a good time, laughing, and I try to walk across a field to get to it. The field turns out to be quicksand – and there are many people all around on solid ground. If only one – just one – turned to me and threw me a rope or extended a hand, a helpful hand to help me across. But there does not seem to be one.

Here the patient stated:

> The future possibility? My feeling of being stuck? The impotence of my analysis? Nothing fair or just! Of course, it's how I felt while growing up. All out of reach. No family connection. No hand-up. My analyst is not the savior I expect. Nor can he be. I remain isolated, feeling connected to no one.

> *The Ice Skater Fantasy*
>
> I go to a country club near Boston, where my parents belonged, to play tennis. I look into my bag for my tennis sneakers. My mother has put in ice skates. What would be the possible response for other people? (1) Call mother and tell her she made a mistake, and ask her to bring down the sneakers. (2) Borrow a pair of sneakers. (3) Apologize and beg off playing. Not for me. I must put on the skates and walk onto the court and have everyone laugh and humiliate me. That is all that is possible in my system. That's who I am. That's where I'm at. I can't be functional.

The analyst pointed out that in the humiliating wearing of skates the dysfunctionality of the mother will be exposed, but this was ignored.

> *The Case Against Psychoanalysis*
>
> We (the community) assume it's a privilege to be allowed to watch the installation ceremony of the Emperor and Empress of Japan. Why it's occurring in a seventeenth-century fortress-like palace surrounding an enclosed courtyard in Parma, Italy, or in a city like Parma, instead of in a sacred forest near Kyoto is never explained. In fact, the balcony on which the Shinto priests are reciting the ancient rituals in a language known only to themselves, and their majesties – and which we can't hear anyway – is so high above the courtyard that we can only glimpse the strange, magisterial head-gear amid the cacophony of brightly colored priestly robes.
>
> The most interesting part of the ceremony – in fact, the only part we can really know anything about – occurs when men dressed in costumes and make-up resembling base, demonic spirits are thrown into the courtyard below from the balcony above on which the installation is occurring. They somersault in the air and land at our feet with the skill of the acrobats they must be, as well as represent the demonic aspects of the Emperor's character which he is now 'unloading,' though not destroying, as he assumes the Chrysanthemum Throne.

The patient says that in the actual dream the demons really needed no masks. It was only when writing these contemplative paragraphs that he put in the masks, probably to protect the analyst and himself. He also pointed out that the analyst has two antique Japanese teapots on his shelf. He says that he keeps the Emperor-analyst way up on a balcony to idealize him, and to protect him.

> Parma is a place for a Duke; a ducal system where one can get protection if one cooperates, but never release. Parma is also a place for gourmands. Everyone eats well, under the protection of the Duke. Notice, not an emperor or king – just a Duke.

He says that the demons let loose during the enshrining ceremony probably are the analyst's demons, and they are terrifyingly frightening. There are two: the analyst's capacity for thought and feeling, and his passion for both. The patient fears that these will engulf him. That is why they are seen as demonic. His own sense of his dysfunctionality, or his deserving of this from others, make him experience the analyst's 'demons' this way. The dream then is an opportunity for the patient to express his fears – historically, his fears of his parents, particularly his mother's irrationality, and its alienating quality, her threats of dissembling, and his father's disappointing protection of her, that evoked the patient's confusion and rage. Now, it is his fear of analytic limitations or even failure, and the lack of analytic justice. The dreamer sees psychoanalysis as duplicitous in promising a release from turmoil, along with an implicitly promised justice. It cannot and does not happen – clearly not the way it is promulgated or promised. The dreamer says that the two majesties, once having been enshrined, release their demons that magically fall to earth landing upright, so that the emperor and the empress are far removed from the ordinary ways of his own experience. It is like his parents historically, and his analyst currently. Psychoanalysis is 'in' Parma, a ducal system, where one pays for protection. By contrast, there are no allies, no helping hands that are given in pure altruism.

The patient says that he found the academic and literary worlds corrupt, in the sense that all participants are self-serving or opportunistic. He thought that the publication of his first book (there is a second in progress) would demonstrate that he is not the piece of shit his parents led him to believe he is. He thought it proved his value. But nothing happened. Nothing changed. Everyone wanted something, something for themselves. All operate in a ducal or feudal system with no justice. This corruption is the same as the mother's corruption. Parma is the metaphor for the seat of the bosses, and the Duke is the boss of bosses. Help should be given altruistically but it does not appear that way. Like therapy, the Duke demands that one pay for protection. In the literary world it is the same. He even admires the candor of the self-serving nature of the world. It would be good if the Duke (the analyst) were really the Emperor. But the realization that he is so far removed releases the patient's demons: disappointment, disillusionment, hostility, rage, murder. No Duke can cure the past, and, after all, all society is based on exchange.

Psychoanalysis promises radical transformation but cannot deliver, according to this patient. This possibility cannot even be imagined. The patient sees only reform. Following some deal, he believes things may be better. The world may have peace, the wife may gratify, the dog may have his bone, and the fisherman his fish. Life will improve in satisfactions and security if the 'duke' permits it. But it is really only a deal. After recognition that release from personal demons does not take place, a profound cynicism sets in, and all the ways the patient has learned to endure return. What can the patient do? What satisfies his own demons that are released when something creative is accomplished? The demons, formerly his mother's, are now his own. And they paralyze him.

How many ways do people respond to their demons? They do so by accepting and forgiving; by raging and avenging; by living in fantasy, or, by dissembling, even going mad; by freezing and limiting their lives, their self-definitions; and, by enduring, that is, by going on in their individual ways. For this patient it was only listening to his music, or playing it that offered some sort of relief.

The patient fears moving on. He expects to be engulfed, and consequently accepts his self-definition. Dysfunctionality will destroy him (as will the demon functionality of the analyst, or his own murder-demon that appears after creative effort). He lives with his mother's demons occupying and directing him. He sees himself as a man who 'deserves' dysfunctionality and nothing more. In fact, he assumes it keeps him less isolated.

For this patient, creativity begets the threat of death since it is a departure. I believe that this derives from the early desire to connect, and still be autonomous or separate, to be able to leave. Early on it would have necessitated making a diagnosis of the parents and, in his realistically dependent context, facing whatever threat to his self-organization that would have meant. It could not be accomplished in childhood, and it is unrealistic to expect it to have happened.

'Where it was,' that is, where living was, unfortunately, is where the patient still is, internally. 'Where it is,' that is, where living is, is where he must be, and continue to go from there. The 'where it was…' and in the present whatever structurally, even remotely, resembles it, for this patient, provide the form and content of current experience. The sequence may be: exposure, loss, then murderous rage. Usually, patients present rage as an emotional product of loss that is out-of-awareness. Where, then, is salvation? Near the end of *Faust*, Part II, Goethe has the angels say, 'for him whose striving never ceases/we can provide redemption'.

But, there is no justice. For this patient, dysfunctionality is the only way to be safe. Otherwise, he faces demons, the demons of the other, or of himself. The world is corrupt because, lacking reliable altruism, it is based on exchange values. Psychoanalysis is unwittingly deceitful in that it functions – as a product of its culture – in contradiction with altruism. It offers help, but on condition of a fee. The exchange of coin determines the existence of the relationship. It requires payment of fees like the rest of the commercial world of service enterprises. The duplicitousness of psychoanalysis is that it proselytizes and propagandizes that it is selfless. But, like all contradictions in a non-static world the patient must come to terms with that.

At the moment the patient identifies the duplicitous nature of the therapeutic connection and the therapist forthrightly agrees with the validity of the observation, the relationship and the process is no longer duplicitous. But, it is only for the moment. Another contradiction shows itself around the time of change. The patient comes to the appropriate conclusion that the curious, non-judgmental, empathic analyst is a participant in his expansive exploration of himself. It is as if the patient were a fledgling peregrine, precariously poised in some remote aerie on the side of a steep mountain, with an adult falcon urging him to let go and join the updraft. The analyst seems to be intoning two things, 'Leap, you'll fly!' and 'I'll be with you as you try.' The patient would like to bank on the latter, but knows somehow that he will be on his own. The former is a matter of conjecture. In the light of his restless past experience, the patient knows that the probability of his success is increased neither by any amount of urging by his analyst, nor by his own reasoning. The decision to let go, that is a triumph of the non-rational aspect of his restless passion, must be his own.

And yet it is true that the confrontation of these paradoxes facilitates the leap into something new, a transformation. Thus, if the 'restless spirit' of a patient gets him into trouble – as it accounted for the sins of Faust – then surely it may get him out of trouble, as Goethe indicated what was necessary for Faust's change (Bloom 1991). The move from 'where it was…' to 'where I am…' is a move from an invading and dominating, fixed history that is foreboding, and determining the present, to the possibility of current novelty.

When the analytic experience helps the patient become curious about feelings about things as they are (which, of course, includes the embedding of feelings of the way they 'were'), the patient can see things as they might have been, or might be, but as a hopeful derivation of an accepted organic process with all the tensions of uncertainty. In this way transformative change is not an add-on, an idealized imitation, or the magical result of the simplistic experience of having been listened to. No creative effort, reward or prize suffices. It is a leap of faith, with inner conditions having changed.

What is in the analytic relationship that is special about it? There is the patient's imaginative narrative, and his and the therapist's commentary. There is their co-participating curiosity and discussion. There is the scrutiny of their own relationship and behavior with each other. And there is the communal, authentically articulated, interpersonal connectedness (Levenson 1996). In this way, enlivened change comes from inside outward, after having been stimulated or facilitated by the interpenetrating experience of an imperfect analytic world-view, in a world that is not fair, where there is no justice. A new self-definition of relevance and non-dismissiveness comes into being. Psychoanalytic phenomena include the object of our curiosity; the observer's curiosity about himself; the object's curiosity about himself and the observer; and the mode of observation. When all these interpenetrating elements are contemplated by patient and analyst in the session, interpersonal psychoanalysis is made manifest (Levenson 1996).

As McElroy (1973) points out, at the end of *King Lear*, Shakespeare has Gloucester despairingly say, 'A man may rot even here.' Edgar, his son, counters with, 'What, in ill thoughts again? Men must endure.' Gloucester (whose eyes have been gouged) replies, 'And that's true too' (Act V, Scene 2, 8–11). Shakespeare irrefutably offers both possibilities.

The interpersonal psychoanalyst agrees, emphasizing the word 'and' in consciousness, always asserting that differentiatedness is possible. Tragedy, hurt, and damage are never denied, nor seen as inexorable and as defeating as one assumes.

The concept 'and' is a difficult one for psychoanalysts. We are brought up on 'but.' 'But' indicates a conflict in which one element or idea ultimately eliminates the other or some compromise is achieved. Yet, reality does mean complimentary, multiple histories, multiple meanings, and multiple measurements, all viable, depending on points of view and contexts. All of this is in flux, in which opposites move in combination toward some more complex, organized level.

The challenge for all is how to endure what is evidently unjust and may seem to be unendurable. How can patients create, or reimpose, some order and meaning in their lives if an unjust world is to be endurable? How can one come to terms with a complex, uncertain, multifaceted, painful reality where one's basic assumptions and necessities have been denied or destroyed, or one's self-definition has been organized around mystification, inauthenticity, irrelevance, dismissal and inner vacancy, so that one rages and mourns over what was never there, what was absent? Therein – to keep on enduring, to keep on exploring, searching and expanding – lies salvation.

References

Bloom, H. (1991) *The Western Canon.* New York: Harcourt Brace.

Damasio, A. (1994) *Descartes' Error.* New York: G.P. Putnam.

Feiner, A. (1995) "Laughter among the pear trees." *Contemporary Psychoanalysis 31,* 381–397.

Fromm, E. (circa 1954) Presentation to William Alanson White Psychoanalytic Society.

Hallie, P. (1994) *Lest Innocent Blood be Shed.* New York: HarperCollins (reprint).

Kanwal, G. (1995) "Hope, respect and flexibility." Manuscript.

Levenson, E. (1996) "Aspects of self-revelation and self-disclosure." *Contemporary Psychoanalysis 32*, 237–248.

McElroy, B. (1973) *Shakespeare's Mature Tragedies.* Princeton, NJ: Princeton University Press.

Pagels, E. (1995) *The Origin of Satan.* New York: Random House.

Note

1 All dream material and quoted associations were typed by the patient. They appear with permission after severe editing for obvious reasons.

Chapter 5

Touch and the Genesis of Hope[1]

Touch is an area of interest that analyst and patient rarely explore directly. And for good reason. It is part of the minutiae of interpersonal relatedness, like smiling, greeting, muscle tension, and tone of voice. We usually do not comment about it. Furthermore, there are all kinds of cultural differences in attitude about touch, in addition to the traditional taboo laid down by Freud regarding physical contact between patient and analyst. But the topic can emerge, somewhat organically, out of an inquiry about other matters.

I once asked a patient what special moment, or event, or happening, might effect some relief from her persistent feelings of dreariness, her helplessness and hopelessness – feelings that made it so painful for her to be alone. She replied that were she to be noticed, particularly by a man, someone who would say she was pretty, she would indeed feel better. (The patient is married, 65 years old, bright, attractive, and markedly overweight.) Then she said:

> But I know that would only last a few seconds. I respond to little else. I know nothing would ever come of such a remark, I would be too frightened. I would act like a fool and it would be humiliating.

She followed this with a comment that she did get pleasure from her 5-year-old grandson, from listening to music tapes in her car, and from watching videos of ballet performances. She said she never went to the theater, concerts, movies, or museums, because she would have to go alone. Her husband, her son, her sister, and her few friends were conspicuously absent from her comments. When she said something about being 'noticed,' I was sure she was alluding to me.

In fact, I asked, as I had many times on other occasions, whether she thought that I had not 'noticed' her, perhaps in some special way, that special way she was searching for. Her response, as it had always been previously, was negative. I was not getting it. Not only had I noticed her, appropriately, as her analyst, she asserted, but also I had made her feel relevant here in the therapy, a feeling that despite her endless struggle, she had failed to achieve elsewhere. I had never dismissed any of her feelings, she said. No, 'noticing,' as she meant it this time, had implications of more than relevance and non-dismissiveness. It meant ultimately, a romantic relationship that would necessitate a change within herself. 'Is that, perhaps, what is on your mind here?' I asked. 'Of course not,' was the quick retort.

On several occasions I had tried to explore her feelings about my participation in our relationship, or her expectations of me in fantasy or reverie, and had been met with her confusion ('But you're the doctor, why would I have thoughts about you?') or her denial – idealized of course, but denial nevertheless. My feelings were not hurt. I was comfortable doing my analytic job. So I surmised this notion was too dangerous for her to contemplate when I queried about it. What was evident to me this time, however, was the relatively sophisticated way she attributed different meanings to 'being noticed' in different contexts – and I told her so.

The ballet, she continued, had unique significance for her. She found the expertise that is necessary in executing the various steps stimulating, but the leaps, she said, during which someone catches the ballerina, had special appeal. It is that kind of thing that makes her feel it might be all right for her to be who she is. It is the element of trust, the reliability of a partner, concurrent with freedom in movement. And this feeling is somewhat similar, she emphasized, to the kind she gets watching her favorite professional tennis players, whose speed, looseness, and integrated gestures are enviable.

The patient then went on to talk about her experience as a child in ballet school. She remembers that she thought she might become a professional dancer, but that she knew she really was not good enough to be a star. Good, she said, but just not good enough. And she had had little encouragement. It seemed to her that no one cared, that she was just a 'burden,' a 'bother' to her family. Her father was totally uninterested, usually drunk, or preoccupied with his failing business, and her mother cared only for the elder brother, or her own satisfactions and pleasures, and grandiose posturing. So she felt she was on her own, feeling 'unfit, confused, even grotesque, and stupid.' She became fat when she was 13, she said sadly, 'a lump, a blob – they called me stupid cow,' and was convinced that she always would be. If she had shown a modicum of athletic ability it was never encouraged, let alone complimented. Even at camp, it was attributed to her size, or strength, or luck. She seemed to be left always with a feeling of being grotesque. And she still felt that way. Her breasts were too large and pendulous, so she had them reduced surgically. But her self-definition was tenacious. Following the breast reduction she remembers she thought of herself as grotesque because of her girth, the wrinkles on her face, the imperfections of her skin. There seemed to be no end to it. There was no sense in moving, trying something new – nothing would come of it. She couldn't change, she said, with sad resignation. That is, she couldn't change her self-definition.

The depressive triad was painfully evident: her tautological thinking, with its flattened, impoverished communication; her motor retardation; her persistent dreariness. These accompanied a pervasive sense of powerlessness and pointlessness (Spiegel 1960). Even her dreams were replete with images of blocked roads; her car being missing from a parking lot; taxi drivers not being able to find the way; a ubiquitous inaccessibility of lovely landscapes. All these reflected her feelings of defeat and hopelessness about her life, her future, her therapy, and the impotence of her analyst.

After several years of work, it did not look like I had been much use in getting to the depth of her distress, that is, in terms of having had some radical effect on it. Of course, the cure of the past is illusory, and it would be duplicitous to suggest otherwise. But the past's ossified grip on the patient's self-definition had to be loosened, and apparently, despite my efforts, my hope, and intentions, I had had minimal effect. Even the therapy itself was often 'something for her to do, something to give [her] shape or direction for the day.' Over the years I had learned to tolerate the sense of gloom and defeat I felt at the end of each session, after her cynical, refuting responses to anything positive that had occurred between us. Now, feeling helpless before all this, I wondered how I was going to facilitate some change in this woman who felt so hopelessly blocked.

She insisted she had few, more likely no resources, despite her evident intelligence, sensitivity, and sense of humor. (She said once that she was going to get a face lift so as to be noticed, but she was not expecting 'rave notices.') Her past achievements and current assets were persistently ignored or denigrated. ('I was a fake in C. College. I did no work. I got away with it. I was just smart in class and could write reports that I knew would please the instructors.')

Most of her language exchanges were shaped to expose her self-definition of an irrelevant person. She spoke the way she did because her rhetoric, its cadences and tone, reflected what she stood for, and needed. She presented herself as someone who had hid her bank book in the secret recesses of some closet and had forgotten she ever had had an account, so that she had no idea of the accrued interest. I was feeling that I had been engaged in something like trying to start a fire with wet paper. In fact, my feeling futile probably had sparked the question I asked about her potential relief, though I am sure this was not in my tone, nor was its relationship to my query readily in awareness. Still, I could have inquired – perhaps should have, but did not – how she heard it. I did not have to.

Suddenly, there came a remarkable memory. She said that when she was about 18 months old she 'remembers' there had been a small, smoldering fire in her bedroom, possibly caused by a baby-sitter being careless with a cigarette. Her brother (two years older) was also in the room. The baby-sitters (there were two, who happened to be her mother's younger sisters) tried to hide the small burned spot on the rug by moving some of the furniture. She 'remembers' her mother screaming at the young girls, something to the effect that if one hair on Jimmy's head had been burned she would have murdered them.

> But, as for me, I was ignored. Only Jimmy was my mother's concern. All I can think of now is my standing in the crib feeling terribly confused and frightened.

After a brief silence, she went on to comment that all during childhood and adolescence she had dreams of Jimmy's head being on fire.

> And to this day, when feeling terribly distressed, I still think of the ovens connected with the Holocaust, and how those poor people were put in, some of them alive. How could people do that to someone?

I then asked her what she thought she would have liked to have happened with her mother. Plaintively she said:

> She should have picked me up and held me tight to reassure me. When my 4-year-old son got lost – so I thought – I ran down the street frantically, and there he was, not far away, sitting on a step with his hands on his face. I picked him up and held him and patted him. It is odd, he doesn't remember this at all.

Her childhood anecdote, as she remembered it, seemed to echo Winnicott's (1971) insight that the early mother–child relationship, that includes the whole business of mothering (particularly tender holding), engenders the illusion that mother and child are one. And, he adds, percipiently, that the mother's eventual task gradually to disillusion the infant of this alleged symbiosis, so as to encourage differentiatedness, has no chance of success unless there has been sufficient opportunity for illusion (Winnicott 1971, p.11). Apparently my patient missed this experience of reassuring safety, according to her memory.

I asked her what she thought might be in the holding or the patting. She said:

> It is the touch of skin, the touch of body. Did you know my skin is always dry? My fingers crack. I've spent a fortune on dermatologists. I have to use a cream all over my hands and arms and legs every night. I used to have my husband do my back, but I do not ask him anymore. Anyway, he's useless and crazy. He would take it as an opportunity to be hurtful or insulting about my weight. Occasionally I have a massage, but that doesn't last. I look forward to it though, and it is relieving, more so than relaxing. But it is too impersonal to mean anything to me.

While the patient was talking this way, thoughts I had had in connection with two recent cataract operations intruded. The cataracts were removed on different occasions about a month apart. The surgeries were entirely uneventful, except that in my subjective view the second was different. I had remarked to the surgeon that the second surgery (same surgeon, same staff, same procedure, same facility) seemed dissimilar to the first. The surgeon told me they were identical procedurally, and added that many patients, in his experience, say something similar, usually reporting that the second seemed to vary. Then I told him why I thought so.

I was certain that the nerve block used in the second operation was of a different kind, or of a different strength; perhaps it had not been applied precisely the same way, or my face was not symmetrical. What made me think this, he asked. I replied that for whatever reason, I could feel two things in my eye that I hadn't the first time. These were the coldness of the irrigation, and some pressure on the lens. These two things had caused a considerable amount of anxiety and tension.

Despite his insistence that the procedures had been the same, I stood by my feeling – whatever the reason, I knew my experiences were different.

During the surgery I had been connected to an automatic sphygmomanometer. In this way my blood pressure was monitored automatically at intervals of approximately five minutes. I could predict that my blood pressure was about to be measured because the machine made a slight whirring sound when going into operation. Then I felt three separate pressures around my arm. The rhythm is important. There was one slight pressure, and then rapidly, two typically heavy impulses, after which my blood pressure was noted. After that, there was complete depressurizing.

I note this in some detail because it relates to my mounting anxiety in response to what I felt was the traumatic invasiveness of the procedure. Despite my increasing muscle tension, however, at the first mild impulse of the pressure cuff I relaxed, with the coincident fantasy that it must be someone, probably a nurse, gently touching my arm. The nurse must have been reassuring me because my increased tension and stress were noticed. So I thought. But as soon as the machine made the two subsequent pressure impulses, I realized that this was sheer fantasy. This would not be worth commenting about except that the fantasy occurred repeatedly during the entire procedure, despite my awareness of its non-actuality.

The sequence was: sense of traumatic invasion; increasing anxiety and muscle tension; the first felt impulse of the blood pressure machine; the fantasy that it was a reassuring touch, with subsequent relaxation; second and third impulses of the machine, coincident with the realization that my interpretation was, indeed, fantasy; then, a prompt return to the anxious state. I want to emphasize that despite the awareness of the unreality of my interpretation, I kept making it each time I felt the first impulse. It distracted me from my anxiety, and it became obvious to me that I kept wishing it were real. It was as though my hope for safety, or for the reassurance of safety and well-being, transcended rationality. Without it there probably would have been more and more tension, and, ultimately, complete despair (Kanwal 1997).

Now, there is no surprise to the idea that touching can have a reassuring, reparative influence. At this stage in our professional history it is a rather banal, and conventionally informed idea. Freud (1913) commented that touching is the first step in obtaining some sort of control over, or attempting to make use of a person (pp.33–34). Michelangelo's painting on the Sistine Chapel ceiling depicts God almost touching Adam with an extended forefinger. Steinberg (1983) writes that many Renaissance painters used the touching of or the pointing to the genitals of the infant Jesus, and His chin-chucking of the Virgin, as ways of demonstrating His incarnate reality. We are familiar with the mutual back-scratching of apes, during which individual relief, the exchange of protein occurs, and communal existence is established, simultaneously.

Common in experience are our picking up children who have fallen, and have been hurt, or frightened, and our patting them to reassure them; our clinging to each other in times of mourning; our putting an arm around someone in moments of stress; our encouraging the petting of animals such as cats and dogs so as to reduce the blood pressure of senile patients; our sensual fondling and stroking gestures of affection and tenderness; and our elbow nudges and pats in camaraderie. My patient refers to her feelings of relief from massage. All these are commonplace in our experience and knowledge. Yet oddly, 'touch,' especially its relation to hope, is not common in the indices of psychoanalytic texts. In the operating room, when the touch experience became personal, despite my awareness that it was hallucinatory, it had ineluctable presence because it repetitively stimulated the sense of my connectedness and/or well-being (Kanwal 1997, p.138).

The description of my experience suggests there was some anticipation and expectation of the reparative, reassuring aspects of touch. For me, there was a positive historical referent that enhanced their probable potential. In my history, I remember that touching was neither forbidden nor hurtful – and usually pleasurable. I assume, therefore, that my hallucination derived from a hopefulness based on 'preconceptions of how things...should be' (Boris 1976, p.143). These preconceptions structure, and are shaped in turn, by reality. They reflect an expectation of well-being, of connectedness to others in which 'the whole world is kin' (Shakespeare, *Troilus and Cressida*, Act III, Scene 3, 175). My not giving up the illusion, despite knowing that it was not real, suggests the development of a compelling need. And surely there was one in my experience in the operating room. Therein lies hope's genesis (see Kanwal 1997, pp.138–141). My patient's interminable quest is similar.

To state it so, however, does not do justice to the interpenetrating aspects of the evolution of the feeling of hope in the individual. One's preconceptions never have separate existence from the environment. The organism and its environment are never alienated from each other. Mature individuals are the result of their experience with the environment, which is profoundly and persistently interpersonal; and their environment does not shift or change without their influencing it. So the two are not simply interactive, in that people cannot be alien from their surround in the process of maturation and development. A preconception of the way things should be initiates a unique response to the way things are, which, in turn, reinforces it or warps it. At any stage of development we do what we believe, which is a product of the entire growth process that has preceded. Our behavior is not evidence of our belief about ourselves and others. It is identical with it. A person is not evil because of evil acts. Evil acts are identical with evil self-definition. Change of self is, in part, a change in the restoration of preconception. The result is change in behavior, especially in response to variety.

Boris (1976) remarks that the depression, or the emptiness of a patient's experience, lies in that 'concave configuration left from where the breast (mother's) was supposed to be' (p.143). In an analysis of Psalm 22, Fromm (1966) points out that the poet moves from despair to hope in his thinking, only to fall into a state of deeper desperation until he recites, 'thou made me trust in my mother's breasts.' He comments that it is a most reassuring memory for someone who feels lost and abandoned to remember the mother's love, and express it in the language of the body (Fromm 1966, p.218). These examples from Boris and Fromm are both 'touch' images. Balint (1959) writes that for someone who feels uncertain in the 'spaces between objects,' the touch of one evokes a feeling of safety (p.34). Thus the capacity for hoping, and the genesis of its functioning, derive from the experience of the gratification of an early skin-to-skin relationship that reinforces and anchors the sense of one's location and connectedness.

My patient's lifelong struggle with depression embodies a profound loss of hope – really, hope abandoned – with repetitive but failed attempts at its restoration. It is a slippery thing. She does have a preconception of how things should be today, and what they should have been. Unfortunately they are not, and they were not, at least as she says, after age 4 or 5. After that, after her parents stopped seeing her as cute, she reports, she felt she was always in the way. (So things were not all bad, of course.) There will be mourning in her analysis, especially over the absence, over the what-might-have-been.

Without the experience of touch, she says, there is vacancy for her (experienced as emptiness), with the consequent need for fillers: fashionable clothing; attentive looks and compliments from men, and the cosmetic surgeries that are supposed to guarantee them; food; passive entertainment, and conspicuous, indulgent consumption.

Typical in her therapy sessions is her extreme discomfort if she has 'nothing' to say. She then feels inadequate. She needs to be 'invited' into the room, she insists, with an initial query or remark by the therapist. In this way, she believes there will be some structure, some shape she might assume, or concrete place or mold into which she could fit. She is furious when it does not happen. She is terrified of the therapist's silence, which, in anxiety, she perceives as an ambiguity, and perhaps – she conjectures – she is in the way, and silence is his disdain for her, or his punishing her for being a bad patient. This quickly is transformed by her into feeling 'stupid, or like a blob,' with the additional feelings of not belonging and disconnection, or of failure and humiliation. There is anger, but her full rage never surfaces. At least, not yet. It is a rage about dismissal and irrelevance, and about not having been given what she should have, about not having been 'touched' or 'held' and supported, literally and figuratively. It will be expressed ultimately toward the analyst, because he has held out the promise of non-dismissal, of being noticed, perhaps even the promise of touch, and his silences reaffirm the fulfillment of her self-definition. When that begins to change she will expect more, and she will have to be queried whether 'nothing-to-say' is a metaphoric appeal for 'touch,' and his silence – the absence of 'touch' – is, to her, the apparent repetition of her early experience.

Having 'nothing-to-say' also follows a creative or autonomous impulse, as though she has dared be something she is not, or do something she should not, so that 'nothing-to-say' is a tense, anxious, waiting for judgment, or validation. She anticipates humiliation if she makes a mistake, so she tries to avoid the possibility by limiting her contacts. And making a correction is equally unavailable to her. In fact, the expectation of humiliation is a self-ordered explanation for her feelings of tension and distress. It almost seems that she struggles for the right to exist, for being itself, something she dare not assert. She often answers a query with a question. If I were to ask what she felt, or what she feels, she often replies quickly, 'What do you feel?' It is not resistance or reluctance in the conventionally analytic sense. She wants a guide to know what is typical, permissible and acceptable. In this way, she believes, she may be different, but at least she will not be deviant. Her own spontaneous thought processes are not safe enough. She wants to read books, like biographies, so she asks why I am reading the biography that lies on my table.

It is the same with people she meets, or in conversations with friends. Without some structure provided by rules, guidelines, directions, or implicit signals, she says she feels dumb, alien, and consequently 'lost' or 'in a fog,' sort of like a 'lump of dough needing a cookie cutter to give it shape.' Her two friends treat her as though she were abysmally ignorant, the group's clown, or a consummate fool – which she is not (she has had a text on social studies dedicated to her as the author's 'best graduate student'). She says:

> I am what they need me to be, a simpleton, a dope. My husband needed someone to take care of, and he's a great 'take-carer.' So we married. But I do not need that anymore. I've changed. He and my friends really do not know me. I do not let them.

The flip side of her being an 'empty vessel' is occasional arrogance in taste, opinion, values, in areas such as style, clothing design, architecture, politics, entertainment, and child rearing. She 'knows' the way these things should be. Perhaps the word 'officious' would better describe her opinionated communication, which often resulted in my silent disdain, not so much because of the information, which, as I recall was often incorrect, but for what I perceived as the smug tone of the delivery. Her assertion was that she knew better than anyone.

In essence, her idea of fillers is a good idea gone bad. Her intention is reasonable. Her transient gratifications (real and pseudo) are substitutes for what she feels is missing, purposive of what she hopes to obtain, with no result.

She has wondered, countless times, what the plumber's helper had in mind when he said it was a pleasure to see her, or what the airline clerk was thinking when he held her passport for what seemed to her interminable moments; or what the handsome stranger had in mind, when, in a hotel lobby in Verona, he asked her for directions to the amphitheatre which was two or three blocks away.

She has even contemplated a third face-lift so that she will not be 'mistaken for [her] son's mother.' But there is a danger in the romantic sense of being 'noticed,' the danger of humiliation, due to her assumption of what she says will be her probable silly, stupid, or slovenly behavior. She often creates scenarios in her mind of others' thoughts – sort of an interior monologue – that somehow explain to her why she is feeling the way she does. What were they really thinking, she muses. If she knew that, she would know more about her vague feeling of excitement, or at least have some understanding why she is having it. It is a variation of the 'cookie cutter' metaphor. Feelings, when she is vaguely aware of them, just seem to occur, as though they were disembodied. To her, they are hardly interpersonal. (This has changed considerably with analysis.)

One time long ago, when she had done poorly on an arithmetic test, her mother said, addressing no one, and looking at the wall, 'At least she's pretty.' She was 7 or 8 years old then. Today she wants to know if it is true. But still, she does not want to live as though her mother were right. That would prove that that is all she is good for – romance or marriage – as her mother once commented. Therefore she does not lose weight, which she says she wants to do. She describes her weight as a protective wall preventing exposure to others. It is a bind from which she cannot extricate herself expressing her differentiatedness and autonomy. She has been seen and treated as an object, and she sees herself that way. She once told me that stuffing her mouth with food – junk food – often prevents her from screaming. But her weight is mixed up with an attempt at honesty. She said once, that the only person with whom she is completely straightforward is her trainer, who, while being a friendly, warm, professional, is very unattractive. The attractiveness of any man rattles her, so she 'plays a part.' If she is to be authentic, she believes, she need not care about how she looks. Otherwise she fulfills her mother's expectation of her. With me, attractiveness is of little concern. She fears that she will appear 'dumb.' And more important, she will see it in herself.

She has not been 'noticed' as a separate person, so she is never free to notice a separate world around her, that is, free to use her imagination to engage it in all its nuances, and to establish relationships the way she would like. She believes, she says, she should have been given something, some tender touch. This would have given her the confirmation that she is worth something, but she was left with vacancy. Still, she has a glim of the way things should be, and like myself in the operating room, this expectation of rightness continues to prevail over actual experience (Boris 1976, pp.141–142). She waits for a validation that never comes.

The idea of touching in therapy has been dealt with by many others, beginning with Freud's (1915) admonition about responding to a patient's professed love in any nonanalytic way. When we think of 'touch' in connection with analysis, we immediately think of a modality of treatment. It is tempting to go into it, but its exploration is not my purpose. My interest here is about hope's genesis. Briefly, however, there is a literature concerning its possible value, and its difficulties and hazards in the course of psychotherapy (see Smith, Clance and Imes 1998). Casement (1985) labored over his dilemma of gratifying a patient's request to hold his hand. He reasoned that were he to do that he would risk losing the patient analytically. Still, if he ignored her request he would seemingly avoid those painful elements in her history relevant to her request, which might then become encapsulated as too terrible to confront (Casement 1985, p.163). My patient never asked me to touch her, nor have I ever had the desire, for any assumed reason, therapeutic or extratherapeutic. In fact, the idea turns me off. Casement resolved his dilemma about touching his patient on the basis of his searching for the function of the patient's communication, and sharing with her his own helplessness. Her response, gratifying to him, was to shift the word 'touch' into metaphor. From a demand to hold hands with him, she asserted, hopefully, that she believed, now, that he was 'in touch' with her feelings. Perhaps if my patient screwed up her courage to express the same demand, I might deal with it similarly. My being turned off needs to be confronted by both of us in session, as possibly retarding the patient's progress toward becoming a desirable human being.

When we write of preconceptions, are we referring to the alleged 'thinking' of infants, which is what psychoanalysts often try to describe (Boris 1976), or are we referring to how a person interprets or translates his or her past, attempting some correction? I would guess it is both – past alleged 'thinking' and current interpretation – but not necessarily in the lingua franca of psychoanalysts (e.g., Bion, as cited by Boris 1976).

A preconception of well-being is probably part of our biological make-up that is accountable by evolution. It is one aspect of total consciousness, which includes conscious and out-of-awareness processes. In the course of development, consciousness is not an instructional mechanism, but a selectional one. It does not develop by simple alterations of inner experience, insightful or otherwise, but by selectionist processes that eliminate or ignore some possibilities, or strengthen others, with regard to feelings and behavior, so that in the course of development, self-definition comes into being. One can readily appreciate the functionality of selective inattention (to avoid stress), and of course, selective attention (to gratify needs), in the evolution of the self-system (Sullivan 1953). The self-system, as Sullivan described it, has to do with the avoidance of anxiety. Self-definition involves more than that. It includes all of one's beliefs based on feeling experiences. It is somewhat like an ideology, most of which is integrated out-of-awareness, and involves a world-view, and a concept of causality, as well as feelings, attitudes and values.

I believe interpersonal experiences, via these processes, are registered in neuronal groups. It is not a matter of hard or soft wiring. I think it is a matter of being genetically or congenitally equipped from birth onward with neuronal groups, some of which die out and some of which survive. What is selected in experience is one neuronal group or another. This is part of the processes that give rise to our values and beliefs, our categorizations and generalizations, that are the manifestations of our self-definitions. It is accomplished in an ambiguous world of shapes, colors, textures, temperatures, movements, sounds, smells, things, and relationships and their emotional attributes. In this way, abstract concepts and all that is relevant to self-definition are formed, in a world that is not already labeled, that is without categories, and in which there are no advance programs nor an inner structure to guide one (Edelman 1987).

Thus the formidable task for the interpersonal analyst is to facilitate change in self-definition. But how is that possible when self-definition is never not expressed? If ideology is never on vacation, then self-definition can never be absent. It is sort of like there being no such thing as 'no communication' or 'no relationship.' Our questioning 'In what way?' clues us to this truism. It is the 'how' of interpersonal inquiry. A patient who says she has 'nothing to say' is showing a part of a self that has nothing-to-say. One might wonder who or where the 'I' is when someone says, 'I'm empty, I have nothing to say.' It is in keeping with the consistency and reliability of self-definition. It is like the many facets of the Hope diamond, each interrelated and interdependent, giving the stone its particular characteristic brilliance. The evolving sequence of preconception, touch, and hope is probably organized this way. It is all part of self-definition along with the necessity for relevance and nondismissal.

Another patient (40 years old, with one child of 4), early in analysis, after having been abandoned by her husband of eleven years, dreamt that she 'met President Clinton as some function and he took her by the hand in a friendly way, which made her feel hopeful.' And then, in a second scene in the dream, she called her sister only to hear her brother-in-law's voice on the answering machine saying, 'Don't call back unless someone has died or been murdered.' The theme of extreme unavailability and utter rejection, of having been shut out by her mother, sister, and husband, was noted by her as coincident now with a rekindling of hopefulness via the contact in therapy.

One final speculative note: It is hypothesized that touch, like light, may affect the production of nitric oxide, a neural transmitter, which, carried by the hemoglobin to the brain, stimulates the production of endorphins, so that one feels good. But only in a positive context. By that I mean a perception of, or, expectation of, safety in touch.

What is not speculative is the body's fight-flight response in a threatening context, during which cortisol is released by the adrenals after a complex chain of biochemical events. Cortisol usually sustains the body's response under stress, and then slows so that the body can return to normal functioning. But it may go awry and fail to turn off. Particularly, under conditions of chronic stress, instead of protecting the immune system, it may suppress it, as well as the further production of certain brain cells (in the hippocampus).

I believe there is some continuous, integrative necessity for living beings, some organic lawfulness, perhaps reflective of the 'deep' structures referred to in disciplines like linguistics, anthropology, developmental psychology, and neural science. That is, I think we are so made up that from the start, we are integrative at successively more complex levels of organization. It is the one compelling thing that we, like all matter in this universe, do. We organize. We do it any way we can – with our best foot forward, despite its not looking that way. But it is the best we can do at the moment. It is who we are. My analyst used the image of a tree growing around a boulder that blocked its way on the side of a mountain.

Someone's sense of what should have been reflects today's evaluation of what actually happened in the past. From the point of view of an ongoing analysis, the accuracy of the patient's memory is less important than her translation of the past. The communication of what feelings have been experienced, for example, dismissal and nonrelevance, is what is significant. (In my first patient's case, according to her memory, her mother did prefer her brother.) I think this is more important than what the actual event was that one experienced with feeling. It is not that the actual event should be ignored, but the patient's memory is a function of her view of previous relationships, and perhaps a reflection of how the current one – the analytic – is experienced. At least, it clues us as to how the patient defines herself. If we ask, 'Tell me a "daddy" (or any other figure) story,' we shall hear part of a self-definition in relation to that person.

When feelings are brought into awareness, explored thoroughly, and commented about, along with what the patient 'sees' in the session, particularly in terms of the inherent contradictions in the analytic relationship, the experience of the past experience changes (Boris 1976; Laing, 1960). My first patient's chronically depressive response has been fraught with failure. Her early experiences, freighted with self-denigration, fear and confusion, have blocked the development of processes that would have been useful in expressing desire, and the understanding and resolving of frustration (Gut 1982). The therapeutic engagement is one of non-dismissiveness, always with the potential for the non-duplicitous examination of the analyst's feelings when appropriate, if, of course, they are available for scrutiny. This way, in the analytic relationship patients can learn to trust their perceptions, so that their appraisals can be differentiated from their apprisals, something my patient has rarely done successfully (C. Rabinowitz, personal communication, c.1954).

When the patient's view of the analytic relationship changes, the interpretation of the past begins to do so as well. If the experience of the old experience becomes different, current situations, however homologously similar to, or actually repetitive of, old interactions, also can be seen differently.

Spontaneity is a function of one's being available to oneself and connected to others at the same time. When the self is known to oneself, the world becomes less austere and foreboding. Of course, this is part of a process, not a sudden state that one arrives at, like those rats in Gestalt learning experiments. They quit searching for food and suddenly said, 'Aha!' to themselves, running for the hidden reward. Change means that self-definition, or self-conception, has changed. Suddenly, there are choices. A self no longer self-defined as vacant does not need, nor does it look for, an appropriately safety-producing shape. Nor is there any more need for filler to dispel the distress of vacancy, since the feeling of vacancy vanishes.

There is no magic in it, but it may seem so, in the light of our inability to describe it precisely. For one thing, it has little to do with conventionally so-called 'understanding' oneself; particularly with regard to some set of theoretical constructs, that kind of labeling that is long on metaphoric coloration, and short on felt experience (Levenson 1998). For another, behavioral change is like a leap of faith. It creeps up on you. You do it, and there you are, like learning to walk or ride a bicycle. Change has to do with how one experiences oneself, defines oneself, and the way one functions. Variations of anti-self self-definitions are abandoned. There is no expectation of dismissal or nonrelevance. The preconception of well-being, the embodiment of hope, is expectable and becomes demonstrable.

There is a transforming power to touch that helps us feel part of the commonweal. It is most succinctly and elegantly captured by I. Levin's and M. Schafer's 1965 ballad, 'She Touched Me.' The last bars are, 'She touched me, she touched me/And suddenly/Nothing is the same.' It is evident in our noticing the difference between the how of the past and present and the what. And it is the how, not the what, that makes all the difference.

References

Balint, M. (1959) *Thrills and Regressions.* New York: International Universities Press.

Boris, H. (1976) "On hope: its nature and psychotherapy." *International Review of Psycho-Analysis 3,* 139–150.

Casement, P. (1985) *On Learning from the Patient.* London: Tavistock.

Edelman, G. (1987) *Neuronal Darwinism.* New York: Basic Books.

Freud, S. (1913) "Totem and taboo." *Standard Edition 13,* 1–161. London: Hogarth Press.

Freud, S. (1915) "Observations on transference love." *Standard Edition 12,* 159–171. London: Hogarth Press.

Fromm, E. (1966) *You Shall be as Gods.* New York: Holt, Rinehart and Winston.

Gut, E. (1982) "Cause and function of the depressed response: a hypothesis." *International Review of Psycho-Analysis 69,* 179–181.

Kanwal, G.S. (1997) "Hope, respect, and flexibility in the psychotherapy of schizophrenia." *Contemporary Psychoanalysis 33,* 133–150.

Laing, R.D. (1960) *The Divided Self.* London: Tavistock.

Levenson, E. (1998) "Awareness, insight, and learning." *Contemporary Psychoanalysis 34,* 239–249.

Levin, I. And Schafer, M. (1965) 'She Touched Me.' Milton and Nina Music.

Smith, E., Clance, P. and Imes, S. (1998) *Touch in Psychotherapy.* New York: Guilford Press.

Spiegel, R. (1960) "Communication in the psychoanalysis of depressions." In J. Masserman (ed) *Psycho-analysis and human values.* New York: Grune and Stratton.

Steinberg, L. (1983) *The Sexuality of Christ in Renaissance Art and Modern Oblivion.* New York: Pantheon.

Sullivan, H. (1953) *The Interpersonal Theory of Psychiatry.* New York: W.W. Norton.

Winnicott, D.W. (1971) *Playing and Reality.* New York: Basic Books.

Note

1 In its original form, this chapter was an essay dedicated to the memory of Harold Boris.

PART TWO

The Analyst

Chapter 6

Countertransference and Misreading

The Influence of the Anxiety of Influence[1]

Io sol uno
di nostra vita.

(Dante)

In a casual conversation, a young analyst tells me that a patient of his, finally, after years of tedious work with her, became affectively engaged with him, and immediately began getting seductive. Then, in her next session, he confesses, much to his astonishment and resentment, she announced that she was terminating analysis. I tell him it sounds like a lot of people I know, patients and non-patients. As soon as they feel safe with you and become connected, they let you know what they want, or believe they need. It may have little to do with sex. Perhaps it was a sign of some affirmation of herself as a woman, as a person, as an equal, or even as a loving, loved, or desirable object. In effect, she may have been saying, in a strong desire for some affective response, 'I'm here, are you?' Alas, in his stunned disbelief, and perhaps his resentment about her leaving after all the hard work they had done together, he did not answer. In response to my conjecture, he said, painfully, he had no answer. He thought of her behavior as manipulative, power oriented, or even demandingly dependent.

He may lose the patient because, it appears, he was rigid about questioning her seductiveness. He may lose her if he fails to respond affectively in a constructively analytic way because that would be a dismissal. Even her sensitivity to his anxiety, of which he had not a shred of awareness, may have stimulated her withdrawal.

Did he fear that he would be seduced? I doubt it! Was he distressed over not knowing what to do? Apparently. What were his choices? What should he have done analytically? How could he have avoided being seduced and still respond respectfully, supporting the seriousness of her feeling? That was his task. After all,

Freud (1915) advised that the patient's erotic feelings toward the analyst be treated as real, even though they are not to be responded to in kind.

In other words, our psychiatrist somehow is to express, 'I won't love you madam, but I love you.' Unless he acknowledges that something is going on between them, which is the result of his impact or influence on her, and hers on him, the therapy probably will be lost. But apparently he could not do that without thinking about nomenclature? That will give no lasting comfort to him, nor to the patient. In fact, the diagnostic labeling is a foreclosure, a defense against the anxiety stirred up by the necessity for an exploratory process. It can be a sort of hidden countertransference under the guise of expertise.

If the psychiatrist reasons, justifiably, that he will not be seduced, but that some spark is beginning to glow in his patient, and that his task is to make it flame, the therapy may have a chance of continuing. He could query about what she thought she was asking for, perhaps using words like 'open' or 'warm,' maybe even 'available.'

Now, after the interaction, his task is a little more difficult. The flash of spontaneity is lost, but it still is possible to save the situation. If he asks baldly about her quitting, he is probably going to get all the rational and irrational reasons – money, time, school, job, or doing it on one's own. In my experience, I never know what that 'it' means, although I surmise it may have something to do with some aspect of resistance to therapeutic influence. For example, it may have something to do with not wanting to be scrutinized, i.e., not wanting to be objectified as a 'patient'; not wanting to be responsible for facing oneself; or perhaps even wanting to experience the confidence of having the freedom to leave. A patient once told me, after I inquired about her wanting to do 'it' on her own, 'I can leave, so I'll stay. There's so much to do.'

Suppose he addresses the interaction itself with:

> Do you think I might have failed you in some way, recently? In our last session, perhaps? Did I fail to hear something or affirm something, in some way that was hurtful, perhaps suggesting I dismissed you?

And who knows, maybe he can save it by re-engaging her. After all, the actual inquiry, his willingness to be open, taking the onus on himself, would communicate something in response to her, 'I'm here.' It would be saying in essence, 'I'm here too!' But I do not mean being lubricious. I do mean there has to be a common language for them to proceed. The analyst has to search for that so that the patient is not self-abusive or self-denigrating.

Any situation, event, or object has many possible interpretations. Speech imposes a particular interpretation, and creates a temporarily shared social reality. The choice of words emphasizes this. Here's Sullivan (1953), for example:

> The child gradually learns the 'consensually validated' meaning of language – in the widest sense of language. These meanings have been acquired from group activities, interpersonal activities, social experience. Consensually validated symbol activity involves an appeal to principles which are accepted as true by the hearer. And when this happens, the youngster has acquired or learned the syntaxic mode of experience. (Sullivan 1953, pp. 28–29 note)

Still, what any particular observer 'sees' going on in a situation is an entirely private affair. One semiotician comments:

> [However,] *it [the event] can be talked about* and hence...become a temporarily shared social reality. The solitary observer may thus try to transform his 'private' outlook on the situation into a social reality simply by telling some other person about it... From that moment on the two of them are jointly committed to a temporarily shared social world, established and continually modified by acts of communication. (Rommetveit 1979, p.10, my italics)

A long time ago, during a visit to Chestnut Lodge, I listened to one of the resident psychiatrists present a patient with a comment, spoken in a denigrating way, that she had been very seductive with him. There were no details about the interaction the two had in session, but there were many data about the young woman's tenderless, unsatisfying, unsupportive, sexless marriage, and the severe depression that overtook her when her lover appeared to have abandoned her. Later, I commented to his supervisor about the student's remark, and, it seemed to me, the apparent lack of data to back it up, in the midst of a wealth of detail that might have contributed to an understanding of the interaction. 'Could the young psychiatrist have had an overinflated idea about himself, *vis-à-vis* this attractive young woman?' I asked. Could his judgment have been an oversimplification of a complex encounter? Could it be that the eager doctor had some values which were reflected in his private opinions about fidelity, and the compulsory, legalistic part of a marriage? Or, in a word, could it be that the psychiatrist's own person was all too nakedly present in his summary about the patient? The supervisor's answer was, 'Well, she was showing a lot of thigh.'

One way of thinking about it is that one troubled woman's depressed sloppiness, her not caring about how she looked in hospital garb, could be one doctor's seduction. But, suppose the patient intended to be seductive. To what could an analyst think the patient was drawing him astray? Does the woman believe she can seduce anyone with her magnificent thigh? Is it really to be an adjournment to bed? Is it to be men only, or anyone, so that sex is no end in itself (and probably not fun or not pleasurable at all), perhaps more likely a step on the way to conquering, possessing, collecting, or self-validating? We do not know because we never learned what to do with the message.

The subtitle of this chapter is an amalgam of the title of an early paper on anxiety and countertransference by Mabel Cohen (1952), 'Countertransference and anxiety,' and a paper of mine (Feiner 1979), 'Countertransference and the anxiety of influence.'

My phrasing could be seen as poorly imitating the form of the last sentence of James Joyce's book of the dark – that willfully obscure *Finnegans Wake* (1939) – which ends the volume but does not finish it because the sentence continues on the first page, opening up the tale. That sentence, which completes the great circle is, 'A way, a lone, a last, a loved, a long the [and then the first page begins] riverrun past Eve and Adam's…' My point is that we get some kind of reciprocal, circular stirring, some kind of anxiety, sometimes, because, as analysts, we are pushed to remind ourselves of our being alone, autonomous and differentiated, and wanting to be relevant, and have impact at the same time. This occurs under the influence of our patients, the influence of any ambiguity. There is a circle of tension, usually mild, although sometimes powerfully intimidating, that may influence us to abandon our technically neutral position, abandon an analytic attitude, or prevent us from clearing some imaginative space for ourselves and doing something useful.

We are, under these conditions, primed for personal change, if we are sensitive to ourselves (Franklin 1994). We become aware of our interaction with patients, and can, if possible, try to understand ourselves in these interactions the same way, and to the same degree, try to understand the patient. For example, Franklin (1994) noticed, in an attempt to encourage a patient to explore something, that his choice of the word 'we' in contrast to the word 'you' indicated how much more he had become involved and invested in the patient's analysis than previously, and that this had represented a marked change in himself. Defensive gestures, on the other hand, usually manifested in typical countertransferential responses, are automatic, if the awareness of one's aloneness and one's autonomy is threatening. They can be shaped as idealizing and/or imitating; or abusing ourselves or others; or even isolating ourselves, sometimes sacrificing our sanity or even our safety.

Or, we may be moved to make some viable, strong expression of ourselves, our openness, and our availability, and appropriate accessibility. In an analytic context can we 'misread' our patients, our own way, giving patients' struggle a new affirmative expression, so that they can reabsorb this and reread themselves?

To characterize patients' striving for perfection their 'need' is to imply (almost adversarily) that they must give up an observed aspect of themselves with no guide to facilitate a change that remains in the abstract, and is about something that is possibly pejorative. To suggest that possibly they are staving off some perceived disasters with their attempts at perfectionism gives patients a way of exploring the purposiveness of their efforts with others, as well as its history.

Reading the data, to regard themselves, and the other, analysts ask themselves: 'What is going on?', without foreclosure on the development and evolution of the interaction (Levenson 1988).

In the 1979 paper on countertransference, I suggested that therapist's desire to be original, that is, to be themselves, required that they clear some imaginative space so that they could shape a response, using the patient's metaphors and history. I did not mean this as an interpretation in the traditional sense. And I want to differentiate it from the 'role-responsive' concept of countertransference (Sandler 1976). 'Role reflex,' as I understand it, is reactive, in that the analyst, in feelings, fantasy, attitudes, and behavior, is complementary to the role in which patients cast themselves. In this view, the irrational nature – if any – of the analyst's response reflects the compromise between the analyst's self, and his or her reflexive acceptance of the role in which the patient casts the analyst. Sandler's assumption is that the analyst's countertransference, which is not interpreted, must be irrational.

All views of countertransference, not as hindrance, but rather as useful data, are constructive misreadings of Freud's (1912b) suggestion that the analyst 'turn his own unconscious like a receptive organ toward the transmitting unconscious of the patient.' I believe misreading suggests a new way for the analyst to understand or comprehend – a revision, a looking-over-again at what is being presented. It is based on the idea of 'misreading' used in literary theory (Bloom 1973, 1975a), from where it was borrowed.

Misreading analytically, or misprision, as it is sometimes called in literary theory of criticism, is a deliberate reworking of what is offered (by the patient) for the purpose of understanding the data as well as oneself. In this way we can make some creative response. This is not the conventional sense of the word 'misread,' which refers to error, usually due to misunderstanding. As the concept is used here, in a misread we exercise judgment in that the analyst believes the patient could profitably go in another direction. In this sense, 'misreading' refers to reworking. It is a translation.

'Misprision' in literary theory means to have disagreement with something the way it is. Bloom (1973) uses it as an indication of a swerve in poetry needed to make creative change. Thus, it is a corrective movement in a new work, which implies that a precursor poem took its ideas 'accurately,' up to a certain point, but then should have swerved, precisely in the direction toward which the new poem moves. By so reading, the parent poem – its terms, its metaphors, its vocabulary – are retained, but are now meant in a new sense (Bloom 1973, p.14). Therefore, misprision, or misreading, the poet's struggle with a precursor poem, as used here, is similar to an analyst's interaction with the survival achievements of the patient.

That is, it is a struggle with the form the patient has imposed on life out of the necessities of personal history. It is for this reason that I have borrowed the term.

By reworking their vocabulary, patients' reality and struggle are made relevant. The patient's integrative forces lying below the surface, transforming the patient's thoughts, beliefs, feelings, fantasies, i.e., their total experience, into words, can be addressed.

Interpersonalists are familiar with this when they view a patient's presentation, not as concealing some 'truth,' but as revealing what is desired or needed for growth and expansiveness. It is not a matter of shared meanings, one text leading to another text, or, discontinuously, an allegedly more rational text, the analyst's being substituted for the patient's, but more a matter of a relationship between texts, the patient's and the analyst's.

One of the more obvious ways of misreading the influence of the patient is to scrutinize the content of a fantasy, or the feelings aroused in us coincident with the patient's commentary, or even those which take place in us later in the day or week. It is somewhat similar to linking day fragments to dream metaphors. The relationship between or among the elements, or more precisely, the 'properties' of the fantasy of objects or processes, or between these 'properties' and ourselves, clues us to patterned issues extant in the patient.

The 'property' being used is significant. The 'sun,' for example, is warm, distant, the center of the solar system, the source of life as we know it, irradiates, and is one of Hamlet's hostile puns in response to his uncle, King Claudius (Act I, Scene 2), and so on. We can ask ourselves how is it that we are having such and such an imaginative fantasy or play of feeling at this particular time. What is it about the patient? What is it about ourselves?

In this reflective process, the data are sometimes obvious, sometimes obscure (e.g., with radical shifts in the analyst's posture or muscle tension). It happens, not always, but it is as though something from the patient – about the patient, or for the patient – needs to get heard and recorded, and hints about the patient are there. Sullivan (1954) wrote succinctly in his *The Psychiatric Interview* that patients reveal in their communications to the therapist what they need to communicate, and which should be 'grasped by the therapist, and perhaps finally...by the patient... [I]f the possibility of their existence is ignored, some of the most important things about the psychiatric interview may go by default.'

In the same way, if marginal or parenthetical thoughts of the therapist about the patient are ignored, treated as though they are simply evoked by the patient, or, if it is assumed they are nothing but our own unconscious intrusions, derivative of unanalyzed aspects of ourselves, little is gained. If they are treated as potentially imaginative responses, they can be of immense help in facilitating a necessary intimacy. The patient has influenced us and has stirred something in us beyond our immediate grasp. This can result in some resolution and reconstruction in the analyst (Franklin 1994), in which the therapist's interaction is open to the patient, and in which the patient's statements or gestures are included with the therapist's, but within a new perceptual and conceptual framework – with the patient's authentic desire for growth suffused within the new.

It is probably easier to distance oneself optimally if the patient is severely disturbed, as with the thought disorders. The patient and analyst then do not simply talk different languages. They are in different worlds. When there is this obvious lack of communal feeling, severe discontinuity necessitates a translating process, which, in turn, may serve as a brake on our expanding tension. Then, there is less self-doubting (except, perhaps, as to efficacy), or self-questioning as to how we got where we are, and what we are to do. The 'bad analyst' feeling (Epstein 1986) dissipates. But if there is our conventional expectation of cooperative connection, of continuity, as there is with most of our patients, we are confronted with the limits of our own tolerance for asymmetry, separateness and difference, and a consequent, necessary search for a misread that will bring about the connection we lack. Without it, we are usually reduced to self-denigration.

Surprisingly, embedded within the classicist's view on countertransference (Reich 1951, 1973[1960], 1973[1966]) there is an unrecognized hint of the posture I am describing here. In a severe critique of Reich's assumptions and conclusions about the negative value of the use of countertransference data, Epstein and I took her to task for not giving credence to the constructivist position that countertransference data could be useful tools in analytic work (Epstein and Feiner 1979). We cited, among other things, her criticism of Heimann (1950), in which she insisted that Heimann's report of the use of countertransference data showed that:

> something interfered with the process of immediate intuitive understanding. The analyst [Heimann] reacted to the patient's striving with an emotional response of her own. She did not just 'know' that the patient was involved in an acting out of his transference, since she failed to identify him and to detach herself again from such trial identification. For this process she substituted a *retranslation* of her own feelings into those of the patient. (Reich 1973 [1960], p.279, my italics)

If we 'misread' Reich, who is attacking Heimann's application of the concept projective identification, we notice first Reich's slipping into the apparent use of the same process as Heimann. Reich writes that the analyst 'substituted a *retranslation* of her own feeling into [my italics] those of the patient.'

I would prefer to call Reich's critique of Heimann an accurate 'misread.' For Reich, in the classical framework, the process of identification with the patient and subsequent detachment from him remains crucial, so that what she called 'intuitive' understanding can be accomplished. But, a 'retranslating,' regardless of theoretical orientation, is precisely what is necessary to understand the patient. And that is what Heimann accomplished.

There is more to Bloom's thesis on misreading that I think may be useful for analysts. Following the movement towards discontinuity with the precursor through misreading, there is an opening to a range of being just beyond the precursor (Bloom 1973, p.15). We experience this during an analysis, when we realize we are differentiated from the patient, at the same moment as our being connected, and then in our being able to see just beyond the patient, just beyond the content and point of their sensibility or complaint, to a place where the patient is not, but could go. We recognize thereby that we journey 'our life's way' (*nostra vita*) as Dante wrote, and yet we travel alone (*io sol uno*) at the same time.[2]

Then there is a yielding up of part of individual human endowment. In analytic terms it is seeing patients' individual struggle as part of a larger humanity. Their suspiciousness, their hurt, their loss is everyman's. Someplace we are all like each other. I think this has something to do with compassion, and transcends needs to be special. It reminds us of Sullivan's one-genus principle (1953), that we are all more simply human than otherwise (p.33).

In Bloom's theory, finally, burdened by our imaginative solitude, we hold ourselves so open to the ideas of the precursor that our achievement makes it seem to us as though we had spelled out the precursor's characteristic expression (not as though the precursor were making it) (Bloom 1973, pp.15–16). Patients know, finally, what they already know, but they do not dare to let themselves know that they know what they have been forbidden to know. They no longer remember to forget. In a word the repudiated, the amputated, returns.

Here is an example: After many years in analysis, a 45-year-old investment banker finally recognizes he has a juvenile view of the world, and says, with the air of Ponce de Leon thinking he has discovered the Fountain of Youth (or that it really was a stash of testosterone), 'I guess it does not matter whether I go out again with Sylvia or not, except to me, or whether my family wants me to get married – just married. It's what I want for myself that's important.' Banal words like these had been stated by the analyst innumerable times during the years. This patient had finally made them his own.

Our job, then, is to misread, deliberately to question, so that patients can reshape, reshuffle their own data, their own story, their own metaphors, their own set of explanations. It is what Levenson (1988) has described so elegantly in his description of the act of 'deconstruction', and its application to psychoanalysis. Levenson quotes Norris:

> Critical texts must be read in a radically different way, not so much for their interpretive "insights", as for the symptoms of "blindness" which mark their conceptual limits [Norris 1982, p.23]. (Levenson 1988, p.8)

And he adds, quoting Eco:

> The text does not speak of itself; it speaks of our own experience in reading [deconstructively] it.... The text as symbol is no longer read in order to find in it a truth that lies outside; the only truth is the very play of deconstruction [Eco 1984, pp.154–155]. (Levenson 1988, p.8)

Levenson then comments:

> the forcing of data is to deconstruct the story, to create a chaotic flux of meanings, from which new meanings may emerge, forged in a transferential crucible of considerable tension. From my position, those meanings would be endlessly recursive, a hall of mirrors. However it is inconceivable that, in any psychoanalysis, data could emerge that any one of the present crop of metapsychologies could not satisfactorily encompass. (Levenson 1988, p.12)

In this way the patient may realize that there are many choices. One time, after I had asked impertinently how it all works, that is, what my analyst was doing for me, he said that I talk to him about myself and him, that he talks to me about myself and himself, and that I ultimately might talk to myself about myself. In a luminous discussion, Levenson (1988) remarks:

> however construed, for all of us the enrichment and deconstruction of the patient's story is our most powerful instrumentality. Even those analysts who pursue that Will o'the Wisp, the mutative interpretation, must begin with a free-associative deconstruction. It is not, per se, psychoanalysis, but it is the absolute precondition for psychoanalysis... Psychoanalysis proper is the analysis of resistance and transference; but transference, however strictly or loosely defined, is not an automatic benediction of sitting in the same room with a patient, or having the patient's character structure impinge on you. It is a consequence of the pressure of the inquiry. The transference is not a slice of life; it is a highly intensified, isomorphic version of what the patient is exploring. (Levenson 1988, pp.14–15)

Here are a few simple condensed examples of misreading: The first is from a session with a young, divorced, female lawyer, which was the last before the analyst's vacation.

> Pt: I'm finding myself attracted to women (*sighs*). That's not new but I was off it for awhile. Even had fantasies of men (*sigh*).
>
> Th: Do you think it might have something to do with me?
>
> (I'm thinking 'unavailable me.')
>
> Pt: You're stretching it, you're not womanly. I don't think of you as a mother figure (*sigh*). Why should I feel rejected? Why, because you're going away? No

> more than usual, I never expect anything from you (*sigh*). Never hoped I could attract you. I used to make an effort to look nice. You're bored with me. My clients talk to me so they're interesting. I don't think I'm always relating to you so you're not there (*sigh*). It would be too frustrating. I'd be annoyed, angry. You'd get angry. This way you just get bored... I even had a dream. I was pleased I remembered it (*sigh*).
>
> Th: (I'm thinking silently, 'Jingle Bells,' and she's trying as best as she thinks she can.) (I say:) Maybe it's a gift for me – going away.
>
> Pt: A real gift would be a dream about you and would be interesting. I wonder if I'll miss you. It would mean I'm still dependent on you. I notice I'm going into the office when I don't have to. Weird. It is just not to be lonely. I even smile sometimes.

Now what is the misread in this example? First, the context. The month is August; the patient is facing a separation from the analyst in the midst of her resistance to the awareness of her feelings toward him. He believes this is the most important direction to take. The words of a common children's Christmas song occur to him. There are other Christmas songs with different affective implications that could have been remembered. Why did he suddenly think of this one? Is the mommy-analyst abandoning the 'child'? Or is the mommy-patient giving her 'child' a gift as he goes off to 'camp'? I believe the misread derives from the context and the specificity of the song, and the therapist's understanding, correct or not, of what is of primary significance at this moment in the therapy.

In the second example an analyst talks to colleagues about her most 'fascinating' patient.

> What is the fascination about? Is it a morbid allurement, the look on the patient's face, his manner, his tale? Does he 'need' to be fascinating, recreating some earlier experience? Does fascination emanate from aberration, difference, sameness, success, failure?

Third, a patient says he 'needs [*sic*] to be anxious' and then goes on to describe how he defines himself as a man who is at his best when surmounting troubles, and that without external reasons for fears he thinks he may get panicky. I think he is saying he needs something like a clothes tree upon which to hang his anxious hat, a structure that will hold or contain him. In essence, he needs something to pull him away from some basic terror. He needs to be needed. He thinks of so-called problems as his shell, or skin. In a sense, he is telling a truth. Being needed gives him a feeling of his own self-definition. What is that basic dread about? Is he illustrating a difficulty with what he thinks is his emptiness, or boundarylessness, a problem with spontaneity or just being, being alone? Does being alone equal being anxious? Or does being herald death or some other disaster? And where did that come from in his history? Is it true there was no containing, no 'structure,' no boundaries in his development, so that he now feels the danger of a constant centrifugal pressure? Or was whatever structure there was available (mothering, for example), fraught with tension? He says he learned that his way paid off with success. If he does not surmount 'problems,' he feels bad, even a 'homosexual.' He says his way is what it takes to be a 'man'. If he has a free hour, he 'should' be jogging, or doing constructive things. It is because of his inner law, he says. If he changes his basic assumption will it be like a traumatic separation?

Finally, a patient says that if he concentrates on making a putt, a thought that something terrible might be happening to his girlfriend comes to mind. Is there a confusion between possibility and probability? Is there a feeling of being disconnected if he concentrates on anything, and does 'if' restore the connection? How does the intruding thought help him avoid his anxiety about separation, of being autonomous, and what is its history?

Tauber (1954) wrote, succinctly:

> that the analyst *takes in* more about the patient than he realizes...and that by discussing some of the countertransference fragments, both the analyst and the patient may find out that the analyst has a richer understanding of the patient which can be put to good use. (Tauber 1954, p.331, my italics)

If the analyst does 'take in' as Tauber (1954) suggested there seems to be no reason not to use the data, if processed according to what analysts know about themselves, and not discharged recklessly. Not only is it often a source of insight about the patient, but an awareness and regard for the countertransference material is a further way of demonstrating the relevance of the analyst. Countertransference data are usually seen as derivative of the analyst's unconscious. But there is a lot more in the unconscious than one usually admits. Analysts, like their patients, also have self-definitions, and world views that include social values, attitudes, and categorizations about what is good, bad and acceptable. As one literary critic pointed out long ago:

> Every man...undergoes the inevitable influence of time and place. He imbibes with his mother's milk the principles and the sum of concepts by which his society lives... But mankind has not suddenly leapt from the twelfth to the nineteenth century: it has had to live through a whole six centuries, in the course of which its conception of truth developed in its various stages, and in each of these centuries this conception took on a particular form. (Belinsky 1953–9, Vol II, p.284, quoted by Berlin 1997, p.227)

Whatever the analyst's dynamics, a message has been sent and registered. Something that patients 'think' the analyst should know about them, their relationship to others, or what they are doing. And, in reverse, perhaps it is something the analyst thinks the patient should know about the patient's capacity for availability, accessibility, intimacy, tenderness, generosity, shame, or guilt.

I do not know why this constructivist view was such a radical idea when introduced by Winnicott (1949), Heimann (1950), Little (1951, 1957), Racker (1953, 1968), Crowley (1952), Tower (1956), Tauber (1954), and others. True, there had been forty odd years of the ambivalent, forbidding attitude of Freud. Freud's note about unconscious transmission and reception seemed to have been ignored till Winnicott. But it evidently was a little too hot to handle even in the 1950s. Perhaps it was assumed at the time that analysts were the apotheosis of mental health, and the myth of their objectivity in the search for the hidden truth had to be perpetuated.

In contrast interpersonalists thought it all self-evident. They took seriously Sullivan's definition of the effort of the analyst as being based on participant-observation. Sullivan stated clearly, 'The expertness of the psychiatrist refers to his skill in participant observation of the unfortunate patterns of his *own* and the patient's living' (Sullivan 1949, p.12, my italics). By the 1970s, several interpersonalists were acutely aware of the interactive nature and its potential in the psychoanalytic relationship, and were writing about it (see, for example, Ehrenberg 1974; Epstein and Feiner 1979; Levenson 1972).

If there is a creative misread, a patient's vaguely hopeful goal may be transformed into a real possibility. When this happens a patient is faced with the turbulence of ambiguity, an ambiguity of differentiated aloneness, but with an opportunity for choice. Then the search for alternatives begins.

The view of countertransference as a hindrance can only deter options. Tauber (1979) called this idea a variant of countertransference in its own way, writing clearly:

> The question is how can this analytic process approximate outside reality without the therapist's making pathological claims on the patient. Guarding against unconstructive intrusion is not sufficient to accomplish the mission. The atmosphere is impoverished and unnatural; the atmosphere may unwittingly recreate many of the restrictive elements in the patient's past... My argument in regard to the classical tradition is not to degrade it but to respect its early beginnings... [But] I see the classical technique as unwittingly introducing a countertransference phenomenon by the therapist's failure to use himself in therapy in the fullest and most natural direction... Nonengagement is the therapist's misuse of nonintrusion and may have its roots in neurotic anxiety. (Tauber 1979, pp.67–68)

Only an openness to the patient and to oneself fulfills the remarkable promise and excitement of an interpersonal analytic orientation. It necessitates a misreading of the other, and a constant, vigilant awareness of mutual impact. Two people talking at or to each other may be in proximity but are not necessarily interpersonal. They may even think it is dialogue, and often we call it that, but it could easily be monologue in disguise. The analyst has the responsibility of making it interpersonal. Only when the resistance to mutual influence is recognized is there a viable interpersonal situation for both. The recognition of the influence of influence makes it a special, animated experience for the analyst, and, of course, enriches the analysis.

The patient's response to being in analysis, to what the analyst does or says, and does not say, and to whom they perceive the analyst to be, what they assume the analyst's unconscious is probably like, all contain transferential as well as non-transferential elements. Patients' communications always allude to themselves, that is, their self definition, and to some aspect of the relationship with the analyst, particularly the way the analyst maintains the frame of the therapy (Langs 1981, p.9).

Patients, like analysts, are continuously engaged in self-defining processes of which each immediate interpersonal field serves as metaphor. We bring ourselves, our strivings and our histories to any situation. Therefore we can infer a lot about individuals by the way they respond to us. The synecdochic converse (the part standing for the whole) is equally true. If a relationship has had an affective impact we may behave elsewhere as though it were being replicated. Historically, this is evident. Levenson's thoughtfully pellucid idea that the content of a session can be an allusion to the relationship with the analyst, and homologously, the interaction in the session can be a recapitulation of the content communicated, has impacted the field broadly (Levenson 1972). For example, a patient may bemoan the evident truth that his sometime lover is dismissive and is really not interested in him as an individual, which can be taken as an allusion to what he may assume about his analyst. Not that he believes the analyst is not listening, but he senses the analyst, in some way, is not taking him seriously, or responds to him with generalizations, or relativistic, collective comparisons. Or, a man comments about his trickery and shrewdness in a business deal and then provokes a picayune argument with his analyst about his monthly statement, or about his previous session, which he believes started one minute late. Unless these issues are explored in terms of the field in which they occur, curiosity and movement toward self-understanding will be curtailed. The analytic field is not life, but it can be seen as small culture, a living example of the entire process of life. Getting along with friends can be metaphoric of, or an allusion to getting along with one's analyst. And getting along with one's analyst, metaphoric for getting along.

Freud pointed out: '[We] do not project...into the blue...where there is nothing of the sort already,' but rather on someone who offers some reality basis for the projection. He notes:

> considering, too, the fundamental kinship of the concepts of 'stranger' and 'enemy,' the paranoiac is not so far wrong in regarding...indifference or hate, in contrast to his claim for love. (Freud 1922, p.226)

Freud's words are about paranoia, but projection is no stranger to anyone. Rioch (1943) wrote clearly:

> I believe that the personality of the analyst tends to determine the character of the transference illusions...
>
> There is no such theory as an impersonal analyst, nor is the idea of the analyst's acting as a mirror anything more than the 'neatest trick of the week.' (Rioch 1943, quoted in Mullahy 1949, pp.82, 96)

Gill (1982) comments:

> It would be more correct to say that the patient develops a hypothesis than that he distorts the actual situation...
>
> A more accurate formulation than 'distortion' is that the real situation is subject to interpretations other than the one the patient has reached...since the patient's conclusions are not unequivocally determined by the features of the situation he would be wise to investigate how his interpretation may in part be influenced by what he has brought to the situation.
>
> I see transference as always an amalgam of past and present. Insofar as the present is represented in the transference, it is based on as plausible a response to the immediate analytic situation as the patient can muster... It is often concealed, however, because both the patient and the analyst resist its implications. The most common concealment is by allusion in associations which are not manifestly about the transference. (Gill 1982, pp.117, 118, 177–178)

This in a nutshell is the plausibility or perspectivistic attitude toward transference. What is attractive about 'plausibility' is its congruence with the idea of the interpersonal and its apparent respect for the patient's experience. Since a good part of relatedness occurs in the context of translation, interpretation and exchange, 'plausibility' permits a grasp of one significant aspect of the transferred interaction, exactly as Freud (1922) counseled. But 'plausibility' can lend itself to inauthenticity in that the analyst can accept the patient's plausibility and go on to derogate it via an interpretation that supports only the analyst's version of the 'truth.' So plausibility can be duplicitous and dismissive.

If the dichotomy of subject-object can no longer be maintained, the patient's input is more than an attempt to organize defensively in the light of the influence of the therapist. Suppose we add the idea that it is all an attempt to organize oneself as the result of the experience with ambiguity. This ambiguity results from anyone's being made aware of their differentiatedness or potential autonomy. Part of the analyst's job then is to facilitate an understanding that differentiatedness is not the tragedy that it is often assumed to be, and that we can, if we desire, reconnect at will.

Given the pressure to respond in the face of ambiguity, so as to transcend the imposition of distance, and given the reality of the patient's response, one way of viewing transference is to see it as the kind of use the patient is making of the analyst, since transference is derived from the patient's basic organizing necessity, a revelation of self-definition. In this way the context and patterning of the session get determined, and it takes its own shape.

A patient operating under a fixed aegis of hopelessness or helplessness cannot resolve any issue, since any conflict or attempt at gratification will be conceived in a hopeless or helpless way. We have all heard those tautological, inertial, defeating, despairing, exasperating 'Yes, buts,' or as they say in mental hospitals, 'You say that, doc,' the goal of which, evidently, is safety in the status quo, as painful as that is. The tautological style, patients suggesting that they must do something to feel better, and at the same time intoning there is nothing to do, and they cannot think of anything, actually precludes communicative interaction. At this point it is not only the patient that feels helpless.

The hypothesis of the patient in response to the influence of the analyst is a translation of context, and its elements that are homologously similar to the patient's experience. It reflects a state of feeling. How the analyst responds adds or contributes a new context. Take the following common example:

The patient reports that he likes steak for dinner but his wife serves lamb chops (ergo he is frustrated – and not being flexible, he is angry).

His appraisal is what he wants the analyst to consider, that is, his interpretation of the situation. His anger is appropriate to his perception. This would be so whether his wife is seen as a powerful rival, a hateful sibling, a bad mother figure, a two-headed ogress, or an ungiving anything else. He is not getting what he wants. An interpretation directed outside the room may be correct, but is limited in impact and, ultimately, will be heard as persuasion or suggestion – that he should not get angry, be flexible or eat out, get his wife to change, or get a new wife. A long, virtuous inquiry would confirm the patient's historically repeated inability to get what he wants in certain circumstances, about his impotence in general, or his ineffectuality with women. We learn the astonishing news that his mother served prune juice when he wanted apple; his fourth grade teacher made him read *Fun with Dick, Jane, Carlos and Rosita* when he wanted to read *The Boy Allies*; his girlfriends all insisted on Chinese food when he wanted Italian; and his wife serves these wretched lamb chops. Of course this does not happen in his business office where he is the chief executive officer of a multimillion dollar rare chemical corporation.

Suppose this repetitive theme of non-gratification is assumed to be the defining element of the context of the analytic situation. We can conjecture then about who is being frustrated, and in what way. We are not invalidating the lamb chop business when we ask what is the purpose of the patient talking about this theme of non-gratification at this particular moment. Sure his wife is ungiving but why tell the analyst about it? And we wonder why tell it this way? This day? Is the patient's metaphor implying the therapist does not gratify, or has not cured? Is the patient suggesting indirectly that he does not gratify, his wife or others; that he serves the therapist boring stuff, or that the analyst can expect little from him? If this is reasonable, the analyst might wonder how did this person get to be a non-gratifier? Or business-wise, how did he get to be a success?

To find out that a patient feels rejected and not desirable because her boyfriend did not send a Valentine's Day card, or because he did not want her to interrupt him when he was playing with his computer, is to hear a complaint, which I take as a feeling. It becomes analytic when the examination of our interaction begins. There is evidently some resistance to doing that (Gill, 1982). When this resistance is transcended, we are able to ask ourselves:

> Does she want me not to interrupt her? Have I done that? Am I doing that? Is she telling me she is rejectable? Is she saying she has always been interrupted and consequently felt denigrated? Is she saying I am rushing her like mommy did when she was on the potty? Did daddy shoo her away when he read the newspaper? Was there a sick sibling whose illness was rivalrous? Doesn't anyone give her enough time so she has enough – fun, satiety, orgasm? Am I the rejecting, rushing, abandoning one? Is she telling me that she believes she is so unlovable, so dangerous, so poisonous that I must be careful, and that it is all a waste of time? Does she think I do not want her to use the analytic 'program' with me?

As I see it, this is a situation with infinite allusions to itself, and to the self-evident mutuality of the relationship. When the patient describes a third party in the session I have the patient's picture of the third party. It is only through the filter of the eye of the patient who is in the session. And his report is influenced by my presence. As Stone (1984) puts it:

> it would seem that extra transference interpretations cannot be set aside or underestimated. But the unique effectiveness of transference interpretations is not thereby disestablished. No other interpretation is free, within reason, of the doubt introduced by not really knowing the 'other person's' participation in love, quarrel, criticism, or whatever the issue. And no other situation provides for the patient the combined sense of cognitive acquisition, with the experience of complete personal tolerance and acceptance, that is implicit in an interpretation made by an individual who is an object of the emotions,

> drives, or even defenses, which are active at the same time. (Stone 1984, pp.96–97)

Freud (1912a) stated long ago:

> it is impossible to destroy anyone in absentia or in effigie...this struggle between the doctor and the patient, between intellect and instinctual life, between understanding and seeking to act, is played out almost exclusively in the phenomena of transference. It is on that field that the victory must be won – the victory whose expression is the permanent cure of the neurosis. (Freud 1912a, p.108)

Here is a communication from a patient, a young psychologist:

> Look it seems I have no problems today. That's really new for me. It's like I am floating. And that's scary. I am being appreciated in the hospital since there is input on my part. And I perceive myself differently. But then comes the floating. My good work is a violation of the rules and the history and the tradition of myself...something catastrophic could happen. That is, I'm not supposed to feel good or real. So if I put it outside, just suspend it, it's easier to look at it. It's away from me. So it's less dangerous or scary. So I have to make the world familiar in the old way. It makes a lot of sense to be neurotic but it really does not work. I really don't want to be that way. A spider makes a web and falls back on it, but if you don't know what tomorrow will bring what do you have then? You live with anxiety. That's what it is. And I go on and on.

At the moment this was reported I did not have the foggiest notion what the patient was talking about. It occurred to me hours later that perhaps I was not supposed to, that my feeling of vagueness was what he was feeling. I think now that he was telling me about his view of analysis and how life feels. He was to have no anchor, tiller, or sail, and no point on the horizon to sail to even if he had the equipment. He saw himself and his analysis as a piece of cork on the open sea.

At this remove it is fairly clear. He had had what he considered a good day and then he became anxious. How is it that a 'good day' leaves him feeling so vulnerable? Was I to make a 'web' for him, so he would be contained, safe? Which one of his parents did that for him, robbing him of any autonomy, any comfort with experimentation, or spontaneity? Who is the spider? Father? Mother? Both? Himself? Was he an insect prey? Was I? What about black widows? Are these the women in his life? Mother? Wife? Analyst? If I help with the 'web' am I colluding with the way things are with him? Is it all just a study in the fright of annihilation, the dread of empty space?

The interpersonal field is like the overlapping of red and yellow filters. Analytic interaction is in the orange which is quite different from red, and quite different from yellow, but cannot exist without either. The orange comes into being because of the mix. Anything that happens in the orange area because of changes in the red must be influenced by the presence of the yellow. A description of the perceptual world, of self-definition, can be gathered from so-called relations with 'outsiders,' but patients are usually so busy maintaining themselves that they cannot hear themselves, or look at themselves to achieve any insight.

Patients respond to the influence of the analyst, their verbal and non-verbal input with their own kind of misreading. This would include their need to maintain themselves in keeping with their desire and courage to change. Misreading in this sense, is similar dynamically to Racker's (1968) concept of the 'total' transference. He stresses the importance of paying attention:

> Not only to what has existed and is repeated but also to what has never existed (or has existed only as a hope), that is to say, to the new... Outstanding...are the real new characteristics of this object (of analyst and analysand), the patient-doctor situation...and the situation created by psychoanalytic thought and feeling. (Racker 1968, p.150)

Racker illustrates his point with an example that relates how a male patient, who fears his female analyst will reject him because of his denigration of women, needs an interpretation that includes the patient's desire 'to connect himself with an object emotionally.' Since the patient was indirectly asking whether he might trust the analyst, an interpretation should refer to what has existed and also to what never had existed and was now hoped for in the new experience.

When one's characteristic and traditional way of organizing the world fails in the presence of a new set of ears, the resulting turmoil may be panicky, but it sets up this possibility of something creative. Panic often occurs when something new is required but cannot take place immediately. If the situation remains stagnant with the person not being able to restore his original organization, or creating a new, more appropriate way of being, disorganization may ensue.

Resistances to analysis represent a conservative principle in our nature. They obviously have survival value by helping us to maintain the status quo, and the self-definition that has been achieved. It may be a less than satisfactory, even painful status quo, but it is the only one we know. We have all known privately the poignance of painful words like, 'the songs I know only the lonely know.' The difficulty in leaping into an unknown is that the 'new' is an entirely different and unfamiliar system. Psychoanalysis, in contrast, especially its analysis of resistance to curiosity represents a revolutionary principle in human beings in that it underlies transformation.

It is not enough for patients to express all feelings, say the unsayable, contemplate the unthinkable, and discharge their toxicity in analysis. Patients can do that in an empty room to a wall. In fact, they do all that too often to the blank walls and the barbed wire of the concentration camp of their mind. Analytic therapy must expose a person to the impact and influence of an analytic ear that hears, and to an analytic mind that responds in affirmation, through a constructive misreading. For without this interaction, that encourages the patient to be curious and to think, I do not believe transformation possible.

Therapeutic action has been our profession's concern since its onset. We keep asking ourselves what makes people change, and how this comes about. Perhaps our interest has been so persistent because we believe we have been elusively effective. There is little doubt about that. Since we do define ourselves as healers, we feel a gnawing cynicism when we fail, with a lot of self-abuse and rationalization. I am not referring to the horrendous failures of those predictive diagnoses in mental hospitals – those horrifying occurrences when someone is given exit, and then goes out and pushes someone off a subway platform. Our ubiquitous failure to get any clue as to what we think we ought to know in those situations should give us constant cause enough to doubt ourselves. I am referring to our broad concepts for patients: differentiation, integration, spontaneity, and autonomy – something akin to satisfaction and security, and how we only approximate them in our work.

Freud said that our task was to make the unconscious conscious via a therapy of interpretation. Strachey (1934), introducing the idea of the relationship as a primary source of data, suggested that not only the immediacy or the 'point of urgency' of the interpretation, but also its area of derivation or its specificity was significant. We must reveal the unconscious, he stated, but it was an unconscious participating in the relationship with the therapist as the object of impulse. This really was fresh, perhaps a borrowing, or, let us say a reminder, of something Ferenczi and Rank (1986 [1925]) had introduced ten years earlier. They had written knowingly:

> The...analytic situation...exposes the patient a second time to his infantile trauma...we give the patient the parental image...on which he can emotionally live out his libido.
>
> In every correct analysis the analyst plays all possible roles for the unconscious of the patient; it only depends upon him to recognize this at the proper time and under certain circumstances to consciously make use of it. (Ferenczi and Rank 1986 [1925], pp.20–21, 41)

Addressing the relationship was the power that was mutative, Strachey (1934) insisted, and all else supportive or, at best, introductory to a potential mutative thrust. Note that word 'mutative.' It suggests a process that encompasses a discontinuity as well as a continuity. The patient was to become accordingly, something entirely new, and yet continuous with what he or she had been before. From the point of view of evolution it makes perfectly good sense. Like the chicken that must have come from a mutant egg, which, in its turn, had come from a bird somewhat like, but not quite a chicken, the patient's change was to be transformative. Anything other was less – that is, reformative, and only quantifiably different. With reform one could be less angry, less alone perhaps, even more loving, and perhaps more cooperative with others, and, ultimately, according to our middle-class values, the way one should be, so that one would be better adjusted. It really is a successful salesmanship, packaging kind of orientation. For this one does not need an analyst. A tutor, a counselor, a coach, perhaps, but not an analyst. How Strachey (1934) anticipated mutation from an interpretation of some aspects of transference leading to modifications of the superego within the relationship, for example, one can only speculate. I like to think that he found himself influenced by the popular interest in eugenics in the 1930s, and therefore may have reasoned that if the so-called structures of the mind were real things, they were akin to formations of genes and chromosomes. Therefore, accepting impulses from the patient without retaliation, could affect his superego as though it were a real thing and not a metaphor (Home 1966). It was similar to tinkering with genes, and would produce an equivalent change in the mind, he may have surmised. But the importance of Strachey's work was that he was emphasizing an interpretation in terms of the patient's investment in his relationship with his analyst. He did lay the ground work for our current appreciation of how insight, integrated with an experience with the analyst, does effect change. Much later, even Arlow and Brenner (1988), who have been staunch supporters of the most traditionally classical position, wrote, 'the future teaching of both theory and practice...will...have to emphasize...the centrality of the psychoanalytic situation as the instrument for studying the mind' (Arlow and Brenner 1988, p.8).

The topic lost passionate interest for several years despite some occasional discussion about the relative significance of the therapeutic relationship and interpretation in psychoanalytic treatment (Friedman 1978). The mainstream of psychoanalysis tended to be preoccupied with describing what was in the unconscious, and whatever were its permutations and combinations.

Almost thirty years after Strachey's effort, Loewald (1980a [original publication 1960]), borrowing Strachey's title but never referring to his paper), also addressed the process of change. He emphasized the differentiatedness of the analyst from the patient; and, enlisting Freud's similes, wrote:

> In his interpretations [the analyst]...implies aspects of undistorted reality which the patient begins to grasp step by step or transference is interpreted. This undistorted reality is mediated to the patient by the analyst, mostly by the process of chiseling away the transference distortions, or as Freud has beautifully put it, using an expression of Leonardo da Vinci, per via de levar, as in sculpturing, not per via di porre, as in painting. In sculpturing the figure to be created comes into being by taking away from the material; in painting, by adding something to the canvas. In analysis we bring out the true form by

> taking the neurotic distortions. However, as in sculpture, we must have, if only rudiments, of an image of that which needs to be brought into its own. (Loewald 1980a, pp.225–226)

That is somewhat true for the carvers. For shapers it is different. For them, it is more like breathing life into mud. While this sensuous simile has a grossly aggrandizing quality in its allusion to God and Adam, the fact is that giving amorphous clay a shape does endow it with a life, a vitality, of its own. Sculptors describe different felt experiences for carving, working in wax, or shaping clay. Each material has its own properties, demands and limitations, that influence the experience of the artist.

I do not think it was by accident that Freud borrowed Leonardo's phrase, *per via de levar*, and that it was reiterated by Loewald. It captures perfectly the analytic situation in classical context, especially in terms of the early theory of the blank screen. Loewald also seems to be immersed in a view of transference as patient distortion.

Wet clay modeling, however, in contrast to carving's rhythmic quality, is the more directly sensuous – actually bordering on the erotic – and offers more ambiguity and free tactile contact. The God and Adam myth, whatever else it conveys, says something about the feeling of life flowing from direct contact. For me the shaper metaphor reflects the interpersonal field, wherein the 'hands' of both analyst and patient engage whatever both bring to session. All sculpture enlivens the space around it, compelling movement on the part of the viewers, pulling them into its orbit (Martin 1981). The use of Leonardo's simile is to Freud's credit albeit rooted in a Cartesian view of subject and object. Both these ways, carving and shaping, refer to the therapeutic action as bringing new order, new form where it did not exist before. Both are transformational. While Rodin (1911) said, it is all in the seeing, to sculptors and to interpersonalists 'seeing' is 'not a passive process, by which meaningless impressions are stored up for the use of an organizing mind, which construes forms out of...amorphous data to suit its own purposes' (Tauber and Green 1959, p.26). 'Seeing' is an immediate process of translation, of formulation, and of comprehension, and provides us with our grasp of the world. It indicates that in any setting a kind of mentation operates that is usually regarded as out of awareness. 'Seeing,' for the interpersonalist, in its immediacy, takes place in the realm of symbol translation, imagination, and creativity, that is, in the land of the misread. This borrowed term 'misread' reminds us that an analyst's listening cannot be purely dispassionate, contemplative or theoretical, if it is to impose its influence.

Loewald's basic thesis, like Strachey's, is that progressive change for the patient is built on the new evolving relationship with the analyst. This is characterized by the patient's identification with the analyst's greater maturity and understanding. Furthermore, while Loewald states clearly there is no relationship without transference, nowhere does he indicate how the necessary identification comes about. He obviously does not mean idealization. Evidently he assumes the desire and capacity to make an 'interpretation' (and, of course, his analytic training) is evidence of the analyst's maturity, and that this leitmotif of the relationship, as he sees it, facilitates identification. Processes like projection, countertransference, counter-anxiety, patient's rectification, that is, whatever goes on in the analytic space as a dynamic field of forces, are not explored by him, nor is the issue of the mutual addressing and articulation of all aspects of the relationship, positive and negative. I stress the word 'mutual.'

Ferenczi, Rank, Strachey and Loewald agree that the therapeutic action takes place as a function of the relationship. But an authentic relationship is something of mutual influence, consciousness and expressiveness, not the imposition and/or imputation of the concepts or metaphors of one onto another.

Loewald likens change in the patient to change in the growing child. As the responsible, progressive parenting is internalized by the child, according to Loewald, so are interactions with the analyst of a comparable, analogous nature necessary if the analytic process is to lead to structural change (1980a [1960], pp. 229–230). He cannot mean that he thinks of the patient as a child. He must be alluding to the analogous similarity in growth processes, child's and patient's, so that by 1970, he could write, somewhat gingerly, that 'truth' about a patient is discovered with him. Here are his words:

> To discover truth about the patient is always discovering it with him and for him as well as for ourselves and about ourselves. And it is discovering truth between each other, as the truth of human beings is revealed in their interrelatedness. While this may sound unfamiliar and perhaps too fanciful, it is only an elaboration, in nontechnical terms, of Freud's deepest thoughts about the transference neurosis and its significance in analysis. (Loewald 1980b [1970], pp.297–298)

This, again, is not what I think of as interpersonal, interpenetrating influence. To discover something with someone is to create something new at the edges, like the jars in a Morandi painting that reveal the image's dynamic power precisely where they touch. Analytic work is really in the space shared by, or between, the two people. As T.S. Eliot (1963) wrote: 'The roses in the rose garden which is ours and ours only.' The garden is the shared, prepared, and created area that is used by Eliot as a metaphor for the intimate ways of a marital relationship. It is sort of like salt coming into being via the admixture of chlorine and sodium, with new properties, similar to the old, but really nonexistent before.

Another author does come close to this position. Calling it the 'X-phenomenon,' which is based on what he calls the analyst's 'act of freedom,' Symington

(1983) reports progressive shifts in the analyses of three patients after analyzing his own post-session thoughts about them. In one case he amends the arrangement as to fee, and the patient goes on to 'extricate herself from...[a]...patronizing boss...[and]...a parasitic boyfriend.' With another, the work progresses so that the patient achieves some insight as to his attempt to substitute the thoughts and feelings of Symington for his own. And with the third, the patient's seeming fusion is carefully scrutinized. Symington stresses the inner nature of his acts, and the perceptions by the patient of Symington's communications based on this. He comments:

> the inner act of freedom in the analyst causes a therapeutic shift. The interpretation is essential in that it gives expression to the shift that has already occurred and makes it available to consciousness. (Symington 1983, p.286)

What is 'inner,' apparently, is to have a private thought or fantasy about the patient, or about what the patient is communicating. It is noteworthy, I think, that all of Symington's illustrations have something to do with his sudden awareness of his patients' desires for fusion, and the emergence of what he calls his own need to establish boundaries, or to establish his differentiatedness. His explanation, as I understand him, is something like this. The patient and analyst form, according to Symington (1983), one 'corporate' personality. The two are then caught in a shared 'illusory' system, with the analyst 'lassoed' into the patient's illusory world. Via the analytic work, the analyst proceeds to extricate himself from it. In fact, Symington states, the analysis 'catalyzes' the individuals to individual existent reality. The X-phenomenon is a product of the analytic process. In this sense, transference and countertransference are shared illusions. Psychoanalysis 'catalyzes' that area of the personality that is noncorporate, that is, personal and individual;[3] the result of this is the freeing of the analyst's personal feelings from the illusory feelings emanating from the patient's superego. This superego includes all the components of the common culture. Analyst and patient have fused, according to Symington, via the superegos of each, since the analyst, in his passive role, tends not to assert his own view of the world, and is swept into the personal-cultural contents of the patient's superego. It is rather like a rephrasing of Reich's (1973[1966]) description of the interactive analytic process, in that to her, an identification with the patient is made, and then this is followed by detachment in the service of understanding. To Symington similarly, the X-phenomenon is a product of the process, in that a sudden access of personal feeling in the analyst breaks the bond of the illusory fusion in which both patient and analyst are supposed to be held in thrall.

We might ask, why was there a sudden access to personal feelings? Why at this time? What in the field, the process itself, had held them in check? Is the 'corporate' personality a real entity, or is it a metaphor for a particular interpersonal experience? Does the analyst-individual actually become subsumed under an analytic mass, as Symington describes? And if so, is he or she not changed? Did it have something to do perhaps, with the content or dynamics of the session? Did it have something to do with the analyst's accessibility (Feiner 1979)?

That the very 'newness' of the therapist's 'act of freedom' is derivative of the patient's influence seems to be of no concern, nor is there any regard for mutuality in a field of forces. We are left with so-called accepting, rational analysts and their interpretive impact on the patient's mind structure, and their subsequent release from the analytic artifact of amalgamation. This is like one plus one, first making one, then making two. That they have made 'three' is the interpersonalist's interest, but in this schema that possibility is never considered.

Tauber and Green (1959) address the issue differently. Since the therapist cannot operate in the therapeutic situation as the so-called unemotional, rational, detached, non-participant-observer, assumed by the traditional psychoanalytic ideal, he will always be:

> changing the interaction by virtue of his own problems, prejudices, and perspectives, and the patient will be responding to them. The question then arises: How can the nonrational forms of communication between the patient and therapist be put to use to enrich the understanding of the patient's life problems? This view of the analytic process involves a departure from the traditional concept of the patient–therapist relationship...
>
> A great deal of what we do among one another consists in apprehending nonproportional emotional responses and reacting to them... One must infer that nonverbal subthreshold 'arrangement' is frequently the determining factor in highly significant decisions such as marriage, friendships, and sexual collaboration where unusual or sophisticated nuances are called for. (Tauber and Green 1959, pp.6, 3)

There is something therefore, going on out of awareness, in which an actual exchange of information takes place. It is called tacit knowing, according to Polanyi (1966) and can account for this kind of valid interchange, or understanding of a problem, or a situation. It helps explain our capacity to pursue a problem guided by our sense of approaching a solution; and for a valid anticipation of the undetermined implications of the discovery arrived at in the end. Polanyi says that such an act of knowing is based on:

> interiorizing particulars to which we are not attending and which, therefore, we may not be able to specify, and relies further on our attending from these unspecifiable particulars to a comprehensive entity connecting them in a way we cannot define...
>
> To hold such knowledge is an act deeply committed to the conviction that there is something there to be discovered. It is personal, in the sense of involving the personality of him who holds it, and also in the sense of being,

> as a rule, solitary; but there is no trace in it of self-indulgence. (Polanyi 1966, pp.24, 25)

Here is Polanyi again:

> Consider the situation where two persons share the knowledge of the same comprehensive entity – of an entity which one of them produces and the other apprehends. Such is the case when one person has formed a message and the other has received it. But the characteristic features of the situation are seen more clearly if we consider the way one man comes to understand the skillful performance of another man. He must try to combine mentally the movements which the performer combines practically and he must combine them in a pattern similar to the performer's pattern of movements. Two kinds of indwelling meet here. The performer coordinates his moves by dwelling in them as parts of his body, while the watcher tries to correlate these moves by seeking to dwell in them from outside. He dwells in these moves by interiorizing them...
>
> This is not to say that we gain an understanding of the mind without a process of inquiry. But the inquiry consists, like a scientific inquiry, in picking out clues as such, that is, with a presumed bearing on the presence of something they appear to indicate. And as in a scientific inquiry, many of the clues used will remain unspecificable and may indeed be subliminal. (Polanyi 1966, pp.31, 29–30)

We are all in agreement about the significance of the relationship, its interpenetrating impact on understanding, but we still have not answered the question about what in it facilitates change. We all agree with Strachey that the relationship is where the action is. We agree with Loewald that patients model themselves after or use aspects of the analyst for their own growth purposes, but I do not believe it is the analyst's analogously parental type attention. I think that if anything is taken in by the patient it is the therapist's willingness to hear non-dismissively, to facilitate the patient's feeling of relevance. Patients also absorb therapists' facility in using their imagination in an uncompartmentalized way; their tolerating imperfection and the complications of ambivalence; and their admission of the reality basis for patients' views of them; and, in their ease in looking honestly, courageously at themselves, at their fantasy, at their errors, at what is going on between them and their patient. Finally the patients observe their therapists exposing their pleasure and playfulness in an exploratory process of a great deal of uncertainty – which I think engenders hope, a sense of vitality, possibility, and surely detoxifies the felt banality and the tedium 'of our life's way' (*di nostra vita*), making it excitingly interesting. If anything is taken in by the patient it is the analyst's desire to exist authentically, non-exploitively, non-dismissively and respectfully, in their own highly differentiated manner.

I agree with Symington's desire and attempts, at what I would call misreading, but see his explanation of this event as having a misplaced emphasis. As I see it, Symington did misread his patient, not as a gesture in search of differentiated freedom, but accomplished this because he already had it, asserted it and consequently could tell the patient something that he had absorbed, something he had extracted from the ambiguity that had to be communicated.

If from the patient's point of view, transference is very much like water to the fish, it is a necessity that helps patients organize their world. It is the same for the analyst. Therefore the issue for the analyst is not simply that transference is present in some part of every relationship and every communication. The issue for analysts is how can they help transference to change. From an interpersonalist's position this means that if the therapeutic action relates to the experience, the need for the therapist's presence is not the need for a new description, or even a fresh explanation, although that helps, but for the need of the presence of a new person with new choices, and new possibilities (Levenson 1983). As Harold Bloom (1975b) reminds us, what experience is more valuable than that which shows us how to distinguish real from illusory dangers to the self's survival?

True, Yeats (1965) did assume that there is wisdom in the images, but I think what we need to do is not necessarily translate or interpret the images, or even derive a meaning of the images themselves, but somehow attempt the reverse. I think we have to find out what leads to a mind that develops such an idea, and expresses it with this particular image, at this particular moment. This is done by an examination of the image's properties and misreading them. I believe that through the impact of our counter-imagining, this analysis of historical development and how this history comes to be alive in the present is initiated. We are thus in a search for how a relationship is organized, how it means, not what it means. We are not in a search for causes. This is accompanied by mutual misreadings in creative attempts to maintain oneself – the patient as courageously desirous of change, and the analyst desirous of being an analyst. It seems that with no desire there is no influence. Consequently there is no victimization, no anxiety, nor is there any vulnerability for that matter. Without courage and responsibility there is no change, since there is no risk.

Let me offer an offbeat model for the necessity of the interpersonal dialectic, the interaction – interaction as a basis for life as we experience it. Someone once drugged a spider so that it was not at all sensitive to outside influences (wind, temperature, atmospheric pressure). The result: precise, symmetrical webs. Another drug made the spider overly sensitive to environmental forces. The result: chaotic webs, with no recognizable pattern. Conclusion: normal, ordinary webs are the result of the interaction of the biological pressure of webmaking, and the chance vagaries of weather and of the environmental surround, which, it was concluded, is a Darwinian, interactive model for the development of thinking and desire – in a word, life.

The fun and joy in this work is finding out why something has to be what it is, not what it is. It is an idea we can borrow from the DNA crystallographer Rosalind Franklin. She is reputed to have commented that she was not so much interested in the fact that 'the butler did it,' she sort of figured that out early in the mystery story, but in how it had to be the butler. Psychoanalysis deals with how it came to be the butler, how it had to be the way things are. It is the interpersonal experience of searching for the way things are that rekindles hope and possibility – the possibility of the reality of the way things ought to be, as well as the probability of gratification (Boris 1976). The power of the interpersonal field resides in the awareness that we cannot gain insight into a patient, or even ourselves, by being merely contemplative, that is, by imposing a theory or its constructs on him, but only by being contemplative about the very interpersonal field that we and the patient have made.

References

Arlow, J. and Brenner, C. (1988) "The future of psychoanalysis." *Psychoanalytic Quarterly 57*, 1–14.

Belinsky, V.G. (1955–1959) *Polnoe Sobrainie Sochinenii*, Vol VI. Moscow.

Berlin, I. (1997) *The Sense of Reality*. New York: Farrar, Strauss and Giroux.

Bloom, H. (1973) *The Anxiety of Influence*. New York: Oxford University Press.

Bloom, H. (1975a) *A Map of Misreading*. New York: Oxford University Press.

Bloom, H. (1975b) "The use of poetry." *New York Times*, November 12, p.43.

Boris, H. (1976) "On hope: its nature and psychotherapy." *International Review of Psycho-Analysis 3*, 139–150.

Cohen, M. (1952) "Countertransference and anxiety." *Psychiatry 15*, 231–243.

Crowley, R. (1952) "Human reactions of analysts to patients." *Samiksa 6*, 212–219.

Eco, U. (1984) *Semiotics and the Philosophy of Langauge*. Blodnington: Indiana University Press.

Ehrenberg, D. (1974) "The intimate edge in therapeutic relatedness." *Contemporary Psychoanalysis 11*, 320–331.

Eliot, T.S. (1963) 'A dedication to my wife.' *Collected Poems, 1909–1962*. London: Faber and Faber.

Epstein, L. (1986) "Collusive selective inattention to the negative impact of the supervisory interaction." *Contemporary Psychoanalysis 22*, 389–409.

Epstein, L. and Feiner A. (eds) (1979) *Countertransference: The Therapist's Contribution to Treatment*. New York: Jason Aronson.

Feiner, A. (1979) "Countertransference and the anxiety of influence." In L. Epstein and A. Feiner (eds) *Countertransference: The Therapist's Contribution to the Treatment Situation.* New York: Jason Aronson.

Ferenczi, S. and Rank, O. (1986 [1925]) *The Development of Psychoanalysis.* New York: International Universities Press.

Franklin, G. (1994) "Dual therapy: personality change in the therapist while working with patients." *Israel Journal of Psychiatry 31*, 86–93.

Freud, S. (1912a) "The dynamics of transference." *Standard Edition 12*, 99–108. London: Hogarth Press.

Freud, S. (1912b) "Recommendations to physicians practicing psycho-analysis." *Standard Edition 12*, 111–120. London: Hogarth Press.

Freud, S. (1915) "Observations on transference love." *Standard Edition 12*, 159–171. London: Hogarth Press.

Freud, S. (1922) "Some neurotic mechanisms in jealousy, paranoia and homosexuality." *Standard Edition 18*, 223–232. London: Hogarth Press.

Friedman, L. (1978) "Trends in the psychoanalytic theory of treatment." *Psychoanalytic Quarterly 47*, 524–567.

Gill, M.M. (1982) *The Analysis of Transference*, vol. 1. New York: International Universities Press.

Heimann, P. (1950) "On countertransference." *International Journal of Psycho-Analysis 31*, 81–84.

Home, H.I. (1966) "The concept of mind." *International Journal of Psycho-Analysis 47*, 42–49.

Joyce, J. (1939) *Finnegans Wake.* New York: Viking.

Langs, R. (1981) *Classics in Psychoanalytic Technique.* New York: Jason Aronson.

Levenson, E. (1972) *The Fallacy of Understanding.* New York: Basic Books.

Levenson, E. (1983) *The Ambiguity of Change.* New York: Basic Books.

Levenson, E. (1988) "The pursuit of the particular." *Contemporary Psychoanalysis 24*, 1–19.

Little, M. (1951) "Countertransference and the patient's response to it." *International Journal of Psycho-Analysis 32*, 32–40.

Little, M. (1957) "'R'–The analyst's response to his patient's needs." *International Journal of Psycho-Analysis 38*, 240–254.

Loewald, H. (1980a [1960]) "On the therapeutic action of psycho-analysis." In *Papers on Psychoanalysis.* New Haven, CT: Yale University Press.

Loewald, H. (1980b [1970]) "Psychoanalytic theory and the psycho-analytic process." In *Papers on Psychoanalysis.* New Haven, CT: Yale University Press.

Martin, F.D. (1981) *Sculpture and Enlivened Space.* Lexington: The University Press of Kentucky.

Mullahy, P. (ed) (1949) *A Study of Interpersonal Relations.* New York: Grove Press.

Norris, C. (1982) *Deconstruction, Theory and Practice.* New York: Methuen.

Polanyi, M. (1966) *The Tacit Dimension.* Garden City, NY: Doubleday.

Racker, H. (1953) "Contribution to the problem of countertransference." *International Journal of Psycho-Analysis 38,* 223–239.

Racker, H. (1968) "The meanings and uses of countertransference." In *Transference and Countertransference.* New York: International Universities Press.

Reich, A. (1951) "On countertransference." *International Journal of Psycho-Analysis 32,* 25–31.

Reich, A. (1973[1960]) "Further remarks on countertransference." *International Journal of Psycho-Analysis 41,* 389–395. Also in *Psychoanalytic Contributions.* New York: International Universities Press.

Reich, A. (1973 [1966]) "Empathy and countertransference." In *Psychoanalytic Contributions.* New York: International Universities Press.

Rioch, J. (1943) "The transference phenomena in psychoanalytic therapy." *Psychiatry 6,* 147–156.

Rodin, A. (1911) *Art: Conversations with Paul Gsell.* Los Angeles: University of California Press (1984).

Rommetveit, R. (1979) "On 'meanings' and social control of such meaning in human communication." Paper presented at the Symposium on the Situation in Psychological Theory and Research, Stockholm. Quoted in J. Wertsch (1985) *Vygotsky and the Social Formation of Mind.* Cambridge, MA: Harvard University Press.

Sandler, J. (1976) "Countertransference and role responsiveness." *International Review of Psycho-Analysis 3,* 437.

Stone, L. (1984) *Transference and its Context.* New York: Jason Aronson.

Strachey, J. (1934) "The nature of the therapeutic action of psychoanalysis." *International Journal of Psycho-Analysis 15,* 117–126.

Sullivan, H. (1949) "The theory of anxiety and the nature of psychotherapy." *Psychiatry 12,* 3–12.

Sullivan, H. (1953) *The Interpersonal Theory of Psychiatry.* New York: W.W. Norton.

Sullivan, H. (1954) *The Psychiatric Interview.* New York: W.W. Norton.

Symington, N. (1983) "The analyst's act of freedom as an agent of therapeutic change." *International Review of Psycho-Analysis 10,* 283–291.

Tauber, E.S. (1954) "Exploring the therapeutic use of countertransference data." *Psychiatry 17,* 331–336.

Tauber, E.S. (1979) "Countertransference reexamined." In L. Epstein and A. Feiner (eds) *Countertransference: The Therapist's Contribution to the Treatment Situation.* New York: Jason Aronson.

Tauber, E.S. and Green, M.R. (1959) *Prelogical Experience.* New York: Basic Books.

Tower, L. (1956) "Countertransference." *Journal of the American Psychoanalytic Association 4,* 224–255.

Winnicott, D. (1949) "Hate in the countertransference." *International Journal of Psycho-Analysis 30,* 69–75.

Yeats, W.B. (1965) *The Autobiography of William Butler Yeats.* New York: Macmillan Publishing Co.

Notes

1 This chapter is a revision and expansion of a paper dedicated to the memory of Edward S. Tauber, MD.

2 Dante (c.1308) 'io sol uno' 'I myself alone,' Canto II, 3; 'di nostra vita' 'of our life's way,' Canto I, 1. Dante (1980) *Inferno,* trans. A. Mandelbaum. Berkeley: University of California Press. Mandelbaum writes: "[This is] the first triple repetition of an 'I' in western writing" (Introduction, pxiii). Mandelbaum also reminds us of Dante's use of that 'possessive of human solidarity' as it appears in the first line of the *Inferno,* i.e., 'When I had journeyed half of *our* life's way.' It is this dialectic I am addressing in this chapter. I use it as an epigraph because I believe it is present in all human situations, coloring all choice, and I suppose provides the essential grounding of this chapter.

3 This word is a most curious choice. 'Catalysis' refers to a breakdown, a destruction, a dissolution of matter; or in chemistry it is the name for the effect produced in facilitating a chemical reaction, by the presence of a substance, which itself undergoes no permanent changes. Symington seems to mean it in this sense of 'fomenting' or 'instigating'. Otherwise, it belies his thesis. 'Real' feelings are released having been stirred by the joint effort of analysis, according to Symington. This is why he calls it 'an act of freedom.' This is, the 'real' feelings accordingly were also there.

True, they are potential. But if we follow Symington's discussion, it becomes evident that to Symington, nothing new comes into being. The 'rational' was simply hidden. To Symington, the analysis catalysed it into the open. My point is that Symington's discussion makes it sound like interpretive analysis in some special force, in distinction to a point of view that underscores the interactive nature of the process.

It may seem like nitpicking but the difference lies in whether we see data resulting in emergence, like a vector of forces, or peeping through as a filmy covering is teasingly stripped away.

Chapter 7

The Thrill of Error

Image and Appearance, Articulation, Union – An Experience with Erich Fromm

Many years ago I had the privilege of being in supervision with Dr. Erich Fromm. After an hour of my presentation of work with a patient, Dr. Fromm commented, with mild impatience, but evident exasperation, that I should stop trying to show him how learned and perceptive I was. He suggested that since I was spending what he called my 'hard earned money' for his counsel, I would profit more by showing him my errors and misjudgments, and my problems with the case. In effect, he said that I could learn more were I to share with him my difficulties, my awkwardness, and my failures.

Then Dr. Fromm made a remark that I did not fully appreciate at that time. I am not quoting him exactly, but what follows is based on his words as I remember them. He said that my errors, my failures, and my understanding of them, as well as their eventual rectification, were the keys to learning what the process of psychoanalysis is about. They were the keys to 'union.'

I recall that the word 'union' was one of Dr. Fromm's favorites. As I understood him, it referred to more than the achievements and satisfactions, and the ultimate aspirations of organized labor – and all progressive social movements as well. The word stood for the underlying necessities of individuals in their relationships with each other. I remember I thought Dr. Fromm had embraced this word as though he considered it a drive – basic in all humans – somewhat at the level of animal life. The way Dr. Fromm used the word made it sound as fundamental to psychological existence as food, water and air to biological. The ultimate meaning of 'union' refers to the communal connectedness of humans to each other as a result of intimate ways of engagement.

By 'error' I do not mean simply getting something wrong, or being inappropriate – ideationally or behaviorally. That sort of definition would refer to error as due to misperception, misconception, miscategorization – in essence, error due to ignorance, a lapse in cognition, or ineptitude. The modern sense of the word embodies this sort of error. It implies a Cartesian clear subject/object split, in which things are right or things are wrong. These errors are considered cognitive errors, although they may be motivated conatively. Error in this sense, indicates a separation of one thing from the other, that is, patient objectification.

The way I am using error is a more ancient one. It is somewhat like a straying – sometimes deliberately – from the putative objective. My guess is that Dr. Fromm would have agreed with this.

In any conversation there are two things going on. There is, of course, an exchange of information, as report, or request. Communicated at the same time is a definition of the relationship (Watzlavick, Beavin and Jackson 1967). Someone casually asking for the time is requesting information. He or she is also expressing some related dependence implicit in the question. A patient asking for information in the context of an analytic hour is also expressing an aspect of his or her definition of the relationship.

Psychoanalytic errors can occur on either, or both, of these levels. From the analyst's point of view, errors on the level of the definition of a relationship may be considered empathic errors or failures. While they may be cognitively correct, their effects may be disruptive to the analytic work, even though their contents may have merit. Kumin (1989) gives several examples of this. Typical are those errors by the analyst that include: comments that may be accurate but emotionally overwhelming; comments that are jargonizing; comments limited to the obvious, or simply reflections of what has been shared; comments that are accurate although experienced as abusive, or comments that lower a patient's esteem; comments that are self-serving in their cleverness; and finally, an absence of a comment where one is apparently required (Kumin 1989, p.143). Errors of this sort usually derive from countertransference feelings.

Any kind of error that is a straying has potential value. This resides in its acknowledgment by the analyst, and its reception and interpretation by the patient, regardless of derivation, and however varied from an 'objective' standard. In this way it may become part of the binding processes between human beings, part of 'union.'

Engaging another view enriches experience by bringing us into intimate contact with something different. Addressing this in varied creative literary efforts, Kermode (1991) observes:

> We have always been pretty sure that the literal sense is not enough, and when we try to go beyond it we may err, but sometimes splendidly… We bring ourselves and our conflicts to words, to poems and pictures, as we bring them to the world; and thus we change the poems and the pictures, or perhaps it is ourselves we change. (Kermode 1991, p.432)

Kermode is referring to error in its ambiguous or antithetical sense. Since we may desire to have more of a story than is originally offered, or even wish to go beyond its surface to its very depths, perhaps to realize a new experience in ourselves, this kind of error, a deliberate misunderstanding, may become fruitful (Kermode 1991, p.431). In fact, Kermode points out that the history of interpretation of literature, or art, even our humanity, is, to a large extent, a history of error. Science, too, can be described as an infinite praxis of the correction of error – errors of procedure, conception, conclusion and paradigm, with the only thing ever proved being the null hypothesis.

The awareness of the potential value of error is not new in the sciences. When preparing a set of lectures on the origin of seventeenth-century mechanics, Kuhn (1977) discovered that Galileo and his contemporaries had rejected Aristotelian contributions in this area because the Aristotelian ideas were evidently incorrect. Kuhn asked how could Aristotle, who had been such an astute naturalistic observer, have said so many absurd things? How could Aristotle's characteristic talents have failed him when applied to a theory of motion? Kuhn then points out that there are alternative ways of reading texts. Were we to understand the context in which Aristotle came to his conclusions, Kuhn says, and were we to appreciate Aristotle's subject concern as change-of-quality in general (including both the fall of a stone, and the growth of a child to adulthood), difficulties with Aristotelian textual material would disappear (Kuhn 1977, p.xi). Therefore, Kuhn asserts, not only are there many ways to read a text, but also those ways that are more accessible in our time are more often inappropriate when applied to a context in the past. He concludes that when reading the works of any important thinker, we should be aware of apparent absurdities, but continue to ask ourselves how a reasonable person could have written this, and in what context it had occurred. What was previously understood and accepted may have changed its meaning (Kuhn 1977, p.xii). This is what happens in psychoanalysis when the therapist tries to view the world through the patient's eyes.

If the modern, conventional understanding of error leaves us split apart, or objectified, is it possible that error as interpretative misreading can bring us into union? If so, it adds an additional, possibly expanding view. But can it fulfill Dr. Fromm's promise? And in what way? To follow fully the implication of this idea, we need to scrutinize its articulation with patient, supervisor, or colleague.

The full discussion of error, as a playful examination of ideas, provides the best context for 'union' and learning. I believe this is what Dr. Fromm was getting at with his admonition to me. For him, this was one of the most important goals of psychoanalytic therapy. He believed that intimacy could only be experienced via the sharing of truth. Citing Freud's 1937 paper 'Analysis terminable and interminable':

> we must not forget that the analytic relationship is based on a love of truth – that is, on a recognition of reality – and that it precludes any kind of sham or deceit. (Freud 1937, p.248)

Dr. Fromm insisted that only openness between people could be the condition for union. And it was to come about with him via the discussion of my errors. What I took from Dr. Fromm was the suggestion of the importance of recognizing the image and appearance of psychoanalytic failure; the conditions of its occurrence; the sharing with him its expression and examination; its consequent understanding in the context of its occurrence; and the relation of all these to union.

The word 'error' derives from the Latin word for 'a wandering.' Rothenberg (1988) writes:

> It is because such errors appear in the therapy that the therapist knows that transference exists. And one of the aspects of working through and resolution of the transference is a recognition of his errors and distortions about the therapeutic situation and the therapist. (Rothenberg 1988, pp.159–160)

But does error as a wandering from a particular contour, line, or proper texture necessarily introduce a split or a separateness in a relationship between two people? Do not transferential reactions reflect the way in which an individual necessarily structures a relationship (Feiner 1988)? Surely it is the quality of relatedness that attracts the analyst's ear and eye. It is this that gets analyzed in interpersonal psychoanalysis, with a clear understanding of the analyst's contribution.

There are two traits that need to be accounted for in interpreting anything we know about human beings. They are universals having to do with our ways of orienting ourselves toward our culture, toward people and things around us, as well as the past. One of these is our capacity to bring the past into the present in some way, or to alter the past in the light of the present (Bruner 1990). We see that repeatedly in transferential reactions in therapy, as well as in early memories, or even memories of recent events. As we review our immediate and remote histories we change what is in the past by reconceptualizing it in keeping with how we define ourselves in the present. This means that neither the past nor the present remain fixed. Both are fluid, indicating their many possibilities. Typical are the time, distance and size experiences of childhood, as well as the affective, although these are clearly more obstinate.

Interpretations that imply one truth, that are anachronistic or archeological, can be, at best, only part of the story. They may signify, somewhat, the mystery of how things came to be, in their metaphoric ways, but they dispel that mystery at the same time, at the moment they are made (Schweizer 1990). They fail to reflect the actual nature of the influence of the present on themselves. There is even an arrogance in their explaining the secret of our feelings and their evolution. At the point of discovery of their metaphoric application, the plurality of meanings is foreclosed. Only the patient's and analyst's desires for closure are gratified.

One could say that understanding can be helpful, but the power of analytic effort resides in the process of achieving the so-called understanding, not the understanding itself. In fact, this process is homologue to the fabric of interpersonal experience that brought the patient to psychoanalysis in the first place. The current relationship, however, has the potential of being in sharp contrast to the early experience of non-relevance or dismissiveness (Levenson 1972).

The second trait that Bruner (1990) addresses is our capacity to envision alternatives. That is, we have a capability of conceiving other ways of being, of acting, despite our inertia about it. While it may be that we are creatures of our histories, we are capable of being autonomous agents as well, especially in choices. The point of therapy is to help release this agency in all of us. But even in our histories we were not simply passive recipients of the impact of others. It is true that our choices were limited, channeled by our realistic dependency and, increasingly, by our need for integration, connection, and safety, but we did make them, and we are accountable for them. If this were not so, psychoanalysts would have no way to deal with the dialectics of impact, influence and responsibility. As patients, we could not then renounce our histories if we so wished. And what we assume is automatic and immutable, God-given or attributable to human nature – but is not – would remain so.

There is a prosaic conception of truth which arises from the experience of the present in each moment (Morson and Emerson 1990, p.236). Mikhail Bakhtin (1984) had this in mind in suggesting that every moment of existence is rich in potential. Far from necessarily creating distance, then, we might think of error as individualizing people, and intimate ways of relating would include this. As Bakhtin (1984, p.81) puts it, there is 'only one principle of cognitive individualization: error.' This regard for the individual's 'error' insures anyone's relevance and non-dismissibility. Since psychoanalysis draws its power from the 'eventness' of any analytic moment, that makes it particular, unfinalizable, and open to multiple, unforeseen possibilities, the idea of error as a distortion of an objective truth or standard loses value.

Even Freud (1935) once commented that a mistake gained in purpose after it had been corrected, not by being made. Similarly, Rothenberg (1988) and Langs (1981) tell us that the significance of an error can be realized after the error has been made, specifically in the act of rectification. On examining Freud's reported example, we find that correction itself followed discussion. One implication of this is that Freud had limited his insight due to his belief in an objective truth. That is, discussion led to something already in Freud's mind. But if we discard the idea of a decidable truth, discussion can seen as a viable, radical way of exploration and learning.

Langs (1981) has written persuasively on the desirability of the analyst responding to the patient's implicit suggested corrections of the management and conduct of the therapy. These are seen in the patient's derivative communications and allusions. Frame management, boundary reliability, and erroneous interventions, are typical areas requiring attention. Langs writes:

> Because the ground rules are such basic actualities, alterations in the framework are of the highest order of therapeutic indicators...I refer to the rectification of the disturbed framework – the correction of the deviation in actuality...rectification is essential to any meaningful and accompanying interpretative work; failure to correct an infraction in the ground rules...belies all efforts at interpretation. (Langs 1981, pp.614–615)

Neither Rothenberg nor Langs negates acknowledgment and discussion. Langs (1975) indicates that frank acknowledgment of error, and the exploration and working-through of the patient's reaction can be insightful for patient and therapist. Rothenberg devotes a splendid chapter to this in his book (see Rothenberg 1988, pp.149–168).

With regard to articulation, Rothenberg writes that he is referring to a process in which realization or representation of unconscious meaning occurs after the error is made, and after it is discussed. Rothenberg indicates that the value of the articulation of the analyst's error is more than a matter of rejecting data because they are wrong, or because they are deviations from what could be seen as correct technique. Parts of error may be understood as connected and incorporated within the aim of an intervention, or they may encourage its development into new directions. Unlike what is generally called 'trial and error' thinking, wherein errors are unwanted, and therefore removed or corrected, articulation involves preserving in the whole work new, interesting, even valuable elements that occur within a mistake or perhaps are stimulated by it. To Rothenberg, it involves the dialectic of separateness and connection. Rothenberg comments:

> Like the creative writer or artist, both therapist and patient need to be willing to take chances and commit errors in both the form and substance of their relationship. When errors occur, they need to recognize them and then to clarify them as much as possible. As a 'wandering,' an error provides the beginning of a separation which, through constant clarification, yields up some of its unconscious content and intent. Rather than exhaustive breakdown and analysis – using the term analysis in its precise meaning of systematic dissection – the error is connected, usually through interpretative interventions, to issues in the patient's current and past life. (Rothenberg 1988, pp.161–162)

One artist and teacher told me that all errors were seen by him as opportunities:

> When I teach I try to communicate the fact that mistakes are exhilarating, they lead some place. A mistake is not a failure, it is a step to getting on the road to where you want to go in any 'kind of creative activity.' I'm involved with both art and writing, and inherent in the process is doing things that don't work and correcting them. If you look at any manuscript of a great book or great poem, or play, you'll see the guy's crossed out a lot. And the stuff that's crossed out are not failures, they're 'try-ons' on which the writer builds something else that eventually works. Picasso often started out by succeeding. He would start out magnificently and kept pushing it and pushing it, until the drawing finally collapsed, and he finally ruined it. But it didn't bother him one bit because he didn't see these things as failures. He saw them as explorations that eventually something will come out of. He had no sense of failure. Perhaps they were failures, in some objective sense, meaning that they weren't as good as when he started out, but some of them got to be better. And the casualties that you suffer along the way, is part of the process of getting there. But there's another side of this which is difficult to communicate and that's the acceptance of 'failure.' The fact that some things do not work can lead to a kind of freedom that's very exhilarating. (Holden 1991)

While Rothenberg suggests that countertransference errors are related to the conduct of therapy, he indicates that they are invariably handled in a private way by the analyst. He adds, there are some countertransference errors that generally cannot be managed privately. He refers, for example, to overt mistakes, either in the form of forgetting, distortion, and parapraxis, or in the form of technical inappropriateness. Such mistakes become manifest issues in the therapeutic process (Rothenberg 1988, p.162). As a matter of fact, Rothenberg (1988) clearly recommends that overt failures 'should probably become a manifest issue in the therapy,' following the 'well established maxim of making all issues with emotional charge...a matter of grist for the mill in therapy' (pp.162–163). Langs (1975) would concur.

Rothenberg begins a discussion with the following example:

> What does error have to with creativity or, more complicated than that, with the creative practice of psychotherapy? Some years ago, in one of my research explorations of the creative process in visual art, I met with a woman sculptor who did large scale abstract work in perfectly smooth white plastic material. These sculptures had perfectly clean lines and perfectly even coloration and were obviously proportioned according to exact specification. I marveled at their seeming perfection, and she described to me the detailed engineering process involved in creating such elaborate and elegant works. Then she took me over to look at one of the large surfaces more closely. Pointing to a gnarled and slightly raised blemish on the surface on one of her works, she said, 'Do you see that blip on the surface there? Well, that's me.'... This sculptor's dramatic and metaphoric reference to the single error on an otherwise abso-

> lutely perfect constructed sculpture may readily be related to poetic and philosophical conceptions of the human condition. To err is to be human. The sculptor's equating of herself and her own individuality with the error on her creation is consistent with philosophical emphases on celebration of humanness and of individual style and performance. (Rothenberg 1988, pp.149–150)

But a sculpture is a whole, a product of the work of the artist, and as such its totality represents her. Simply put, it is her creation. Was it really an error? Why did the artist need to indicate that the blemish on the surface, the little blip, refers to herself? What made her think it was necessary to express this to Rothenberg? Could it be that the blip was intended as more than sigil, or signature – as a kind of proof of her presence, and a claim on her impact on an otherwise slick surface, and therefore not error or wandering at all? This possibility fits with Rothenberg's thesis of error as a 'celebration of humanness and individual style.'

A signature is not an error. It is the insistence on, and accountability of presence, and it is understandable that the artist would want the viewer to notice her. And yet, it also may be a bit of self-criticism, even mourning. Perhaps it was an emergent thought that in our society, in our time, the viewer would apppreciate the piece, only to lose the artist, or the identification of the sculpture with her, in its stark sheen and smooth, perfect engineering. It could be that her technical triumph seemed at odds with her view of her artistic sensibility, and elicited a thought that her self-definition included more than that, and she wanted to be sure that that was not lost. There could also be a small element of denial of her engineering expertise. But this is sheer speculation.

What is of significance, as Rothenberg suggests, is that by recognizing and focusing on errors, both learning and correcting inevitably occur in engagement. With requisite skills, catastrophes are less probable, and one should not be afraid of making errors and should allow oneself that freedom that inevitably incurs errors and mistakes (Rothenberg 1988, p.168). Being ready to delineate them, one incorporates into the therapy one's own, and the patient's, individuality as Bakhtin (1984) has suggested with regard to genuine dialogue (Feiner 1998).

Dialogic relationships are much broader phenomena than the usual description of sequential statements. They are more profoundly interpersonal than is readily apparent in successive utterances. It cannot be understood as a function of a set of rules to which an exchange conforms, or even a structure that the events exhibit, since in this way, human beings are reduced to objects and we are blind to the value-laden, cultural influences on their speech and actions. Nor can the issue of verbal interaction be reduced to purely personal idiosyncrasy, that is to conscious or unconscious differences (Morson and Emerson 1990, p.139).

Achieving a dialogue in the discussion of errors was important to Fromm-Reichmann (1959), who affirmed the value of the process. She pointed out:

> Further therapeutic help may be affected by inviting corrections and suggestions on the part of the patient to the doctor's review and vice versa. Discussion of the causes and the nature of omissions, additions, or distortions which may appear in these reviews and the patients' own progress appraisal at times will open up new significant therapeutic avenues. (Fromm-Reichmann 1959, p.144)

The suggestion that the therapist show the schizophrenic patient if and when the analyst understands his communications, and that there be no pretense at understanding, implies that there are times when it is not possible to understand (Fromm-Reichmann 1959). Sometimes this is caused by patients' expressing themselves deliberately in an ambiguous way, perhaps in an effort to mitigate the burden of the anticipation of being misunderstood, or even the opposite. At other times, failure to understand a patient should not be looked upon as a result of unfamiliarity with a schizophrenic's means of communication. Therapists accept the potential meaningfulness of schizophrenic communication as well as their own limitations in understanding. Referring to difficulties in understanding one particular patient, Fromm-Reichmann (1959) reminds us:

> So you see, the patient took over where I was not able to do so. My not understanding her was no obstacle to useful psychotherapeutic interchange, as long as she realized that I was listening alertly, expecting her to make sense. (p.183)

Freud's notion that analysts continuously pursue their own analysis, within the analytic session and without, so that analysts become more available to receiving the unconscious communications of their patients followed from the writings of Goethe – the idea that each human being's life is essentially a roadway to themselves. By applying this insight to analytic experience, Freud meant that to the extent that the analyst is aware of his own unconscious processes, so was he in a position to avoid imposing them upon the patient (Freud 1910).

Following Freud's suggestion, Ferenczi called everything into question – his technique as well as his own blind spots (Torok 1984). What Ferenczi was searching for was an improvement in technique. He introduced what he called 'mutual analysis' after a period of treatment with a refractory patient to whom he had mistakenly, under provocation, stated that therapy, for the analyst, was a 'purely intellectual process.' Ferenczi (1988) notes:

> The shock this provoked was indescribable. The whole experience was of course taken back to the past to her trauma, over and over again, but still the patient would not ever relinquish the transference side...The above mentioned crisis forced me against my sense of duty and probably my sense of guilt as well, to limit my medical superperformances. After a hard inner

> struggle I left the patient by herself during vacations, reduced the number of sessions, etc. The patient's resistance continued unshaken. There was one point over which we came to be at loggerheads. I maintained firmly that she ought to hate me because of my wickedness toward her; she resolutely denied this, yet these denials at times were so ferocious that they always betrayed feelings of hatred. (Ferenczi 1988, pp.98–99)

Ferenczi then adds:

> For her part she maintained that she sensed feelings of hate in me, and began saying that her analysis would never make any progress unless I allowed her to analyze those hidden feelings in me. I resisted this for approximately a year, but then I decided to make this sacrifice. To my enormous surprise, I had to concede that the patient was right in many respects... Mutual analysis appears to provide the solution. It gave me an opportunity to vent my antipathy. Curiously, this had a tranquilizing effect on the patient, who felt vindicated; once I had openly admitted the limitations of my capacity, she even began to reduce her demands on me. (Ferenczi 1988, p.99)

In her introduction to Ferenczi's *Clinical Diary* (Ferenczi 1988), Dupont notes that the technique of mutual analysis rests on the idea that where analysts are unable to offer their patients reliable support (*sic*) (I suppose she means the feeling of safety), they should at least provide their patients with guideposts, by acquainting them, as sincerely as the analysts can with their own weaknesses and feelings. And, Dupont continues, mutual analysis was designed to eliminate those ambiguities, so that each person can understand his or her relation to the analyst with great assurance (pp.xx–xxi).

Ferenczi did not let this technique remain fixed as originally conceived. He had many criticisms of it. Dupont writes:

> Indeed, perhaps all experimentation with mutual analysis is essentially the consequence of training analyses as they were practiced at the time, including that of Ferenczi by Freud: rapid, fitful analyses, often undertaken abroad in a foreign language, during walks or travels together or visits to the home of analysts or patients. Be that as it may, the questions raised by mutual analysis remain relevant, even in these days of carefully worked courses and multiple controls. How can the analyst successfully deal with his weaknesses and blindness? (Dupont, in Ferenczi 1988, p.xxii)

What Ferenczi called blindness or complexes on the part of his own personality we would consider a specific class of 'error,' introduced in a psychoanalysis inadvertently. Ferenczi was concerned with the varying levels of conviction on the part of the patient so that his techniques were usually designed to create conditions which would enable the patient to develop that 'conviction' (or 'self-definition') that would be of greatest therapeutic usefulness (Feiner 1991a; Ferenczi 1913).

With the mutual analysis experiment Ferenczi was trying to help the patient achieve the belief that her analyst understood her feelings. Ferenczi writes:

> At the same moment the patient opens up, is permeated by a feeling that I have at last understood (that is, felt) her suffering, consequently with an increased sense of certainty about (a) the reality of her own experiences, (b) the contrast between the present and the period when the incidence occurred: total isolation instead of the possibility of telling her troubles and of being listened to sympathetically. (Ferenczi 1988, pp.26–27)

Ferenczi's conception of the need for mutuality can be appreciated as the forerunner of ideas about the need to dispel feelings of dismissal and non-relevance, that are key to the understanding of anti-self feelings (Feiner 1991a). For it is only in an atmosphere of safety and relevance that the analyst can adopt the advice and counsel of Winnicott (1963):

> The patient needs to reach back through the transference trauma to the state of affairs that obtained before the original trauma... The reaction to the current failure only makes sense insofar as the current failure is the original environmental failure from the point of view of the child. Reproduction in the treatment of examples as they arise of the original environmental failure, along with the patient's experience of anger that is appropriate, frees the patient's maturational processes; and it must be remembered that the patient is in a dependent state and needing ego support and environmental management (holding) in the treatment setting, and the next phase to be a period of emotional growth in which the character builds up positively and loses its distortions. (Winnicott 1963, p.209)

It is evident that Ferenczi set in motion an entirely unique way of thinking about the practice of psychoanalysis, particularly with regard to the focus on and use of the relationship between analyst and patient.

Searles (1975) reports that during one particular session a patient indicated that she was feeling unusually calm and relaxed, and asked him whether he reacted differently when she was feeling this way. He tells us that indeed he did, although he did not share this with the patient. He writes that he had felt calm and relaxed, and had experienced her as a 'source of nonverbal strength and solidity.' Searles then states that he had much misgiving after that hour, about not having told her or confirmed for her how he was feeling. Regretfully, he says in retrospect:

> I feel that I had withheld from her unwisely and hatefully, a vitally needed confirmation of her at least partially successful mothering of me. Probably wisely, she discontinued our analytic work not many months thereafter.

Earlier Searles (1965) had commented as follows, on the potential usefulness of errors in treating schizophrenics:

> The analyst may vary the amount of friendly discussion of some real life problem or interest – for example, the patient's work. There may be more or less laxity in allowing a session to run beyond its official end. There may be a greater or lesser deviation from previously agreed upon statement as to when the patient would be charged for a missed session and so on. However, it seems it is not really possible for the analyst to be consistently so keenly attuned to the patient as to achieve an accurate dosage of what the patient needs all the time. This 'failing,' if it does not become too marked, probably also plays a part in the therapeutic process. The patient has occasion to experience the reality of a person who dedicates himself to the task of helping him to grow up and who comes through reasonably well in spite of obvious difficulties. (Searles 1965, p.155)

Searles remarks that therapists learn, to their surprise, that there is a kind of chaos and confusion with schizophrenics which is not anxiety-provoking and destructive, but thoroughly pleasurable – the playful chaos that a mother and a little child, or two little children can share, where mutual trust prevails to such a degree that there is no need for self-defensive organization. Searles writes:

> We have the job of becoming more skillful at deciphering the patient's disguised communication; but he has the task of being able, over the long course of therapy, to express himself in more conventional terms. Thus we find that our therapeutic dedication is on several counts misplaced if it is persistently directed toward a sober and selfless racking of our brains to unravel the confusing communications: Not only does it on varying orientation of that kind prevent us from assessing fully the patient's sadism, and from participating subsequently with him a therapeutically valuable phase of playfulness with communicational devices, but also intends to maintain him in a regressive position where he is not held basically responsible for the development of increasing mature forms of communication. (Searles 1965, pp.422–423)

Winnicott viewed the patient's reactions to the analyst's failures, as a new opportunity to rework the patient's experience with past failures. In support of that, Tower (1956) suggested that the actual experiences of the analyst's errors offer the patient special opportunities for the modification of difficult transference resistances. Little (1951) insisted the analyst should communicate, with discretion, something of the nature of his errors. She concluded:

> Not only should the mistake be admitted (and the patient is entitled not only to express his own anger but also to some expression of regret from the analyst for its occurrence, quite as much as an occurrence of a mistake in the amount of his account or the time of his appointment), but its origin in unconscious countertransference may be explained, unless there is some definite contra indication for so doing, in which case it should be postponed until a suitable time comes as it surely will...The subjectivity of the feelings needs to be shown to the patient, though their actual origin may not be gone into. There

> should not be 'confessions'; it should be enough to point out one's own needs to analyze them; but above all the important thing is that they should be recognized by both analyst and patient. (Little 1951, pp.148–149).

Responses of the analyst which are out of line with the patient's point of view are inevitable (Schwaber 1980). However, by constantly monitoring the patient's subtle shifts in affect, by listening carefully to the rhetoric, and maintaining a focus on the context, the sense of injury as well as the patient's particular way of reacting to it can be illuminated. Empathy, Schwaber writes, is not an abstract, objectively based state. It entails the search for the subjective meaning of the patient's communication, and perhaps the acknowledged recognition of the patient's wishes (Schwaber 1980, p.382). Thus one critical aspect of analytic listening is the necessity for the analyst to pay close attention to her own affective states, so as to be sensitive to whether she has shifted her perspective to any place other than the patient's. Often, the analyst's responses that are abstract or theory-bound are clues to such a shift, even though they may be triggered by some affective communication by the patient, or by something arising within the analyst herself.

Empathic error or failure, therefore, refers to an awareness of break within the contextual unit. It is not synonymous with a 'technical error.' That might follow, particularly if there is no attempt made to understand its meaning. But there is no way, even ideally, to prevent empathic failures because the analyst cannot always know what will be experienced by a patient as a 'failure' (Schwaber 1980, p.260).

In this regard, Kramer (1989) writes that on one occasion, he asked a patient who was inhibited about taking flying lessons why she did not, and on another, why she did not take the final exams to complete her graduate degree. To his surprise she took the flying lessons with great satisfaction, but after his question about the final exams, the therapy bogged down. The patient angrily criticized Kramer for failing to discern the difference between flying, that to her was liberating, and the professional degree, that represented her parents' wishes. Kramer notes that he had made 'an outright mistake.' And then he adds:

> But would we have reached her anger so readily if I had not? The meaning of the difference in the two choices (flying versus schooling) was revealed only through the patient's response to my empathic lapse. This is just how we work, piling our errors on patients' errors, lurching from one correction to another composing a symphony of error. (Kramer 1989, p.214)

I agree with Kramer's conclusion and description of his therapeutic endeavor, though I fail to see the alleged error in his attempt at relating to his patient's inhibition. In terms of reticence, there is no difference between not taking flying lessons and not finishing the degree. Her experienced difference lies in her interpretation, based, as it was, on her investment of her parental values, and her assumption of Kramer's dismissal of her conviction. Had Kramer known this about the patient (it is not reported that he did) one might have considered his response an empathic failure. Therein would lie an error. But his question why she did not do one thing or the other seems to follow genuine interest, and a desire for exploration. In fact it is only through his exploratory question that he achieved an understanding of the difference in the patient's experience. Far from an empathic lapse, his questions reveal the woman's literalness about freedom and autonomy. The real power of his engagement with the patient rests on his willingness to assume accountability for his attributed failure, by discussing it, and, in the very nature of that discussion, attempting to rectify it. That is, he did not dismiss the patient. Better, he made her feel relevant (Feiner 1991a).

Kumin (1989) states that the recognition and analysis of negative reactions to incorrect interpretations are as helpful as anything else in advancing treatment, and elucidating the nature of the transference. What is therapeutic, Kumin maintains, is the timely, accurate, and successful working through of the effects of the mistaken or inaccurate intervention. To this end, he describes four phases in this process: (1) the recognition of the patient's perception of an incorrect interpretation, (2) the acknowledgment of the analyst's error, either explicitly or implicitly, (3) the rectification of the error by substitution of what would have been the correct interpretation, and (4) the analysis of the patient's response to the incorrect interpretation. Kumin writes:

> It seems to me...that the analyst must be able to acknowledge his own error; at the very least, to himself. This is a [necessary] step without which no further substitution of a correct interpretation, no exploration of the meaning of the patient's response, no reconstruction of the patient's remote past, no mutative analysis of the transference can occur. (Kumin 1989, p.148)

Kumin sees this as a matter of fact statement about error by the analyst, clearly not as a confession. Agreeing with the recent emphasis 'on the importance of attunement to the patient's subjective experience of the analyst's failures,' Kumin points out that some interpretations may contain tacit acknowledgment of the validity of the patient's perceptions and experience. He cites Winnicott (1963) as follows:

> In this work the failures of the analyst...will be real and they can be shown to reproduce the original failures, in token form. These failures are real indeed, and especially so insofar as the patient is either regressed to the dependence of the appropriate age, or else remembering. The acknowledgment of the analyst's...failure enables the patient to become appropriately angry instead of traumatized. (Winnicott 1963, p.209)

Years later, Winnicott (1987) also remarked:

> [W]ith the patient we must be able to see the failure as something that the patient has enabled us to do in a particular way so as to bring the original environment failure into the present moment. (Winnicott 1987, p.39)

Kumin adds, finally, that every interpretation, even those that are correct, simultaneously reveals the extent as well as the limits of what an analyst has understood. He concludes that if the analyst is aware of the patient's experience of the actuality of the error and rectifies it, the integrity of the patient's self-experience can be restored, and that his response analyzed in the transference (Kumin 1989, p.150).

Earlier, Greenson (1972) had pointed out that technical errors occur in every analysis. He states that errors in technique may be caused by misunderstanding due to insufficient knowledge, or due to inexperience, ignorance, or the clinging rigidly to a narrow set of theoretical beliefs and technical practices. Unrecognized and uncontrolled countertransference reactions are another important source of errors which can lead to technical mistakes.

One could not catalog all the possibilities of analytic error or failure. They range from mistaken uses of silence, mistaken rhetoric, imprecise semantics, inappropriate attitudes and feelings, and inappropriate intentions. The permutations and combinations are infinite. All of them can be seen as aspects of dismissal and nonrelevance. The patient's experience is ignored, and the patient's striving and struggle with the contradictions, dissatisfactions, and insecurities in living, are largely dismissed. In a word, early history is homologously repeated. The analyst's intentionality may be benign, but the patient's experience may demonstrate forcefully the assumption of the validity of remaining where he or she is, maintaining the original definition of self that had to be adopted, and that attempts at its current revision and transformation would be futile, perhaps even dangerous.

In keeping with their own self-definitions that include attitudes of honesty and truth, most analysts agree that some sort of recognition, and communication to the patient, is required to maintain the integrity of the analytic process. Anything other than that is denigrating, anti-analytic, dismissive and adversarial. Levenson (1991) puts the basis for this quite elegantly:

> It is now almost a commonplace that the effectiveness of interpretations depends, not on the correctness of the interpretation, but on the context in which the interpretation takes place. Even the more orthodox institutes are discovering this hoary interpersonal axiom. In a contemporary German text, the authors state that, 'Our leitmotif is the conviction that the analyst's contribution to the therapeutic process should be made the focus of attention...the course of therapy depends on the influence exerted by the therapist' [Toma and Kachele 1985] (quoted in Levenson 1991, p.514).

Levenson (1991c) goes on:

> From my particular interpersonal perspective, the therapist is omnipresent and there is no delineation between the therapist real or imagined, and the 'treatment situation;' they are one and the same. (Levenson 1991c, p.514)

So when Dr. Fromm quoted Freud to me with regard to truth, he evidently meant more than that patients should courageously share their innermost feelings and thoughts with their analyst – and I should do the same with him. That, of course, is literally what Freud meant. Analysts know that takes place only with a concurrent development of the feeling of safety.

A patient of mine, for example, discovered that he was becoming considerably more spontaneous with friends and colleagues, particularly with the growing awareness of his own involvement in the process of therapy. He stated that while the analytic inquiry still 'shook him up,' as it always did, he was recovering much more quickly than he had had in the past. And this he attributed to two things. One was that he seemed to be taking himself more seriously, as a function of the feeling of safety that had emerged in the analytic situation. This not only led to a positive development in terms of his feelings about himself outside of analysis, but also within the analytic session he now could address his history with fresh, renewed interest, without the clichés and platitudes that he had used before. He was now in a position, he said, to look at his experience in his family and question seriously why he needed to repeat the self-definitions that he seemed to have been stuck with. There is nothing like optimism as a context for change. Yet, even in this discussion he tried to attribute the welcomed change only to change in the analyst, hesitating to admit his own significant, active participation.

Dr. Fromm had referred to truth and courage in the context of authenticity. He had a fondness for saying that if a man were going to be a crook, he should be a good crook. I never took this as flip, but more as an ironic, paradoxical indication that Dr. Fromm was concerned with consistency, a lack of sham, or a lack of deceit. This meant to me that the requirement of truth and courage was incumbent on the analyst as well as the patient. By extension, I knew that Dr. Fromm intended this for my relationship with him. And, as I recall, that is how it played out.

I had presented to him a female patient in her thirties, of Eurasian background, whose experiences with men – which included her father, her brother, representatives of the American authorities during wartime, her doctor, her dentist, her lovers, and (unfortunately) her first analyst – had been abusive and exploitative in various ways. In this she had been unsupported by a self-preoccupied mother; ignored by a silent, depressed father; intruded upon by a psychotic brother; treated abusively, along with her family, by the US government; later as a teenager, sexually molested by her gynecologist, then by her dentist, and later by a business colleague; and, as she reported, ultimately exploited by her first analyst. Her needs, her desires, her aspirations and her feelings were never treated as relevant. They were dismissed. Her dream during analysis, of being kept in a quarry by a figure who looked like Richard Nixon, only to be rescued later by a figure who looked like Nelson Rockefeller, was seized by me as a telling, complimenting transferential contrast between previous and current analytic experience, past and current life.

For me it was a valid indication of her perception of my benign, beneficent relationship with her. And, as I smiled like the Cheshire Cat, Dr. Fromm simply affirmed that indeed, I seemed to be more benign, in a relativistic way, but it was quite clear that the patient felt that her analyst (perhaps the Rockefeller person) was not only astronomically distant, by virtue of class, race, and caste, but still met with her in an ambience of unyielding granite (the internment camp?). Furthermore, how had it come to be, he asked, that she had persisted in participating in life this way when she was no longer helpless to resist? Her self-definition as derivative of caste, class, race, and family experience must have been significant.

Dr. Fromm did not intend this comment as denigrating criticism, although at that time I received it that way. Dr. Fromm was addressing, in a straightforward way, what was 'really real' (another favorite expression of his), and pointing out that I had not considered thoughtfully all of the data, something to which I should be dedicated. And that, to him, was the responsibility of the analyst. Finally, more than a lesson in what was actually going on with this particular patient, the dialectical notion (Dr. Fromm often used the word 'paradox') of the principle of the interpenetration of relativistic and absolutist properties was deeply etched in my mind, never to be forgotten. This was a Marxist notion of which Dr. Fromm was fond.

With this particular woman, the analyst would be moved to look for contributions of aspects of his own behavior, which, from the patient's point of view, would have accounted for the imagery in the dream. If this patient were asking to be rescued in this derivative way, the analyst would have had to examine the meaning of her request and her expecting it by meticulously examining her experience of the relationship with him. Had he, in some way, indicated that he would do so? So that she would love him? How was it that she had submitted to the Nixon character (pre-Watergate)? Had he too been solicited for rescue only to fail her abysmally? Did this acting on his own needs represent a potential cynical hazard in the current analytic relationship, and what were its ramifications? Because the analyst was male? Also wielded power as an authority? Behaved similarly? Why, for example, was the analytic situation symbolized as a granite quarry? Was the current analyst cold and unapproachable? Was the analysis conducted in a hard, unyielding, impervious setting, and the analyst, seen as abundantly affluent, but impenetrably elitist, and distant? The properties of the Nixon character and the Rockefeller character, and their differences, should have been thoroughly explored. Was the Nixon character's implicit opportunism and gangsterism representative of her past? And the northeastern Rockefeller a metaphor for a more benign future? Perhaps an image of her mother's ambition? This exploration would have included the figures' origins, their public and private roles, their differences from the patient, their styles of presentation, as well as the kinds of press each had enjoyed, and how each was recorded by the public. What were their similarities to her? Finally, did the analyst's overly cautious attempt not to recreate what had happened in her previous analysis serve to defeat the very thing that was necessary – a positive, warm, non-dismissive relationship with a man who would not imprison or exploit her sexually? Had what was intended as non-invasive become cold (like a quarry) and distancing? Had what was intended as an insistence on the patient's relevance become indicative of the analyst's adamantine presence?

The point of all this, of course, is that it would have addressed the issue of how the patient experiences the analyst and the analysis, as well as herself, as homologous to her life's experience. This would have led to a comprehension of the analyst's influence. With that kind of understanding, the analyst might have responded reciprocally, in terms of what would have been useful so that this patient could contemplate change. Even then an analysis of how that is being experienced would have been in order. Dr. Fromm was completely open to this kind of exploration – an inquiry, an analysis, and an ongoing analysis of that.

I believe Dr. Fromm was interested in getting the error or mistake out in the open. It was not to demonstrate that it is what it is, a wandering or a straying, but that an error is part of a whole pattern of the therapy, and that I should take myself seriously, and think about it that way. The point in this kind of expression was not the supervisor's correct interpretation, his astuteness, or the airing out of his private psyche, but the transformation of the data from an abstract, ideational level to a concrete, material, experiential one, so that I saw clearly that my participation as analyst influenced the patient's response in a real, direct way. With the addition of Dr. Fromm's input, I would have further influence on the contact, and hoped for change in the patient. My patient was to achieve a sense of differentiatedness from me, paradoxically via my intimate connection with her. The dialectic in this kind of union was to follow the discussion, and my experience of union, with Dr. Fromm. In the revelation of error, and the play of ideas about struggles in living, the reality of the experience of an intimate way became clear. In my openness to Dr. Fromm, he could say (sometimes slapping his thigh), 'Look here...if you (or the patient) believe(s) that, or see(s) things that way, or act(s) that way, of course you (she) feel(s)...' Or, 'Let's see,' he would say with grin, 'you like Rockefeller relativistically but not absolutely, right?' On one occasion I said that I did not blame the patient for some feeling or attitude she had (probably in relation to men). I probably meant that I could understand the conditions for her rage. Dr. Fromm smiled and said, 'On Monday you don't blame, but on Tuesday you may. Do you think you are God? Psychoanalysis needs skepticism and inquiry, not judgment.' Dr. Fromm then referred to Marx's favorite motto, 'De omnibus dubitandum' (Of all one must doubt), and favorite maxim, 'Nihil humani a me alienum pub' (Nothing human is alien to me) (Fromm 1961).

Whenever Dr. Fromm spoke of passion, he considered it as a part of relatedness, as a dynamic quality of human faculties. This was an aspect of a person needing to strive for union, i.e., a relationship. This passion, he was fond of asserting, was expressed actively, to be described with verbs, not adjectives or nouns. It was not difficult, therefore, for Dr. Fromm to point out that when my patient had dreamed of the Rockefeller character rescuing her from her unyielding, granite-like internment and isolation from men, my error was in failing to discuss what my active contribution had been to her fantasy, and how she had participated in her unrewarding relationships. This seemed simple enough. But his concept of passion went farther than that.

He suggested that the aim of expression of human faculties is to express one's humanity. Thus, Dr. Fromm pointed out that someone getting lost in a task, like the achievement of some worthwhile goal, or the perfection of some enterprise, was expressing a form of power, and actively establishing boundaries, that would illuminate one's identity for oneself. But it could happen that the person used the task, the perfectionism, the expression of passion, to fill his sense of emptiness, or bypass a feeling of worthlessness. In this way the goal would be subverted to self-enhancement. If this were the case, if the task were not enough as a creative expression by a non-alienated self, the person was prone to do one of two things. He could proceed with his passionate activity only to assume that he was becoming expert, better than all others, with the coincident feeling of grandiosity and arrogance; or he could assume that he was simply not good enough for the task, despite his passionate activity, with the coincident feeling of failure and depression. In this case, any minor imperfection, lapse or error, rejection, or defeat was a stimulus for self-denigration. Either way, Dr. Fromm pointed out, the individual was in the position of alienating himself, by virtue of his need to use the task for his own aggrandizement, rather than as expression of his power and passion, as representative of himself, or his self-definition.

The analyst's task is a revolutionary one, Dr. Fromm insisted. It is to help the patient transform, that is, change his structure, his self-definition, and consequently his ways of living. The patient is not to be satisfied with reformation, adjustment or adaptation. That way leads to what Dr. Fromm called a pathology of normalcy, which is a denial, a subversion of a human's full potential.

What is it about openness in safety – a courage to share and play with ideas about oneself, and a courage to respond – that has this transforming potential in analysis? Does it happen in the contact, the 'union' that Dr. Fromm spoke about? Does it make the union? And the discussion, is not that more than sharing? Surely it involved both of us. There was a feeling of being together, of brothers-in-arms. The play on words, the teasing, as evidenced in his remark to me about Rockefeller, brought home my failure to be curious about the self-serving nature of my limited understanding. We played with what I reported, turning it one way and then another, engendering contact – a clean, uncontaminated, reciprocal contact – serious, vivacious, and most friendly. In the brief time we had with each other, he learned a lot about me as I did about him. It was an exciting, playful, learning experience that expanded, once a feeling of safety was established. The play followed effective work, and at the same time intensified it. It came from the union, and facilitated the union at the same time. Of course it was serious. None of my ideas and feelings was dismissed by Dr. Fromm. Nor did I consider any of his not relevant. He was, obviously, more experienced, more expert. To me, he was a rational authority whose clinical experience and insight I found eminently useful. And still do.

Anything, any image and its appearance, can be followed wherever it leads. In this way, the experience makes relevance manifest. Nothing is dismissed.

Here is the artist again:

> I had a friend who had a wonderful way of teaching people to paint. He told them at the beginning of the day that they would have to destroy the painting. No matter how good it was they couldn't keep it. And some of them groaned, but once they realized that they weren't going to be incriminated by the evidence of the failed painting, they felt wonderful, they felt free to try anything. And even the things that went wrong were exhilarating, the whole process. The whole process was taken out of the realm of failure or success and taken into the realm of let's try it or play.
>
> I think that great art and great writing are the product of some kind of playfulness but that playfulness is very serious. The sculptor Manzu didn't want to know what failures were. He just did it. He said, 'I'm an artisan, I'm not an artist. I am not making a profound statement, I'm just doing it. I do my best and I walk away. And sometimes my best is lousy, and sometimes my best is great, and I don't want to know which is which. Let other people decide.' There's a kind of playfulness in that because you let down all the painful self-observation that may have strangled you but there's also a kind of lack of concern about what the market thinks.

> Play (or playfulness) is the ability to let things happen. But every working artist or writer or composer or performer knows that play is a byproduct of work. You have to earn the ability to let things happen. The dancer knows that freedom is earned by all those hours of practice at the bar. The mystic earns the mystical state by spiritual exercises. Gradually, very gradually, you open the door and maybe it means that the problem-solving mode is the route to the playful mode. Robert Frost says: 'The only way out is through.' (Holden 1991)

The mutual articulation that I experienced with Dr. Fromm was due as much to openness on my part, as it was to Dr. Fromm's response. What I was shown was who I was, and that was all right. But it was the intimate reciprocity that made the union, so that Dr. Fromm and I became connected and could play with alternatives. I, in my errors, remained myself, as he remained himself. If I wished to learn and change, therefore, that could only have been my choice. It was the patient and I that were relevant. And that, after all, was the lesson.

References

Bakhtin, M. (1984) *Problems of Dostoyevsky's Poetics.* Minneapolis, MN: University of Minnesota Press.

Bruner, J. (1990) *Acts of Meaning.* Cambridge, MA: Harvard University Press.

Feiner, A. (1988) "Countertransference and misreading." *Contemporary Psychoanalysis 24,* 612–649.

Feiner, A. (1991a) "The analyst's participation in the patient's transference." *Contemporary Psychoanalysis 27,* 208–241.

Feiner, A. (1998) "The relation of monologue and dialogue to narcissistic states." In J. Fiscalini and A. Grey (eds) *Narcissism and the Interpersonal Self.* New York: Columbia University Press.

Ferenczi, S. (1913) "Belief, disbelief and conviction." In *Further Contributions to the Theory and Technique of Psycho-Analysis.* New York: Brunner-Mazell.

Ferenczi, S. (1988) *The Clinical Diary of Sandor Ferenczi,* ed. J. Dupont. Cambridge, MA: Harvard University Press.

Freud, S. (1910) "The future prospects of psycho-analytic therapy." *Standard Edition 11,* 135–152. London: Hogarth Press.

Freud, S. (1935) "The subtleties of a faulty action." *Standard Edition 22,* 232–235. London: Hogarth Press (1957).

Freud, S. (1937) "Analysis terminable and interminable." *Standard Edition 23,* 211–253. London: Hogarth Press.

Fromm, E. (1961) *Marx's Concept of Man.* New York: Frederick Ungar.

Fromm-Reichmann, F. (1959) *Principles of Intensive Psychotherapy.* Chicago: University of Chicago Press.

Greenson, R. (1972) "Beyond transference and interpretation." *International Journal of Psycho-Analysis 53*, 213–217.

Holden, D. (1991) Interview with A.H. Feiner, June 26.

Kermode, F. (1991) *The Uses of Error.* Cambridge, MA: Harvard University Press.

Kramer, P.D. (1989) *Moments of Engagement.* New York: W.W. Norton.

Kuhn, T. (1977) *The Essential Tension.* Chicago: University of Chicago Press.

Kumin, I. (1989) "The incorrect interpretation." *International Journal of Psycho-Analysis 70*, 141–152.

Langs, R. (1975) "The patient's unconscious perception of the therapist's errors." In P. Giovacchini (ed) *Tactics and Techniques in Psychoanalytic Therapy.* New York: Jason Aronson.

Langs, R. (1981) *Resistances and Interventions.* New York: Jason Aronson.

Levenson, E. (1972) *The Fallacy of Understanding.* New York: Basic Books.

Levenson, E. (1991c) "Standoffs, impasses and stalemates." *Contemporary Psychoanalysis 27*, 511–518.

Little, M. (1951) "Countertransference." *International Journal of Psycho-Analysis 32*, 32–40. In R. Langs (ed) (1981) *Classics in Psychoanalytic Technique.* New York: Jason Aronson.

Morson, G.S. and Emerson, C. (1990) *Mikhail Bakhtin.* Stanford, CA: Stanford University Press.

Rothenberg, A. (1988) *The Creative Process of Psychotherapy.* New York: W.W. Norton.

Schwaber, F. (1980) "Reply to Paul Tolpin." In A. Goldberg (ed) *Advances in Self Psychology.* New York: International Universities Press.

Schweizer, H. (1990) Introduction to F. Kermode, *Poetry, Narrative, History.* Oxford: Basil Blackwell.

Searles, H.F. (1965) *Collected Papers on Schizophrenia and Related Subjects.* New York: International Universities Press.

Searles, H.F. (1975) "The patient as therapist to his analyst." In P.L. Giovacchini with A. Flarsheim and L. Bryce Boyer (eds) *Tactics and Techniques in Psychoanalytic Therapy,* vol. 2. New York: Jason Aronson.

Tomä, H. and Kachele, H. (1985) *Psychoanalytic Practice, Vol I.* Heidelberg: Springer Verlag. Reviewed by L. Wurmser in *Journal of the American Psychoanalytic Association 38*, 815–820.

Torok, M. (1984) "La correspondance, Freud–Ferenczi." *Confrontations.* Fall.

Tower, L.E. (1956) "Countertransference." *Journal of the American Psychoanalytic Association 4*, 224–255.

Watzlavick, P., Beavin, I. and Jackson, D. (1967) *Pragmatics of Human Communication.* New York: W.W. Norton.

Winnicott, D.W. (1963) "Psychotherapy of character disorders." In *The Maturational Processes and the Facilitating Environment.* New York: International Universities Press.

Winnicott, D.W. (1987) *The Spontaneous Gesture: Selected Letters of D. W. Winnicott.* Cambridge, MA: Harvard University Press.

Chapter 8

Contradictions in the Supervisory Process

A long, long time ago when I was growing up I used to come home from elementary school each day for lunch, and then return for afternoon session. My mother was invariably out shopping for food, or cleaning and complaining about her back. Grandma was always reading – as I recall, something about Sacco and Vanzetti. Exchanges with my mother were usually based on her perennial question, 'Were you a good boy?' And so, I learned how to lie.

My maternal grandmother had only one thing to say at lunchtime, which was, 'Did you ask any good questions today?' For years I struggled with not knowing precisely what she meant, hoping that eventually I could report that I had done something in school that would please her. One day I related that the teacher had put six stars on the blackboard in the shape of a pot, and had called it The Big Dipper. Then she said that there was a smaller grouping (I doubt that she used the word 'constellation') called The Little Dipper that she drew, pouring into The Big Dipper. Grandma asked, 'And what was your question?' I said with a little trepidation, 'I asked the teacher whether one could ever see The Big Dipper pouring into The Little Dipper.' And, to my amazement, Grandma said, 'That was a good question.' I didn't know why, although I glowed inwardly in her infinite wisdom.

The anecdotal method, as romantic as it is, despite its reinforcement of hopefulness, its warmth, and its negation of cynicism and despair, is without scientific merit. It is wholly unreliable, and, usually, without an ounce of validity, as careful investigation ultimately demonstrates. For example, my grandmother had a rich store of folk remedies, superstitions, and fanciful tales of unique cures for various ills that she had gathered from natives and other ranchers during her short-lived, western frontier experience as a homesteader during the late 1870s; but she listened, avidly and obediently, to my father's brother, who was her physician. Sometimes her imagistic explanations, that were offered generously, bordered on the bizarre. But if taken metaphorically they made enormous sense. I am not sure but their extravagant imagery may have been intended to stimulate a child's imagination. I remember one time, when I was about 10, asking her why a neighbor had behaved in a crazy way after delivering her first child. Grandma's diagnostic comment, that seemed to be offered with utmost confidence, was that 'the milk went to her head.' I took this obvious old-generational bit of alleged wisdom literally, with great respect, and tried to picture the internal anatomy that could occasion such a catastrophic event, only to give up after querying other adults who just scoffed, and searching the encyclopedia for hours. But, if Grandma said so she must be right, I reasoned, so I concluded then that children like myself could not understand such things. Looking back now, however, as a general metaphor for the etiology of a post-partum psychotic episode, Grandma was not far off.

There have been many creditable pieces written about psychoanalytic supervision. After all it is one of the basic, absolute requirements of the training experience. There have been several valuable books and essays that have examined with lucidity, and in detail, the triadic dimensions of supervision: analyst–patient–supervisor (Ekstein and Wallerstein 1958; Fleming and Benedek, 1966); as well as the dyadic context: student analyst – supervisor (Bromberg 1982; Epstein 1986; Fiscalini 1985; Langs 1979; Levenson 1982). Therefore, when I began to write this chapter, I thought what could I possibly add but some of my own idiosyncratic ramblings? But then I thought of that contrasting lesson of childhood, my grandmother indirectly encouraging me to become curious, and my mother's squelching of initiative, and indirectly teaching me a way to get by. Despite the unreliability of the anecdotal method, the issue of mother's and grandmother's influence is of significance beyond the self-evident value of the content – fibbing and curiosity. Its import lies in its contribution to a comprehending of the interpersonal moment, and seeing what one person's behavior evokes in another.

In homologous fashion, the mutual influence of supervisor and supervisee does determine what goes on in supervision, especially how each participant feels about it, and what results in treatment. Grandma's explanations were always tied to activities, as I recall, not to attributions. To contemplate influence requires that we add 'in what way,' since it is the verb, the enactment, that carries weight in comprehension, not the noun.

I remember a supervisor early in my training, who insisted that I listen to myself, my own expressions, in terms of form, and tone, as well as content, if I were to try to understand a patient's communications in response to them. When I would summarize a patient's comments she might ask, 'What did you say before that and how do you think the patient heard it?' Another always wanted to know my purpose in saying anything to a patient. Embarrassingly, sometimes I could not think of one.

These were the first experiences I had had with a real interpersonal orientation. I had trained in various clinic and hospital situations; it seemed to me that each supervisor I had been assigned to had a specific theoretical attitude, that was not very clear, and a corresponding drawer full of therapeutic gestures and interventions, despite giving some lip-service to an interpersonal position. Therefore, whenever I presented my work with a patient, there was suggested an allegedly appropriate response which was supposed to make the theory and practice fully integrated. This, of course, made me quite passive, little more than a conduit for the supra-analyst who saw all, and knew all, and from whom I sought endless approval. In contrast to my experience with Grandma, I learned nothing about myself, nor did I learn anything about the therapeutic process beyond the usual givens, the ground of the interaction. Perhaps, by osmosis something useful did register with me, but for a long time I did not think so. This is a style of teaching that is probably the easiest way to throttle any vivaciousness and originality in the neophyte. I learned to do 'it' their ways.

As an antidote to this stultifying 'by-the-numbers' method, Levenson (1982) describes what he calls 'Zen' supervision. In this method, one learns the rules, and then, with the guru constantly changing the rules, one learns that it is all right to abandon them. Supposedly, one becomes open and spontaneous.

But spontaneity, I believe, is a function of neural circuitry, self-definition, and feelings of interpersonal relevance. It is hardly a simple discharge, an undisciplined expression. The method may encourage ease, relaxation, and fluidity, but if not taking place in a context of the value of serious self-study, along with the careful, orderly application of knowledge, and relatedness to a social field, and the need to avoid countertransference imposition, it can degenerate into impulsive, self-aggrandized wildness. There is a conspicuous absence of the supervisor insisting on professionalism, with consequent little responsibility and accountability. Anything like the respect a surgeon has for living tissue is sorely absent. This method sometimes accompanies uncritical praise from the guru, the hidden agenda of which is to gather acolytes.

Levenson describes another pattern of teaching that is usually practiced by someone of considerable age, experience, and reputation. There is no structure; the doyen or doyenne just listens, and on occasion some word, or brief, pithy phrase, unusually wise, is emitted from his or her Buddha-like presence. Somehow, the student learns to listen. By virtue of the authoritative setting, the student is forced to contemplate the shared aphorisms so that they sink in, to reappear later as a natural part of the work.

Levenson also refers to what he calls an algorithmic approach to psychotherapy that some senior supervisors inculcate. It is comprised of a series of systematic operational steps that one hopes lead to solutions. My grandmother had a way of getting her canary to sing that had to do with one special brand of seeds. I found out later in life that the product she preferred had marijuana seeds in it, so apparently Grandma enjoyed having her canaries high, but she was not aware of that. All she knew was that with her favorite brand of seeds the canary was more likely to sing, and with the more popular brand it did not sing as much.

While the algorithm may or may not have any theoretical basis, in psychoanalytic supervision the steps actually do reflect the supervisor's idea of the source of pathology. Like most good theory there is an implicit practicality. Since Levenson sees the origin of pathology mostly in mystification, those interactive steps which expand awareness and authenticity can only result in the enhancement of growth, and the release of someone's creative, semiotic potential in negotiating with and broadening one's life. One could hardly say that this is not a kind of theoretical underpinning for practice, albeit implicit, but it is evidently not tautological, which would have the therapy prove the theory. This approach derives, in part at least, from an interpersonal orientation toward human beings and their interactions with each other, and from a study of the interactions themselves. It shows that important trust in verbs and adverbs in contrast to nouns and adjectives. There is no attempt at revealing essences. It is about the how not the what.

There is also a common supervisory posture that makes the supervision an extension of each student's psychoanalysis. Whatever one does or does not do, that is objected to by the supervisor, students are advised to take it back to their analyst. Evidently they are enacting inappropriately some countertransferential feeling or attitude that the supervisor believes needs close scrutiny. A more intrusive and invasive variation of this type is some extemporaneous analytic work on the spot. The poor students, facing their ignorance and/or their malfeasance (better, facing their ineptitude and their unconsciousness), are now confronted with their inadequate psychic insides. Some supervisors of this genre make the naive assumption that institutes are comprised of seniors and juniors similar to well-functioning, integrated families (whatever they may be): all-smiling, generous, charitable, benign brothers and sisters, aunts, uncles and parental figures. Since all members of a training institute community are assumed to be equal family members with similar altruistic purposes, with a surfeit of beneficence and love, common dynamics such as self-serving ambition, a cormorant's thirst for fame and power, competition, envy, hate, resentment, rage, and careerism – as well as the banal political necessities for approval – are ignored. Some of our colleagues achieve black belts in sincerity and manipulation. Their studied posture, seated with hands over their chests, finger-tips touching, head slightly tilted, eyebrows raised, displaying a somewhat beatific smile, along with halting speech, is designed to convey profundity, thoughtfulness and seriousness. Our profession's infamous compulsion for status and celebrity inevitably robs us of a real sense of community. So, in addition to being exposed under an inauthentically misguided aegis like, 'We are all members of the same family and it is in our family interest that you (the student) do better,' the poor students have their sense of well-being challenged. With their self-esteem no higher than a slug, students often conclude that they should have gone into the haberdashery business.

Yet oddly, the fact is, denoting the student's personal issues as potential areas of difficulty with a patient, in a context of safety, along with a dispassionate discussion of them, does somehow help the student's work. Since our persons are our instruments, we should expect that any serious, carefully selected student would respectfully consider their imperfections if described by a senior. After all, they are being told this is what professionalism is about. But in the long run, this approach fails to accomplish the main fundamental task of supervision, which is to facilitate the student's own professional competence.

It seems like a rite of passage. Perhaps all groups demand some form of initiation, from circumcision, through gauntlet running, to hazing. So, if the patients are to have their heads aired, to be members of the tribe of the enlightened, analysts endlessly must have theirs – in their analysis and supervision.

Finally, Levenson mentions one more type. Here the supervisor and the supervisee enact what they come to believe (eventually, via the supervisor's persuasiveness) is going on between the patient and the supervisee. The supervisor is allegedly 'put' (not deliberately) in the position of a proxy therapist, with the supervisee playing the part of the patient. Although out-of-awareness, the enactment is not taken by sophisticated supervisors as a simple, mechanistic repetition of patient–analyst interaction, but more likely representing some sort of homology. It is as though the student were saying, 'Do it with me and I'll know what to do with my patients.' As Bromberg (1982) insightfully points out, while the issues that belong to the patient may seem similar to the issues that the therapist-as-student brings into supervision, clearly, what the supervisee introduces belongs to him or her. The similarity is essentially superficial. It is sort of like the descriptions of a spouse by a patient. The image of the described other cannot be taken as the whole objective truth. The description can be seen only as a derivative of the patient's experience, and, as a matter of fact, conditioned by the immediate context. For example, the deference of a patient and the deference of a supervisee may be appropriate to that class of behavior that occurs in all human beings, deference-in-general; but the patient's deference is historically derived, as is the therapist's; their different histories, as well as how their self-definitions on which their interactions depend, are unique aspects of their respective experiences in the contexts in which they occur. In this regard, the discussions with the supervisor can only be molar at best. To learn that one is defensively deferent so as to avoid disapproval when one's career is at stake, and to apply this banal insight to the persistent deference of the patient, shows a disrespect for the history of the patient, and the survival value of his or her self-system and necessary transferential processes.

It is not a question of clinical annotation. Most of us have learned to be accurate in that respect. Deferent patients may beget student-analysts who are deferential with their supervisors. What is surely questionable is the use of general, abstract concepts as explanation. Simply put, explanations are not found in labels or descriptions. They reside in a comprehending of the properties of the elements in the field, the relationship of these elements to each other, and to their movement. The serious criticism of this method of supervision is that it renders the student passive, limiting the supervisory experience to the general issues of the supervisee, inundating him or her with abstractions. It may even degenerate to the use of simplistic analogy, disregarding the conditions inherent in the patient's field. It is somewhat similar to a wife telling her furious husband that he shouldn't feel the way he does, that she is not his mother – and after all, she loves him and has stood by him these many years. Her consternation at his increased rage is a function of her saying something evidently correct but irritatingly invalid. In fact, if the husband has had early experiences of dismissal and non-relevance, with the additional binding notion that his distress is his own fault, the wife has managed to convey the same thing, in addition to an implicit demand for gratefulness. If something like this takes place in supervision, the goal of drawing out of the therapist his own potentials for creative analytic effort is severely inhibited. After all, that drawing out is what education is all about. To ignore, or even obscure (with disavowal, or, heaven forbid, denial) the supervisor's or the student's contribution to the interaction is antithetical to interpersonalism.

It should be noted that difficulties in psychoanalytic cognition, and, therefore, psychoanalytic supervision, also derive from the prejudices of our various schools of thinking. This means that whether the student or supervisor believes the source of psychopathology is social, interpersonal, biological, or intrapsychic – or even that therapists know best – their rigidity can create difficulties for the work. With one source in mind, other sources of psychopathology are overlooked. Or, as sometimes happens, the significance or importance of the therapeutic relationship becomes subverted because of an unwarranted assumption of authority (Havens 1982).

I do not suppose I have added any great insight or clarity into this highly complex situation, one which mirrors, in its own way, those things that occur in any interpersonal field, therapeutic or otherwise. For one thing, in any interaction there are two things going on. They can be briefly characterized as indicative of a request for information, and a definition of the relationship itself. These are going on at the same time in the sequential utterances. If you ask a colleague for the name of a potential reference you are requesting a citation, and you are defining the moment in terms of your dependency on the colleague for the information.

Imagine an old-fashioned typewriter ribbon (remember them?) which has black and red and colorless (used for mimeograph stencils – remember those?) sections. And now imagine a loose, imperfect carriage, so that when key X is struck it manages to produce black, red and colorless impressions simultaneously. If we let the black refer to the message exchange, the content (or the information), with the red impression referring to the definition of the relationship, and the neutral or colorless impression referring to the state of feeling, perhaps in both people, one has a simplified, mechanical model for what goes on between two persons involved in conversation. We now can imagine further what happens in a supervisory relationship. This could be genuinely dialogic, in which each is accessible to the history, the subculture, the reality of the other. Or, it can be self-serving or aggrandizing – anything, but education for competence.

Now, what is the reality of the student? Students want to do better with their patients. They want to do better with themselves; that is, they want to become professionally capable. And they want to do better in their career as an analyst-in-training (of course, there are broad perversions of these). All of these contribute to their definition of the relationship between themselves and the supervisor. In addition, there are the students' prejudices, the students' assumptions, the notions that they have picked up from their course work and finally, powerfully, the model of psychoanalysis that they have experienced in their own training analysis.

Students' defensiveness, which is stimulated by their knowledge that they are being evaluated, tends to narrow the relationship with the supervisor, limiting it to a safe experience. There is nothing wrong with a quest for safety, but narrowing a relationship for this reason makes for aridity and a loss of the supervisor's experience.

If you entertain the idea of all these and similar issues happening with the supervisor, including the supervisor's own relationship with the student's analyst, placing them all under the rubric of the recurrent contradiction between compassion and standards, you begin to see how complex this relationship can become.

This contradiction between compassion and standards, fellow-feeling and the rules by which one lives, or the way one defines oneself, surfaces everywhere. It is an eternal contradiction which many, many have described throughout our cultural and literary history. The Greeks referred to it as a struggle between the Apollonian and the Dionysian traditions, that paradox epitomized by the Oedipus trilogy. The rule of law, in contradiction to the expression of compassion and empathy, finds no better prototypic expression than in Sophocles's *Antigone.*

This can be seen as one's struggle between otherness, or differentiatedness and autonomy, and the desire to join and merge with others, so as to create a community, a sensuous humanity in which conflictual differences may disappear. While we have desires for separateness and uniqueness, we have these equally powerful desires for union. Often the two desires are experienced in contradiction.

Standards remind us of our particularity, our differentiatedness, the reliability of our boundaries, and separateness. Compassion brings us into connection with others. It is our compassion that prevents elitist, self-centered, insularity. It is our standards, with their emphasis on responsibility and accountability that prevent incoherence and mindlessness. The boundary rules assure safety.

Too often we are painfully aware that we fail on one side or the other and need to compromise. But it is from this exercise of compromise, or balanced integration, that we derive our attitudes of reasonableness and of justice. If we are aware of what goes into our decision making and the reasons for doing so, we suffer less.

Some supervisors assume that their most important ethical responsibility is to the student's patient. This would impel them to make the student a conduit for their own expertise. Others make the assumption that their ultimate responsibility is to the development of the student, that is, to provide the conditions for learning. Since supervisors function at a considerably higher level of abstraction than the report of the therapy that is brought to them by the student, they deal with a class of events, of which the student's process notes are typical. Supervisors naturally see more, know more, and seem to be in the enviable position of bestowing unchallengeable wisdom (Levenson 1982). Supervisors who then relate with the assumption of superior wisdom and objectivity behave in one of two ways. If they are moved toward resolving the endless contradiction between compassion and standards on the side of compassion, they tend to inform the student that the student is a superior therapist or, at least, has the potential for being a great one. Their concern is the possible lowering of the student's self-esteem when confronted by the superwise supervisor, and his or her imminent fantasy that he should become a shoe salesman.

Those supervisors who are perceived as Olympian authorities by the student, and who maintain vigorously the position of the necessity for standards, without regard for the student's experience, indeed do drive their students to the fantasy that they should be in a different profession, along with the corollary feelings of self-scorn. The issue of relevance and dismissiveness is so ubiquitous in our society that anti-self feelings and, in the extreme, anti-self self-definitions, abound in all of us. These self-hateful feelings are ready to show themselves acutely in the defining aspects of the supervisory relationship (Epstein 1986; Feiner 1991a, 1993). They must be attended to with students as well as with patients. In our desire to encourage the conditions for learning, and have students develop at their own rate, it behooves us to communicate our evaluations in a compassionate way.

Now anti-self self-definitions or convictions develop after early extended experiences of being made to feel non-relevant, that is, having one's desires, thoughts, needs, and feelings dismissed. It is as if one has been treated as though these fundamental biological and psychological needs are beyond one's inherent right to have and to be expressed. Out of this kind of background one comes to assume a self-definition of irrelevance, that renews itself over and over with a reassuring fidelity. Any event on the horizon provides an opportunity for its expression. It is typical with those situations we have come to call abuse, or inner-city disadvantageousness.

Irrelevantly defined people believe they have no positive impact. No wonder there is so much mindless, destructive behavior in our society that we fail to comprehend or influence. We make polar diagnoses of our social ills. In trying to be compassionate, to ingather what we think of as lost souls, we fail to hold people accountable. We excuse outrageous abominations in our rush to 'understand.' Then we suffer cynicism after our revulsion. Or, we declare behavior savage, monstrous, animal-like, and see it emanating from those we think of as sub-human. Either way shows little respect for the potential growth of others and their necessity to participate constructively and responsibly in a communal process. We might note briefly that the United States' Constitution is based on the opposite assumption. In contrast to most constitutions in the world, the American document uniquely asserts rights, and thereby limits governmental action. In other words, people are relevant. It is a given, and people grant power to the US government with severe limitations. Our relevance, non-dismissiveness, impact, and responsibility are taken for granted. Anything else is a perversion or a subversion of this idea. Unfortunately the subverting of our relevance is what happens to many of us with caretakers, teachers, and other authorities.

What of the converse? What happens when it is demanded that someone be relevant, or take themselves, their feelings and their behavior seriously? It is then that issues of acknowledgment, responsibility and accountability show themselves, sometimes with the dread of exposure and the panic of vulnerability. With the experience of dismissal one feels useless. In this system when one is expected to perform or produce, in keeping with one's participation in a relationship, one covers up, with disavowing. A patient will accuse his wife of being self-righteous, needing to be correct, and not accepting him. But he cannot accept her self-righteousness, nor does he have the facility to deal with it. A wife will yell at her husband, and when he complains about her yelling, she says, 'Don't be so technical.' He is talking form, she concerned with content. And so is it with the supervisee, who will fail to inquire, fail to engage, fail to discuss, fail to function, and then blame the weather, the economy, rhinitis, a malfunctioning car, or even the supervisor's lack of humor, all of which may be correct.

Our structural self-definition is laid down neurally quite early in life, since it is on the neural mapping where early interpersonal experience is registered, and gets to be expressed later as a function of the dynamics of all relationships (Feiner 1993). Connectedness offers the timely chance for revelation. Relationship can be comprised of people, sensations, things, events, anticipations, possibilities, or experiences. Learning in an anti-self system cannot be an exciting, exploratory achievement. It is only a humiliating reminder that one did not know something beforehand, or should not now. It opens the way for all kinds of destructive, antagonistic, disjunctive feelings to show themselves, instead of the celebration of discovery. There is no way to step back and sensuously enjoy what one has struggled to accomplish (like our math professors at the blackboard), and then step in again to deepen the experience, immersing oneself in learning and development.

Both supervisor and supervisee are subject to this kind of human experience, as, obviously, is the patient (Epstein 1986). Supervisors functioning with the assumption of superior wisdom, struggling unconsciously with their own anti-self self-definition, now further influenced by the umbrella struggle between compassion and standards, may ask themselves how they can deal effectively with their supervisees without hurting them, or precipitating the very thing that they themselves struggle with. After all, eight times eight equals sixty-four, regardless of how our parents treated us, or how dysfunctional our family of origin (Crouch 1993). How is a supervisor to get that across to the unsophisticated?

The simplistic solution has been those broad, unrestricted, overgeneralized compliments, without any discrimination based on professional standards. We do have a raft of clinically inexperienced, inadequately trained, and ill-informed, so-called therapists, reminding their friends and relatives that they are indeed superior because their alleged supervisors or consultants have said so. We can spot them by their triteness, their platitudinous homilies, their jargon, and their ever-ready response, 'What you really mean is…' The trenchant, delicate precision of what psychoanalysis could be, that is, its contemplation, its inquiry, and its articulation, is ignored. Even with those who are more clever their talk is little more than rhetorical flourish. Their advertisements for themselves are more public relations and marketeering than statements of fact.

An additional dynamic related to this is the issue of coaching and how some people relate to it. There seem to be gender differences in one's response to coaching and criticism. Briefly, those who have tried to teach members of their families how to drive a car or play tennis recognize what I am referring to. In our society if one tells one's spouse that she does not keep her eye on the road, or that she should get the lead out of her ass, she may assume she is not being loved. If one says the same thing to a male companion, he invariably makes the assumption that he is loved. Indeed one would not be saying this if one were not loving, since the friend knows that love's opposite is indifference.

I think the gender issue is of some minor import but the actual asymmetry of the student being one down in an institutional setting, and realistically needing and relying upon some evaluation is the more important point. In an asymmetrical relationship, too often, a criticism, a rectification, a suggestion, can be seen as an attack, and the encouragement of responsibility and accountability is taken as blame. The student responds with some defense. We do have this enormous dread of exposure. It is this that inhibits the expansion of awareness, retards the procedure in its distraction, wastes energy on the trivial, and renders the supervisor irrelevant. One could easily say that this is what the difficult patient has done to the therapist, this evocation of assumed denigration, but describing it like that doesn't transcend the common or garden-variety elements of any relationship. If supervision is seen as a specific example of continuous interaction, which is no different dynamically than anything else, there must be those moments during which anxiety rises and defensive operations take place in both participants of the relationship (Levenson 1993, p.395). But this should not interfere with learning. Unfortunately, it does.

I suppose the context determines the choice of supervisory methods. I think it is reasonable to assume that these change over time, and from student to student. Obviously, there are beginning student analysts who are of limited sophistication and who need the evident support of someone more experienced. There is also the appropriate concern of the supervisor trying to avoid this student feeling intimidated by the experience, or over-idealizing it. But, later, we should question why the student needs to learn the same lesson over and over as he or she proceeds through training, from supervisor to supervisor.

With all this in mind, we might infer that supervisors, just like their students, need the feeling of relevance. And their own defensiveness serves the purpose of achieving this, albeit non-rationally. As they advise their students to acknowledge and be responsible for their participation in their engagement with their patients, so might supervisors acknowledge and think about their own participation with the student. The supervisor who, in his or her own language, functions as my mother did, asking metaphorically if the student were 'a good boy,' will beget liars and impostors. The student will learn nothing, or, at least, only those skills that gratify that supervisor maintaining his lofty image of himself.

The entire enterprise of supervision rests on the contradiction between learning openly and being evaluated at the same time. Being drawn out – it is really learning how to draw on one's resources – to develop a professional psychoanalytic competence that is unfettered and spontaneous, is inhibited by the requirements of evaluation. Students best learn through the scrutiny of their and others' errors and, obviously, are expected to make them (Feiner 1991b). Yet, at the same time, students' being evaluated and rated has an effect on their status, their own image of themselves, and their career in their institute. There is a natural tendency, therefore, to ensure a positive evaluation. Unfortunately, this is done at the expense of learning by showing error and discussing it thoroughly.

Students often cover their ignorance or helplessness by introducing issues with an au courant phrase like, 'I guess it is my countertransference.' Indeed, that might be getting in the way of their effort. But the use of that fashionable word 'countertransference' has a tendency to preclude the topic for examination, not open it up at all. Few supervisors take a discussion beyond the level of 'If it is your countertransference, take it to your analyst.' What is necessary are queries about the derailing of the process, the aim of which being the mutual discovery of possible valid interventions which would serve the interests of the patient, and how students feel about their work, and what kinds of problems they have with it. It can be accomplished only in an atmosphere of safety, one where errors are expected and welcomed as opportunities for learning.

An interpersonal description of an interaction is as difficult for the supervisor as for the student-therapist. Both need to extract from the student's report those necessary elements which would help explain the participation of the two people in the therapy. What has happened can be seen as a vector of patient A. and therapist B. But B., the student, now describes the resultant interaction C. to supervisor D. This puts D. in the position of trying to do two things at the same time. D. needs to delineate C., the interaction, and to evaluate B. in such a way that it will facilitate B.'s growth to B. prime.

This is inhibited by B.'s expectations, and the student's need to guarantee the quality of vector E., which is the resultant of the interaction with the supervisor. Consequently, the student's report may be colored. Showing one's work in an expressed verbal exchange in supervision presents an almost insurmountable contradiction. It is not like playing the violin in a master class where technique is taken for granted and one is learning interpretive shadings. Words are surely imprecise, but their imprecision may be due less to semantic limitations than defensiveness. Furthermore, like the patient's report of a dream, the student's summary of an analytic hour leaves out those subtle events that are part of the process but marginal to it. I mean parenthetical thoughts, muscle tensions, voice tonality, bodily gestures, anything that doesn't get into a verbal report. Tape transcriptions never fully capture these nuances. And queries about them may be threatening.

Let us say B. is imbued with the latest fashion in our trade and B. says something like, 'I suppose my countertransference, my fear of my sadism, kept me from saying something.'

(It could be that not saying anything was the best thing that could have happened. Why attribute what happened to some theoretical construct? Is one supposed to say something?)

What is the supervisor to do with that?

- Query about the alleged sadism? (And what is that?) Or join it?
- Query about the fear? (Join the fear?)
- Query about the effect of the silence? (Well let's see what happened?)
- Query about the source of the feeling in therapeutic interaction? What prompted it?
- Query about the need to tell it the way it is being told?
- Other?
- All of the above, focusing on the immediate interaction?

Supervisors are not without their own responsibility and accountability. They may believe they are encouraging self-scrutiny, but their comments – like 'It's curious that,' 'It's interesting that,' 'It's fascinating that' – evoke only helplessness in students who must attentively listen; then fantasize their own response:

> Yes Dr. X, it is curious that I forgot my process notes, but curious in what way? The dog didn't eat them. I'm just intimidated here. Why should that be? You're supposed to be helping me grow professionally and all you say is, 'It's curious that I did this, interesting that I said that, and so forth.' If you believe in the unconscious and respect its power, why do you query me in such a way that I feel I'm supposed to be aware of all this? And that I have misbehaved? Do you not have words to help me explore my passions?

Some supervisors (and of course, students as well) cannot tolerate ambiguities or moments of incomprehensibility. One might say it is like being faced with the dreadful fact of finiteness, or death. So interpretations or translations are made forcibly to fill in that gaping hole of ignorance which we contemplate in terror. We use what we have been taught, and with what we are familiar, to give shape to our response, sometimes before we have the data. Sometimes, after session, therapists are left with distressing, uncomfortable feelings of confusion, a confusion that has been engendered by the patient's twists and turns of logic, omissions, lapses, or inaccuracies in communication, and a mystical conception of causality, which surely make the patient difficult to follow. The therapist is made responsible for feelings by the patient without reasonable basis; or a feeling is explained by the patient using evidence that logically supports its contradiction, or at least, its absence. It is as if a person complains of hunger, is given a sandwich, and then complains of anger at the person who gave the sandwich, because he was reminded of having been hungry in the past. The linkage is missing. Is gratitude threatening? It simply makes no sense. Further elaborations are necessary, but they are not forthcoming, and, if available, their expression collaboratively would effectively change the state. It remains incomprehensible. But, for the supervisor, because of distress about the unknown, to 'round up the usual suspects,' as Police Chief Louis was prone to doing in the film *Casablanca*, is of no help to a student who needs to learn how to tolerate ambiguity, irrationality, and the confusion that goes with it. The usual suspects may have a glib romance about them but, ultimately, they provoke our wrestling with stereotypes.

Sometimes, fleeing in dread from mystery, we may come up with clichés and platitudes. It is one source of countertransferential feelings and gestures. Related to this is our lack of wonder at motivation. Our traditional learning leaves out everything but sex and aggression, when perhaps the most important thing is to grasp what in the interaction triggered irrationality. The supervisor and student may fail to capture those many passions that move poets. With a reductionistic lesson guiding them, student-analysts miss the opportunity to enrich patients' view of themselves, and both fail to transcend the poverty of their vocabularies which would have helped them luxuriate in union.

How can the student-analyst, realistically dependent on the potential evaluation by the supervisor, engage in dialogue? Despite the supervisor's reassuring claim for open discussion, this structured role tends to be monologic, even though he or she assumes that the apparent dialogue is real. Alas, it can only be monologue in disguise, and therefore inauthentic.

If the ghost of my grandmother were hovering in the room, she might drop the hint that both were there to find out about asking a good question, and that there was a world of difference between labeling something curious and someone's being curious about it. It is a difference between an attribution and an avowal of feeling. One way implies that there is some arcane poison circulating in the student's veins and it has been discerned by the authoritative supervisor. The other way communicates the supervisor's feeling, and is an invitation to a mutual search.

That supervisor who in his or her own way functions as my grandmother did, wondering whether the student 'asked any good questions,' introduces the student-analyst to a scientific universe of curiosity. In so doing the supervisor invites the student to participate in as meaningful a way as is possible. There is nothing more encouraging to relevance and feelings of esteem than one's productive participation in a communal effort. We see this often in the altruistic voluntarism during some social disasters.

The 'good boy,' on the other hand, will necessarily repeat dogma, the supervisor's dogma to be sure, and ultimately will find his growth not relevant at all. This student will get a good report card. The 'good questions attitude' will stimulate a search for a good question; the reason why it is a good question, and how and when it is to be used in practice. Furthermore, the supervisor coaches the student in exercising one step in the algorithmic approach. This is a journeyman experience which can only stimulate the pleasures in exploration in a rather inexact science, maintaining and spurring the development of the student's individual style. It facilitates the leap from craft to art, and in so doing emphasizes the values that we profess to represent in our profession – authenticity, individuality, spontaneity, and truth as we best know it to be. It helps too in attempting to resolve the contradiction between compassion and standards.

What I have not heard or read much about, either in individual or group supervision, is a discussion of mourning. Perhaps profound feelings of mourning and their expression arrive late in the psychoanalytic process, and this contributes to their infrequent appearance in supervision. Since candidates tend to graduate or complete their supervision before these feelings need to be worked through with their patients, patients' mourning tends to be brought in rarely to the supervisory relationship. Still, mourning is an appropriate, or one could say integrative, response to any kind of loss – persons, relationships, ideals, values, esteem – whether due to logistics, disappointments, betrayal, or tragedy. I wonder why discussions of these feelings do not appear more regularly in supervision. Perhaps they do for others, but I have not heard much about it with my students. Maybe my students seek to protect me from mourning feelings without my awareness or theirs. But no one would disagree with the idea that a comprehensive appreciation of mourning makes the impact of people on each other more than a faint blur on time and space.

When I was a candidate we used to say that if one were graduated it was of no great moment, but if one did not that was indeed a tragedy. It was said that one could learn the basic principles of psychoanalysis in six months but that it took ten years, at least, to become an analyst. The many useful supervisory opportunities or therapeutic experiences account for this, with differing points of view enriching one's thought with different images or mental pictures. The formal aspects of training, the ongoing rectifications by patients, and especially the experiences of life's disappointments and losses and their articulation, do impinge. But one must have a mind for it to be able to receive it all and make use of it. It must have a place to register and there must be a willingness to let it happen. Unfortunately, too little time is given to the expression.

Asking the right question has led to progress in science. In fact, it is the questions that drive science, not the answers. Sullivan's 'detailed inquiry', his careful scrutiny of the patient's interactions with other people – past, present and in fantasy – follows this dictum (Sullivan 1954). In psychoanalytic supervision there may be more than one good question to suggest, but formulating one stimulates optimism in students since it helps them feel relevant to any potential movement in their patient. Under the conditions of optimism, for student as well as patient, things can change. That one can matter and belong is an essential part of anyone's esteem. Of course it is the same for students. Levenson once pointed out that senior analysts of different schools were quite similar in that they all asked good questions, despite the astronomical differences of their metapsychologies.

If we really care about our students, their future, their curiosity, their development, their professional competence, we should encourage them to discover the good question, the how, and when to ask it, the point of which is the search for meaning in appearances, rather than meaning behind them. To restate Levenson's apt description of the difference between interpersonalism and the Freudian position, we want to know 'what's going on, not what does it truly mean' (Levenson 1985, p.53).

But we will eschew our own idealization. After all, it is the ultimate accolade that all good teachers and their theories are overthrown by their good students. This happens because the good teacher has educated the student to ask good questions.

Supervision, perhaps the whole of psychoanalytic practice, can be likened to the well-meaning, sensual attempts of an eager, naive lover who, anticipating low moans of grateful pleasure, hears only, 'Darling, here, not there!' We will be compassionate, yet we will, out of respect, attend to standards. It is no credit to ourselves nor our profession to encourage inept therapists for the sake of not lowering their self-esteem without some attempt at teaching a procedure that calls forth an efficacious process (Levenson 1982). We should know who the student is, how much of a professional he or she has become, at our moments of engagement. And this should be in keeping with our knowledge of and respect for those refreshing aspects of time.

Our students walk after us, and we trust they will do the work better. It is what my analyst's analyst (who was an analysand of Freud) told him, and he told me.

References

Bromberg, P.M. (1982) "The supervisory process and parallel process in psychoanalysis." *Contemporary Psychoanalysis 18*, 92–111.

Crouch, S. (1993) Quoted in the *New York Times* August 28.

Ekstein, R. and Wallerstein, R.S. (1958) *The Teaching and Learning of Psychotherapy.* New York: International Universities Press.

Epstein, L. (1986) "Collusive selection inattention to the negative impact of the supervisory situation." *Contemporary Psychoanalysis 22*, 389–409.

Feiner, A.H. (1991a) "The analyst's participation in the patient's transference." *Contemporary Psychoanalysis 27*, 208–241.

Feiner, A.H. (1991b) "The thrill of error." *Contemporary Psychoanalysis 27*, 624–653.

Feiner, A.H. (1993) "Out of our minds." *Contemporary Psychoanalysis 29*, 453–478.

Fiscalini, J. (1985) "On supervisory parataxis and dialogue." *Contemporary Psychoanalysis 21*, 591–608.

Fleming, J. and Benedek, T. (1966) *Psychoanalytic Supervision.* New York: Grune and Stratton.

Havens, L. (1982) "The choice of clinical methods." *Contemporary Psychoanalysis 18*, 16–42.

Langs, R. (1979) *The Supervisory Experience.* New York: Jason Aronson.

Levenson, E. (1982) "Follow the fox." *Contemporary Psychoanalysis 18*, 1–15.

Levenson, E. (1985) "The interpersonal model." In A. Rothstein (ed) *Models of the Mind.* New York: International Universities Press.

Levenson, E. (1993) "Shoot the messenger." *Contemporary Psychoanalysis 29*, 383–396.

Sullivan H. (1954) *The Psychiatric Interview.* New York: W.W. Norton.

Subject Index

Author Index